Control Systems for Live Entertainment

Second Edition

CONTROL SYSTEMS FOR LIVE ENTERTAINMENT

Second Edition

JOHN HUNTINGTON

**Focal
Press**

Boston • Oxford • Auckland • Johannesburg • Melbourne • New Delhi

Butterworth–Heinemann supports the efforts of
American Forests and the Global ReLeaf program in
its campaign for the betterment of trees, forests, and
our environment.

Cover photograph is a scene from *The Eighth Voyage of Sindbad*
at Islands Adventure, Universal Orlando. Photo by Kevin
Kolczynski, © 2000 Universal Orlando.

Library of Congress Cataloging-in-Publication Data

Huntington, John.
    Control systems for live entertainment / John Huntington.— 2nd ed.
      p.   cm.
    Includes bibliographical references and index.
    ISBN 0-240-80348-5 (pbk. : alk. paper)
    1. Theaters—Electronic sound control. 2. Stage lighting. 3. Electronic
control. I. Title.
    TK7881.9 .H86 2000   00-039407
    621.389'7—dc21   CIP

British Library Cataloguing-in-Publication Data
A catalogue record for this book is available from the British Library.

The publisher offers special discounts on bulk orders of this book.
For information, please contact:
Manager of Special Sales
Butterworth–Heinemann
225 Wildwood Avenue
Woburn, MA 01801-2041
Tel: 781-904-2500
Fax: 781-904-2620

For information on all Focal Press publications available, contact our World
Wide Web home page at: http://www.focalpress.com

10 9 8 7 6 5 4 3 2 1

Printed in the United States of America

To my parents,
for making it all possible.
(And for making me possible!)
And the second edition especially to my mother,
who didn't live to see it.

Contents

III Production Element Control 67

Table of Figures

Foreword to the Second Edition

Not long ago, show control seemed like a black art, practiced by a select group of magicians in utmost secrecy. Many of us mortals wanted to know the secret rituals, but who knew where to search? Stumped, we resorted to reinventing the wheel for every production to get the show going.

Although "the mystery of it all" might be a slight exaggeration, the fact remains that the art and science of show control in its early days developed behind the closed doors of the major theme park players and their subcontractors. In other entertainment venues, audio, lighting, motion control, video, and every other technical production discipline existed each in its own universe. Veritable armies of technicians sat at outrageous numbers of control consoles practicing the fine art of button pushing on cue—sometimes with variable levels of success. The performance where every technical element was perfectly synchronized to the stage manager's call was rare indeed, an elusive goal. Of course the synchronization was *almost* perfect a lot of the time, and the audiences were certainly not complaining. And *almost* was probably within a quarter second. Nonetheless, the goal of a perfectly synchronized performance, where a single control system reached out to touch every production element or its "expert system," remained firmly in the minds of many production people, from designers to technicians to systems engineers.

As shows moved out of the theatre and into restaurants, casinos, cruise ships, and other nontraditional venues, the industry began to realize that linking the various production elements was becoming a necessity, rather than just an engineering goal that would be nice.

That realization did not lead to quick or obvious solutions. Show-control experts tended to guard their knowledge jealously, since it was usually attached to proprietary products that paid the rent. There were no show-control generalists to disseminate the basics of the craft and identify the available tools. And the tools were often custom designs; there were very few standard show-control products. In short, life with show control was a challenge.

Which brings me to *Control Systems for Live Entertainment* and its author. I had been a reader on John Huntington's Master's thesis at Yale, the precursor to the first edition of this book. As soon as I read that marvelous document, I jumped on the phone to try and hire him. Unfortunately for me and fortunately for publisher Pat MacKay, John had committed to a job at *Lighting Dimensions (LD)* and *Theatre Crafts International* (now *Entertainment Design*) magazines. During John's tenure there, he taught all of us in the entertainment technology industry a thing or two—or six—about show control in his articles. He was already emerging as one of the leaders in a new breed of entertainment engineers—the show-control specialists who had the tools in their back pocket to "glue" together the technical elements of a production—*and* he delighted in teaching the craft to his colleagues and readers. As soon as John's stint at *LD* was up, I managed to pull him in to my company, Production Arts (PA).

I still remember the great relief I felt in 1993 when John took over the task of show-control integration for Production Arts on the lighting systems for the "Buccaneer Bay" Pirate Battle at the Treasure Island Hotel in Las Vegas. At the time, John was an engineer at PA, designing lighting control systems for a wide variety of projects. Imagine my surprise when I learned, unfortunately *after* the contract had been signed, that PA would need to implement multidisciplinary show-control elements on the project. Out jumped my newly acquired superhero of show control—John Huntington. Thus began a relationship that has lasted ever since and follows a basic tenet: when I have a show-control problem, I either pick up *Control Systems for Live Entertainment,* or I exercise the privilege of a long friendship and pick up the phone to call John. And when colleagues or students call for show-control advice, the first thing I do is send them to this book.

Quite a lot of water has gone under the bridge since the first edition of *Control Systems* was published in 1994. Perhaps the most important change is not in the technology itself, but the depth of its penetration into venues and productions that would have seemed totally improbable six years ago. When the first edition was published, the skill set required to be a competent lighting, audio, or scenery automation technician was much, much smaller. Today, in order to claim competence in even one of those disciplines, a technician must have good grounding in an alphabet soup of control technology. On any given project, he or she may be problem-solving with Ethernet distribution, TCP/IP networking, a bewildering array of obscure serial protocols, DMX512, SMPTE Time Code, or MIDI—just glance at the Table of Contents of this book for the full menu!

Those are not technologies that can be learned in the same *ad hoc* way that most entertainment technicians absorbed their craft in the past. Because the entertainment industry has always been an adopter of other industries' technologies, substantive information on the full spectrum of knowledge is spread out over a huge variety of resources. Those diverse resources are simply not much help to the technician trying to get the show going in the inevitable entertainment time frame, which is *now*! That's where this book comes in, and what John Huntington has contributed to our industry by compiling all the diverse information in one place, glued together by his insight and teaching ability.

At the current rate of acceleration, I calculate that by 2010, at least the fourth edition of this book will be required to keep up with the technology advances. I for one am looking forward to what John does with that one as much as I have enjoyed and used the first and second editions!

Steve Terry
President, PRG Lighting Systems
New York City
March 2000

Preface

As a child, I drew huge machines made up of motors, sprockets, gears, belts, and control panels. When my mother asked how a machine worked, I replied, "You just press a button!" Many years later, I am still fascinated by what you can make happen by pressing a button; now, instead of machines, I draw entertainment control systems. When asked how they work, I still answer, "You just press a button!"

Engineers in other industries—food processing, automobile manufacturing, robotics—get to make lots of cool things happen by pressing a button; they have vastly larger budgets and bigger and better toys with which to play. But not many food-processing engineers get the satisfaction of helping create a beautiful moment on a stage; not many auto manufacturers take part in the excitement of creating a theme-park stunt show; not many robotics engineers see the wild and woolly backstage world of rock and roll.

WHY DOES THIS BOOK EXIST?

In 1993, when I started work on the first edition of this book,[1] I couldn't find a single lighting text that even explained DMX512, the most widely used control standard in all of entertainment lighting, much less any book that covered topics like MIDI, MIDI Show Control, or SMPTE Time Code in ways that made sense for our industry. Moreover, no book talked about how you might connect show systems together. Today's shows are more

---

[1] In WordPerfect for DOS on a 286 PC with a whopping 2MB of RAM!

complex than ever, and the need for even the average technician to have a working understanding of the control systems that lie at the core of live entertainment technology is also greater than ever.

HOW HAS THE MARKET CHANGED SINCE THE FIRST EDITION?

When the first edition of this book was released in 1994, shows like *George Lucas Super Live Adventure* in Japan, Roger Waters' *The Wall* in Berlin, *EFX* in Las Vegas, and the U2 *Zoo TV* tour seemed to be the start of a trend. They all were huge live shows that exploited the power of Show Control not to reduce labor costs, as had been done for many years in the world of theme parks, but instead to do things live on a stage that couldn't be done any other way.

As we enter the new century, that trend has, at least for the time being, ended. Cirque Du Soleil® is producing the biggest live shows as of this writing, with *"O"* in Las Vegas being the most spectacular technological example. On *"O,"* there are many control systems, but *none* of them are connected together. Compare that to *EFX*, also in Las Vegas, which opened in 1995 and has a hugely complex show-control system that passes master control from department to department as necessary throughout the show.[2] The big concerts today are likely to have a lot of control and even automation inside departments, but little if any *show control* that crosses departmental lines. *The Lion King* opened on Broadway in 1997, and even though Disney would have probably highly automated this show if it had been done in one of its theme parks, on Broadway they are using a huge, traditional, backstage crew. I would guess the crew backstage is as big (if not bigger) than classic musicals of yesteryear,[3] but the crews backstage at *The Lion King* or *"O"* are working with extremely sophisticated systems, more powerful than anyone imagined even ten years ago.

Of course, show control is still an important part of shows in theme parks and some live shows, and show-control technology has also created new markets by bringing sophisticated shows to new venues (themed retail, etc.) with less sophisticated running (and more sophisticated installation) crews. The growth areas for show control as of this writing are: theme parks, "Location-Based Entertainments" (LBE), themed retail, cruise ships, corporate theatre/meetings, and museums. There are more and bigger theme parks now, without a doubt, but there also are many smaller theme parks and LBEs with smaller shows using very sophisticated show-control

---

[2] I'll let you compare these two shows in terms of their artistic merit—I'm just talking technology here!

[3] This large crew size likely had little to do with the common scapegoat: unions. *The Lion King* is in Disney's own theatre, and they negotiated their own contract directly with the stage unions, independently of other Broadway producers.

technology. Themed retail is an area that simply would not exist without show control. Themed restaurants have been having trouble recently— although it's interesting that some using show control have been expanding, while the ones with bad food, loud music, and memorabilia screwed to the walls (and no *show*) have been going bankrupt. Cruise ship shows would never be as complex as they are without the labor efficiencies created by the use of show control—less berths for crew mean more for passengers. Many ships still have the same number of stage crew as in past years, but use show control to increase productivity and do more with the same resources (this is happening in all sectors of the economy, of course). Museums are exploiting and integrating all the new technologies in many ways, riding a wave of "Edutainment."

THE IMPACT OF THE CONSUMER COMPUTER INDUSTRY

Today, consumers accept that the technologies they use every day are flawed. They take for granted system crashes, unreliable equipment, and bad cell phone transmission, but they accept those flaws to get the features they want at a price they're willing to pay. However, those same consumers would be demanding a refund of their $100 event ticket if a moving light system crashed, mechanized scenery failed in the middle of a show, or the sound system cut in and out like a digital cell phone does today. And we in the industry are squeezed from the other side as well: Show producers often have a dual mindset—they don't want to pay for reliability, but they won't tolerate a system failure either.

Most of our technology in entertainment has always been borrowed from other, better-funded industries with bigger R&D budgets; the best-funded industry today is, of course, the computer industry. Our little entertainment industry is being dragged along for the ride, and we are being forced to accept Ethernet, Windows®, RJ-45 connectors, and many other things never intended or designed for the "show must go on" nature of our industry. But we cannot match the economies of scale found in the computer industry, so we are increasingly forced to adapt consumer—rather than industrial—equipment and technologies for our purposes. That has probably been the biggest change we've seen in the industry since 1994. We used to be a tiny little industry adapting industrial control standards to the purposes of entertainment, and now we're a slightly larger, more consolidated industry adapting office-computing standards to the harsh environment backstage. So our challenge now is not only to adapt these technologies to purposes for which they were never designed, but also to adapt them in ways that will still allow the show to go on no matter what. But we are not alone in this endeavor. The industrial and process control industries, from which we have historically adapted our control technologies, are now in the same boat: they too are adapting Ethernet to industrial purposes and running factories using consumer-oriented operating systems.

The explosion of personal computers and networks has impacted us in other ways as well. Twenty years ago, most lighting control systems used simple analog voltages to represent the level to which a dimmer should be set and used one wire per dimmer. Audio systems used simple analog distribution systems, in traditional topologies. Machinery systems used simple limit switches and relays. These systems were easy to understand on an intuitive level, and few people needed to deal with the technical, in-depth side of the systems anyway. Today, there are computerized controllers unimaginable twenty-five years ago, buried inside many show devices both onstage and throughout a performance facility. All these devices need to be controlled somehow, and increasingly, that control data is carried via common computer-industry networks. A medium-size lighting system in a permanent facility, an audio system in a large facility, and a machinery control system developed today are all likely to use the same computer-industry network: Ethernet.

Because of networks like Ethernet, entertainment control methods and practices are shifting away from direct association with types of equipment—a lighting control standard for a lighting system, a sound control standard for audio systems—to being far more abstract. Ethernet might be used by multiple departments on the same show to do very different things.

WHAT'S NEW IN THE SECOND EDITION?

Because of all these changes in the industry, I've completely revised, reorganized, and updated this book. Today, not only do experts need to know more, but beginners and intermediate technicians also need at least a basic understanding of entertainment control systems. So I've actually expanded this edition both upwards *and* downwards—you'll see coverage of Ethernet, but also an expansion of Part 1, "The Basics," which discusses basic control concepts, hexadecimal, and so on.

Very little of what was covered in the first edition is actually obsolete, except for MediaLink, an early attempt at a universal entertainment-industry network. MediaLink's developer, Lone Wolf, failed spectacularly, leaving many in the audio industry holding the bag. That section has been deleted, but I've kept the sections on many of the other now less used standards, in case you encounter them in the field in an older installation. I'm continuing to focus here on techniques and standards and not on equipment, since the equipment changes so quickly (the equipment photos in the original book were out of date before the books left the printing press).

I've also tried to streamline the second edition, removing some of the overwhelming detail in which many readers got bogged down. In this edition, for standards like MIDI Machine Control that are somewhat tangential to our industry, I've included only the basic commands. For further information and complete documentation, you should consult the appropriate specifications and standards.

WHO IS THIS BOOK WRITTEN FOR?

I've kept two groups of readers in mind while writing this book: technicians, engineers, designers, and technical managers currently working in or studying the entertainment industry; and technically literate folks outside the business who want to learn more about entertainment control. This second group might include an electrical engineer hired to help create an entertainment lighting product, or a computer specialist interested in interfacing her software with "theatrical" production elements.

Though I've tried not to be extremely technical, this is a technological field: some technical knowledge is assumed of the reader. I assume that you know the difference between analog and digital, what a volt is, and so on. Many other books cover electronic technology and the basics of sound, lighting, and other technical aspects of the entertainment industry; a number of these are listed in the Bibliography. While this information is easier to digest if you have an electronics background, you don't need to be an expert. One of the things that differentiates the entertainment industry from other fields is that we deal with issues and systems very practically. It's nice to understand electronics at a component-level, but it's even more valuable for the average technician to have the ability to put together a reliable system and make something actually happen on a show.[4] So in entertainment controls, we generally deal with systems, not components, and, in general, this book is geared for end-users.

HOW SHOULD THIS BOOK BE USED?

I've tried to make this book readable for motivated, working professionals who may not have a teacher for guidance, while still keeping it useful for class purposes.[5] When I wrote the first edition, the topics covered really might only have been part of a graduate curriculum intended for serious technicians and engineers. Today, however, the technologies have become so ubiquitous that they are important even for the training of undergraduate

---

[4]Entertainment service technicians, of course, do need this in-depth electronic knowledge.

[5]I use it myself in my classes!

technicians. However, I would recommend these topics primarily for upper-level students—with so much of the book now covering networking and data communications, beginning students may have some difficulty finding the relevance of these topics until they have been introduced to the basics of lighting, sound, machinery, and so on.

One important note: Please, if you get bogged down in technical details in any chapter, and nothing is making sense, skip *ahead* and read the chapters in Part 7, "Show Control System Examples." Many of the foundation concepts will make sense only in context, and you can always go back and reread the details later.

NORTH AMERICAN PERSPECTIVE

I live and work in New York City. While I try to keep up with what is happening in other markets throughout the world, the fact is that it is nearly impossible for me to be thorough in this book on an international basis. So, I apologize in advance for any North American (or New York) bias (perceived or real) in this book!

DISCLAIMER

Now here's the "It's not my fault!" disclaimer: While I've made every effort to ensure that the information in this book is accurate, *DO NOT* implement MIDI in your lighting console (or anything in any product for that matter) based on the information in this book. The goal here is understanding; if you want to go to the next level—implementation—you should obtain information from the appropriate standards organizations or manufacturers (see the Appendixes or my Web page at http://www.zircondesigns.com for contact information). They have the newest, most up-to-date information and are worthy of your support.

Additionally, safety is the responsibility of system designers and operators. I include some general safety principles in this book; these are based on the way I do things, and not necessarily on any industry standard. It is *your* responsibility to ensure safety in any system with which you deal!

INEVITABLE (NOT PLANNED) OBSOLESCENCE

As I wrote this book, live entertainment control technology continued to evolve. The only thing I can guarantee and accurately predict is that things will change, and the most important thing you can learn today is how to learn. I've tried here to give you as many basic terms and tools as possible, so that five years, five months, or five days from now you will be able to read information about the next big thing and have some basis from which to understand it.

To counteract obsolescence as much as possible, I have not dwelled here on specific equipment or systems; in today's world, these systems age very quickly. This book focuses on the underlying concepts of entertainment control systems, which will survive a lot longer than the newest, greatest piece of gear. Of course, there's always the third edition. . . .

WEB PAGE

Things today change incredibly rapidly, and this is especially true with the topics covered in this book. For this reason, in this edition I have removed the manufacturer contact information—that information, errata, and much more is available on my Web site at http://www.zircondesigns.com.

John Huntington
New York City
March 2000

Acknowledgments

The book you are reading has been in the works for over seven years, and my interest in the topic started even further back, in 1981, when I entered college. Throughout this period, a number of people offered help that has been invaluable (in alphabetical order):

FIRST EDITION

Cy Becker at SMPTE, for information on the latest time-code standard.

David Bertenshaw, Tony Brown, and Andy Collier at Strand UK, for information about Strand's European standards.

Dr. John Bracewell of Ithaca College, for guidance and inspiration.

Margaret Cooley at Audio Visual Labs, for information on AVL products and protocols.

Sound designer Jonathan Deans, for help on my Master's thesis.

Tom DeWille of Luna Tech and Ken Nixon of PyroDigital Consultants, for their guidance on the pyro chapter.

Anders Ekval at Avab, for information about Avab's protocol.

Bran Ferren, for inspiration and information.

Tony Gottelier, for giving me the European perspective.

Richard Gray of R. A. Gray, for information about SDX and for reading my Master's thesis.

Alan Hendrickson, Ben Sammler, and the rest of the faculty at the Yale School of Drama, for their help and guidance on the thesis and throughout graduate school.

Mike Issacs at Lone Wolf for up-to-the-minute information about MediaLink.

George Kindler of Thoughtful Designs, for checking the book for completeness.

Bob Moses of Rane, for information on the AES-24 effort and for reviewing the manuscript.

Pat MacKay, publisher, and Karl Ruling, technical editor, at *TCI* and *Lighting Dimensions,* for their help.

Charlie Richmond, for the MIDI Show Control standard, answers to countless questions, continued support, and for reviewing the manuscript with a fine-tooth comb.

Paul Shiner at Crest, for information on NexSys.

Lou Shapiro of Erskine-Shapiro, for help early on in the process.

Karen Speerstra, Sharon Falter, John Fuller, and everyone at Focal Press, for all their help.

Steve Terry of Production Arts Lighting, for his support, encouragement, employment, information about DMX 512, and for reviewing the manuscript. Also thanks to John McGraw of Production Arts.

Laurel Vieaux at QSC, for information on QSControl.

Ralph O. Weber, of Digital Equipment Corporation for information on Two-Phase Commit MIDI Show Control.

Kevin Kolczynski at Universal Studios, Florida, for supplying the cover photograph.

SECOND EDITION

Everyone listed above, and:

Tom Lenz and Barbara Wohlsen for assisting me on this edition. Tom did and/or redid many of the line drawings, and Barbara found and gathered most of the photos and screen captures.

Jerry Durand, Philip Nye, and Dave Barnett, for finding typos in the first edition.

Marie Lee, Lauren Lavery, Terri Jadick, Charles McEnerney, Maura Kelly, and everyone at Focal Press.

JoAnne Dow of Wizardess Designs, Tom DeWille of PyroPak/LunaTech, Kevin Gross of Peak Audio, Robert Harvey of White Rabbit/RA Gray, Chuck Harrison of Far Field Associates, Dennis Hebert of Gilderfluke, Alan Hendrickson of the Yale School of Drama, Jim Janninck of TimberSpring, Michael Karagosian of MKPE, George Kindler and Kevin Ruud of Thoughtful Designs, Mike Lay and Steve Terry of Production Arts, Jeff Long of Granite Precision, Lars Pedersen of Scharff/Weisberg, Mike Rives of TDA, Charlie Richmond of Richmond Sound Design, David Scheirman of JBL Professional, and David Smith of the New York City Technical College, for reviewing sections of the draft manuscript.

Extra thanks to Chuck Harrison for his knowledge and inspiration for the first edition all the way back in 1985 at Associates & Ferren, and to Steve Terry for the nice foreword and for encouragement along the way.

Everyone at all the companies who provided me with information on and photos of their systems.

Gardiner Cleaves at Production Arts Lighting, for converting the first edition FastCAD drawings to DXF.

Jim Kellner and Mike Fahl of Dataton, for providing information on many video and projection standards.

Kevin Kolczynski at Universal Studios, Florida, for once again supplying the cover photograph.

Caroline Bailey for putting up with me during the whole second edition process, and for the "Ten-Pin Alley" title.

And everyone I forgot to thank!

Introduction

Live entertainment control systems are simultaneously in their infancy and well established: our industry lags years behind other better-funded industries, so many methods that are new to us have been used extensively in other industries for many years. The first Ethernet specification was released in 1980, and you'll come across it backstage at many shows today, but how many people in the live entertainment industry have any idea how it works?

WHAT ARE LIVE ENTERTAINMENT CONTROL SYSTEMS?

The answer to this question is important, because it defines what will and will not be included in this book. I'm using the rather unwieldy phrase "live entertainment control systems" to cover the control of all the elements in the show environment: the connection between a lighting control console and a dimmer rack, the link between a computer and a number of audio amplifiers, the connection between a pyro controller and some flash pots, or anything in between. I've included the word "live" here because I'm limiting discussion in this book to systems, standards, and practices used to present some form of entertainment to a group of people in a room at the same time. This is meant to include any show that is presented in front of a live audience, including live theatre, theme parks, corporate meetings, special events, cruise ship shows, themed retail, Location-Based Entertainments, museums, concerts, and even special-venue film projection, but excludes film, video, audio or other types of "non-live" media production, postproduction, or presentation. Of course, the show-control technologies covered in this book can be applied to (or may have come from) other disciplines, but if I didn't narrow the topic, this book would be an encyclopedia—the scope of information really is that broad.

WHAT IS SHOW CONTROL?

"Show control," a much maligned and misused phrase, means connecting separate entertainment control systems together into a "meta system."[1] A computer that controls fog machines to regulate the amount of fog in a harbor scene doesn't amount to show control; a system that *links* the control of the fog machine with an audio playback system generating maritime sound effects does. The signals sent between a lighting console and a group of dimmers is an entertainment control system, but it is not show control. If the lighting cues were triggered from a system that also controlled the scenery that was being lit, this would be show control. You don't have a show-control system unless control for more than one production element is linked *together*. So show control is part of entertainment control, but not all entertainment control is show control.

WHAT IS A STANDARD?

Markets often demand that control devices or components—hardware or software—be connected together. The methods developed to allow such linkages make up the bulk of this book and are often referred to as "standards."

Proprietary Standards

As a manufacturer, you could design a connection method yourself: pick the connector, transmission media, and signaling levels; then create the necessary control protocols, messages, data formats, and so forth. With this approach, you have complete control over the way a system works, and you can optimize the connection method for your applications and for your products' idiosyncrasies. However, you also have complete *responsibility* for getting everything working: you have to design every part of the system, debug it, develop test equipment and procedures, and then support your system after the product is released and used in ways you never imagined. Your customers are locked into a complete solution from you or from a competitor; they can't take your best

---

[1]Thanks to Bob Moses for this term.

products and mix and match them with the best devices from another manufacturer.[2] Such a control method is a "proprietary" standard.

De Facto Standards

If a manufacturer is lucky enough, their products come to dominate an industry so thoroughly that their proprietary solutions become "de facto" standards. The proprietary solution is used, legitimately or illegitimately, in many products, and passed around while the owner only occasionally cracks down on misuse when they perceive it to be in their interest.[3] This situation is prevalent in some market segments covered in this book, such as video.

Open Standards

Alternatively, a group of manufacturers, consultants, designers, and concerned end-users can get together and agree on an "open" standard or "recommended practice." The group typically works under the auspices of an engineering society or trade association, which itself works under the umbrella of one or more organizations such as the American National Standards Institute (ANSI), or the International Electro-technical Committee (IEC). The group of concerned participants forms "working groups" or "task groups," develops a draft of the proposed standard in language that is as precise as possible, and then releases the draft to the public for a period of review and comment.[4] Under procedures established by the sanctioning body, the group resolves the comments and issues the final standard, which is typically sold to help reimburse some of the administrative costs of development. The group then takes on the responsibility for maintenance, support, and future upgrades.

Unless there is clear market pressure, and support exists from the highest levels of the contributing organizations' management, the standards process often proceeds excruciatingly slowly, taking many months or even years, with members essentially (or actually) volunteering their time. However, these efforts are typically rewarded: Once the standard is released, a customer or systems integrator can choose the best equipment from each manufacturer for his or her application and still be more or less

---

[2]Some companies see this situation as a competitive advantage.

[3]De facto standards are often the most difficult type of standard to deal with—getting permission to use them legally, or getting accurate information, particularly from big companies, is often difficult.

[4]Sometimes, the work of a standards group is based on one manufacturer's proprietary approach, with that manufacturer releasing or donating their work to the industry in the hopes of spurring growth in the market.

assured that the equipment will work together. Cables and components can be standardized, sourced from multiple manufacturers, and made in bulk, reducing cost; and new equipment such as processors and test equipment often becomes available, since the existence of a standard gives even small companies a big enough market to make the creation of such devices economically feasible. This situation has repeatedly led to industry growth and expanded markets, and the development of new equipment never imagined by the standard's creators. There are many examples in this book of successful open standards that have expanded markets—DMX512, MIDI, SMPTE, TCP/IP, and Ethernet are a few.

Of course, there are downsides to open standards—they usually end up being "Lowest-Common-Denominator" solutions, standardizing only the most common and therefore the simplest and least sophisticated aspects of a control system, often at a low rate of performance. But the benefits of open solutions generally far outweigh the possible performance benefits of closed solutions.

SHOW DISCIPLINES

A production or entertainment installation is typically departmentalized by discipline—scenery, costumes, lighting, sound, and so on. These disciplines are typically organized by "department," each having a separate crew, budget, and so on. Here is a quick overview of and introduction to the disciplines or departments covered in this book.

Lighting

Lighting, one of the oldest design elements, for most productions today is almost always controlled with the aid of one or more control computers.[5] Control interconnection of lighting systems today has become standardized to the point that just about any modern lighting control console can reliably control any manufacturer's dimmer, color scroller, or many other devices. Chapter 7, "Lighting," covers lighting control.

Lasers

Lasers are used in everything from huge rock concerts to corporate theatre productions. Many laser systems are custom-made, but the parts that have been standardized are covered in Chapter 8, "Lasers."

---

[5]The ancient Greeks used the sun in their productions, although the lighting then controlled the show, instead of the other way around!

Sound

Sound plays a critical role in many productions and has been a huge beneficiary of the explosion of digital technology. Because sound is so complex and significantly affected by environmental conditions, many audio systems are totally manual, but many others use computers extensively. However, even in manual systems, sound control is important, either for triggering the playback of sounds, for recalling routing and level presets, or for live-remote operation of digital mixers. Sound is covered in Chapter 9, "Sound."

Video

Video has been booming in recent years, as the digital video explosion drives prices down and sophistication up. This has brought professional-quality gear and techniques into reach for ever-smaller productions, and video is being increasingly integrated into a variety of live shows. There are few open industry standards for control of video equipment used in the live market, but there are several widely used de facto standards. Control for video is covered in Chapter 10, "Video."

Computer Presentation

This discipline is encountered frequently by those who work in the corporate meeting and special event markets. Software-based presentation systems incorporate text, graphics, and sometimes sound, and some can be linked in limited ways to outside systems. Control of these systems is covered in Chapter 11, "Computer Presentation."

Film Projection

This category includes both still and motion-picture film technologies. Still "slides" have been a staple of corporate theatre presentations for a long time; large-format slides are frequently used to create high-resolution images for large-scale events, either outdoors (i.e., projecting on the side of a building), or indoors (projecting huge and highly detailed images). Motion-picture projection is often used in mega-spectacles and concert tours. While these technologies are prevalent today, they are likely to be displaced by digital presentation technologies in the near future, simply because digital images are so flexible, easy to manipulate, and cheaper to transmit and transport. Chapter 12, "Film Projection," covers film projection control.

Machinery

"Machinery" here covers a very broad range, including stage elevators, set pieces, props, or theme park "show action equipment." As in many other departments, the computer has permeated the machinery control business in a big way; some kind of computer now controls scenic machinery in almost every type of show, from small regional theatre productions to major concert tours. Because of the custom nature of much of the work, and because of safety concerns, much of what goes on in entertainment machinery control is proprietary or custom. General standards are covered in Chapter 13, "Stage Machinery."

Animatronics

Animatronics, or "character animation," is a sort of entertainment robotics, where an electromechanical character simulates a living being. The term comes from "Audio Animatronics," which was first used by Disney in their early theme parks. Animatronic devices tend to be controlled by specialty equipment, and the topic is covered in Chapter 14, "Animatronics."

Fog, Smoke, Fire, and Water

This category contains a variety of production elements often found in theme parks: fog, flammable gas, water fountains, and so on. Most such systems are purpose-built, with a custom interface to other show systems. This category is sometimes also called "process control," but this term has specific meanings in industry.[6] Chapter 15, "Fog, Smoke, Fire, and Water," covers these topics.

Pyrotechnics

We're talking here about chemical pyrotechnics: flash pots, sparkle devices, concussion mortars—things that go boom. Pyrotechnic systems, because of the danger involved, have almost always been run separately from other show elements; somewhat recently, though, the introduction of dedicated computer-based pyro controllers has allowed these systems to be integrated and computerized for synchronization purposes. Pyro is covered in Chapter 16, "Pyrotechnics." Pyro substitutes such as air cannons would go into other categories, depending on their construction.

---

[6] In industry, "process control" means the control of processes in chemical, wastewater, refinery, and other facilities.

Show Control

Show control, discussed in detail in Part 4, "Putting It Together: Standards for Connecting Systems," is the newest and, therefore, least well-defined production category. For many years, show-control systems were custom-engineered, supplied in a turn-key fashion by one company, and programmed by "gurus." Today, however, show-control systems can be bought off-the-shelf, and a number of companies offer systems that can control and link a huge variety of gear.

PART I

The Basics

Because control systems are increasingly abstract and networked, the basic information that is common to all systems is increasingly extensive. This is good, because the more advanced chapters in this book simply build on the foundation we build here in Part 1. The bad part is that you have to muddle through all these basic sections before we get to the seemingly more relevant sections dealing with specific production disciplines. So bear with me for a few chapters of basics (or feel free to skip ahead if you already understand these topics).

General Control Concepts

When we design a control system—or part of one—we have to make some decisions about how the system should work, based on what exactly we are controlling, what we want the system to do, and some basic characteristics of the system's application.

OUTPUTS AND INPUTS

Breaking a system down to its simplest level, we have outputs, inputs, and signal connection methods. An output sends some sort of signal, state, information, or data to an input, using some sort of connection method. Outputs are always connected to inputs: a lighting console control output would connect to a dimmer control input; a machinery computer output would connect to the input of a motor drive, and so on. Connecting a number of outputs to inputs gives us signal (or control) flow through a system.

CUES OR CONTINUOUS CONTROL

Entertainment control breaks down into two general approaches: cues or continuous control.

Cues

In most forms of live entertainment control, many of the technical elements are not actually "live," but are in fact being controlled through the recall of a series of preprogrammed "presets," predefined states, or, as we refer to them in the world of live performance, "cues." A cue can be a number of different things, depending on the production element to which one is referring. A cue can be self-contained: once started it runs until completion (such as an explosion). On the other hand, a cue can modify something that is continuing: a lighting cue is generally a transition from one light "look" to another, but "light cue 18" refers to both the *transition* from light cue 17 and the resulting new look, which will continue onstage after execution of the cue transition.

In live performance, each production element—lighting, sound, scenery, and so on—has a cue number assigned for each of the predefined states executed during the show. Depending on the production element, these cues may be prerecorded using a computerized control console, or executed manually. The human "stage manager" is in charge of running the show, and generally uses a headset system to communicate with individual system operators. Warnings are given for each cue: "Sound cue 326 stand by." If ready, the sound operator then replies, "Sound standing by." At the appropriate point in the production, the stage manager initiates the cue by saying, "Sound cue 326 go." When the cue is completed, the sound operator replies, "Sound complete."[1] Alternatively, "cue lights" are used to signal actor entrances and to communicate with run crew members who cannot easily or safely use a headset (for example, a person flying scenery over the stage might not wear a headset because it might get tangled in the rigging). The stage manager turns on a cue light to indicate to an operator to stand by for the next cue. When the stage manager turns the cue light *off*, the operator executes the cue.

Continuous Control

Some forms of entertainment control, such as animatronics or lighting dimmer levels, are more "continuous" in nature. Even though almost all control methods discussed in this book are digital, some techniques are in fact digital, "sampled" representations of continuous, analog-like control value streams.[2] The position of an animatronic figure's arm is probably

---

[1] The "standing by" and "complete" steps are often omitted with experienced crews.

[2] Sampling refers to the repeated numeric "sampling" of a continuous waveform. The numeric samples can later be reconstructed to create a digital approximation of the original analog stream.

better represented as a series of points in a continuous stream of values, rather than by a series of preset positions; the continuous stream gives us smoother control over the position of the arm. A dimmer level may remain unchanged for some time, but then it may have to make a 20-minute fade-out to represent a sunset. While it would certainly be possible to design each dimmer so that it contains all the intelligence needed to store and execute such a fade based on cues, it is generally more cost-effective to have a "dumb" dimmer, which simply sets the light level or other parameter to the value represented by the incoming control stream at that instant. Digital systems that use this continuous approach generally update the values continuously, sending out a static value over and over, or a changing value if the control data is changing.

EVENT-BASED OR TIME-BASED

States or cues in entertainment control systems must somehow be triggered or executed. Generally, systems fall into three categories: event-based, time-based, or hybrids of the two.

Event-Based

A live performance is generally event-based: the stage manager calls cues based on an event's occurrence—the speaking of a certain line of dialogue, an actor's movement, and the like. For instance, when an actor screams "Run for your life!" the stage manager gives a "go" command over the headset to lighting and sound operators. The lighting operator, who has been standing by for this cue, presses the "next cue go" button on her control console, triggering the explosion lighting effects, while the sound operator triggers the sound effects in a similar fashion.

A tremendous amount of intelligence exists in this human-controlled, event-based system. The explosion effect is triggered on the event—the actor's line—regardless of when in time he says it, where he is standing, what day of the week it is, the phase of the moon, and so on. Event-based systems allow performers to vary their timing, to improvise, and even to make mistakes. If the actor is having a bad night and simply runs screaming off the stage without saying his line, the stage manager can improvise and still trigger the explosion effects by giving the go commands. This type of intelligence is not easily built into automated systems: if a voice-recognition system were triggering the effects off the actor's "Run for your life!" line and the actor forgot to say it, such a system could get hopelessly out of whack.

Here are some examples of events that might trigger something in an entertainment control system:

- An operator presses a button on a control console.
- An actor sits on an onstage sofa.
- The sun rises over the horizon.
- An actor speaks a line of text.
- An audience member passes a sensor.

Time-Based

In a time-based system, all elements, including human performers, are synchronized by some means to a master clock. A time-based system is less forgiving to human performers: if explosion effects were triggered at 14 minutes and 35 seconds into every performance, the actor would be out of luck if his performance varied much. He becomes simply another slave to the master clock, synchronizing himself to the system, instead of the other way around. However, time-based systems have a major advantage over event-based systems: once assembled and programmed, they are easy to run automatically and reliably, eliminating many variables. Such a system may sound limiting, but scores of theme-park shows, halftime spectaculars, and industrial theatre productions have successfully run this way for many years.[3]

Here are some examples of time-based triggers in entertainment control systems:

- The show starts at 3:00 P.M. Eastern Standard Time.
- A light cue is triggered at 10 seconds after 3:00 P.M.
- A film is shown, and at 2 minutes, 22 seconds, and 12 frames, a strobe is fired.

Hybrid Systems

Most entertainment control systems are hybrids of event- and time-based systems. Systems that are primarily event-based can have built-in time-based sequences; conversely, a time-based system can stop and wait for an event-trigger before continuing. In our example show detailed above, if complex explosion effects were built into a 5 second long time-based sequence, the system would then be hybrid. Most of the show would be event-based, with the stage manager calling cues off various actions. When the actor yells, "Run for your life!" the stage manager commands a time-

---

[3] At least technically, if not artistically!

based sequence consisting of the lighting and sound cues for the explosion sequence. The actors synchronize their movements to the time-based sequence—which is relatively easy, since the sequence is exactly the same every night. At the conclusion of the time-based sequence (itself an event), the stage manager returns to a normal, event-based operating mode and continues to call cues based on the script, an actor's position on the stage, or other events.

RELATIVE OR ABSOLUTE

Another important control system concept is the difference between "absolute" and "relative." In *The American Heritage Dictionary*, absolute is defined as "pertaining to measurements or units of measurement derived from fundamental relationships of space, mass, and time." Conversely, relative is defined as "dependent upon or interconnected with something else for intelligibility or significance; not absolute."

To illustrate the difference, let's imagine a bicoastal live video event, staged simultaneously in both New York and Los Angeles. Sam, the scenic designer, has designed a series of ten 3-foot square platforms laid out on 6-foot centers, which line up with overhead lighting trusses. A scene shop in Toronto has constructed two identical sets of platforms, and they have been delivered to both New York and L.A.; a lighting company has installed all the trussing.

We have two stage carpenters, Allison and Roger, each installing an identical set in two similar spaces; Allison is in New York, Roger is in Los Angeles. The designer has specified that the first platform should be 6 feet from the edge of the stage, so Roger starts, measures 6 feet from the edge of the stage, and then lays in the first platform. Since the platforms are each specified as 3 feet wide, and they are supposed to be on 6-foot centers, Roger simply measures 3 feet from the edge of the first platform to the edge of the next, places a platform, and does the same for each of the platforms (see Figure 1.1). He wraps up the job quickly because the surf is up.

Allison starts, measures 6 feet from the edge of the stage, and then lays in the first platform. However, instead of measuring from the edge of the first platform to the edge of the second platform as Roger did, she goes back to the edge of the stage and measures 12 feet (6 feet to the first platform, plus 6 feet to the edge of the second platform). Then she measures from the edge of the stage to platform 3 at 18 feet, and so on (see Figure 1.2). It takes a little longer, but Allison finishes up and heads home.

The set designer shows up in L.A., and goes ballistic. Each platform in the series is increasingly misaligned with the overhead pipes. The set designer's assistant in New York, however, checks Allison's work and everything is fine. What happened?

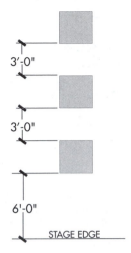

Figure 1.1 Roger's Measurements

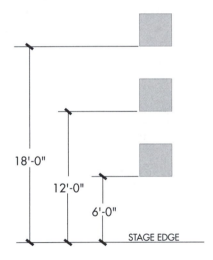

Figure 1.2 Allison's Measurements

It turns out that the scene shop made a mistake in construction (English/metric error), and the platforms are actually 3 feet and 3 inches wide. With Roger's relative measurements—from the edge of one platform to the edge of the next—he never noticed that each platform after the first was off by 3 inches. The error accumulated, and platform 10 was off by nearly 30 inches. Allison, however, used absolute measurements, referring back to the edge of the stage as a reference each time. Even though the distance between the platforms is 3 inches short, the platforms line up exactly with the overhead pipes as intended.

Relative

In a relative system, we only know where something is in relation to the things before and after it. A signal sent to a lighting console containing the message "next cue go" would be relative—if such a message in the middle of a series of cues was lost, the system would get out of whack, running behind the other elements to which it is connected. Conversely, if an erroneous "next cue go" message was somehow accepted by a lighting console, it would now be ahead of the other devices in the system.

Data integrity is extremely important in relative systems, because if data is lost, the system will be in error. If a relative system loses power, at power-up the system must first reinitialize, find a predefined starting point, and then figure out where to go from there. But relative messages do have their place—they are easy to implement and take up less data space, since they carry less information.

Absolute

A control message of "cue 17 go" would be absolute—the absolute signal contains all the information necessary to place the cue in the show. If one absolute message in a series is lost, the system would simply be off track until the next absolute cue is received; well-designed absolute systems will eventually realign themselves. Absolute systems are generally more robust and can recover from data corruption, but are correspondingly more complicated (and therefore expensive).

OPEN LOOP OR CLOSED LOOP

Another key concept in control systems is the difference between open and closed loops.

Open Loop

Let's say someone sends you an E-mail, asking you to send a copy of this book to a client. Months later, the person who sent you the E-mail runs into the client on the street and asks how she liked the book. "What book?" she says. This was an open-loop system—someone asked you to do something, but never got any feedback from you confirming that you did it, and he or she never followed up. Open loop systems are simple and fast—only one message had to be sent, but in this case, the system did not work. If you were asked ten times a day to send out books, and the requester trusted both the communications medium (E-mail) and the target device (you), an open-loop system might be fine. Open-loop approaches are simpler to implement, and are good for systems with high reliability and where an occasional error might not be a problem.

Closed Loop

Now, let's say that each time the sender sent you an E-mail asking you to ship a book, you reply and say, "The book is on its way." We have now added a form of feedback to this system, "closing the loop." Closed-loop systems are generally more reliable, since the system can detect and compensate for errors. If you never reply to one of the request E-mails, the sender can follow up and send another request. However, closed-loop systems are more complex than open-loop systems and are correspondingly more difficult to implement. Many systems consist of closed- and open-loop components: critical functions are equipped with feedback; less important functions are left open-loop.

CENTRALIZED OR DISTRIBUTED

There are two basic structures for control systems: centralized and distributed. In a centralized system, one central controller is responsible for the operation of the entire system; in a distributed system, control intelligence is spread throughout the network. Centralized and distributed often are used to refer both to the physical arrangement of the system and its control hierarchy. However, in these days of networks, the physical arrangement and control structure are more often separate, as we'll see later.

Centralized

In a centralized system, all control functions are run from a single machine or machines, located in a central location. Sometimes this is cheaper because less control hardware is required. However, because the control is centralized, such systems can be a nightmare to program, because many departments may want to make changes simultaneously, bottlenecking the programmer.

Distributed

A distributed system is made up of a number of "subsystems," each optimized for its task. Each subsystem decides, or is told by another system, when and how to execute its tasks. This approach is often desirable in entertainment control applications, since a lighting console's interface can be optimized for lighting, a machinery console for machinery, and so on. Such systems can still be linked to a single master controller, but the work of control is distributed throughout the system. With the distributed load, if one controller stops working, the show could continue on with the other elements.

CONTROL HIERARCHY

When designing a system, a control system designer must decide on a structure that determines how, if, and when each device has control over another. There are three primary control structures: master/slave or primary/secondary, peer-to-peer, and client/server.

Master/Slave or Primary/Secondary

In a master/slave or primary/secondary system, one device has direct, unilateral control over another. The secondary device can be fairly simple, since it only does what it is told to do. This type of control structure often works best in less complex systems, and because one and only one device is in control at all times, design, implementation, and troubleshooting is fairly straightforward.

Peer-to-Peer

In some applications, it's better to spread the control intelligence throughout a system, connecting intelligent controllers or "peers." In such a system, each peer device has equal access to—or even control over—all the other devices in a system. This control structure allows powerful and sophisticated systems, but also can be more complicated to design and troubleshoot, since contention issues—who gets control over the system at any given time—must be resolved by the system designers.

Client/Server

The client/server model has developed in recent years with the rise of the computer network and powerful workstations. Such a structure is a step beyond a peer-to-peer system, dealing with issues of control contention by allowing many simultaneous transactions simultaneously. In a client/server system, one part of a system (or one entire device) is set up as a "server," which offers some sort of service to one or more "clients." Multiple clients can make requests of the same server, and the server can resolve contention issues.

LOGIC FUNCTIONS

In a control system, we typically take information from some number of inputs, process that information through one or more logic functions, and create an output state.

If-Then

Although "If-Then" isn't really a logical function, it is very important for control applications. If-Then says that if the input condition equals some value (like true, 7, or red), then the output condition will now equal some predetermined value. This function is very useful in entertainment systems. For instance, *If* the actor is in place, *Then* execute light cue 1, or *If* the time is 1 minute and 35 seconds, *Then* fade out the sound cue.

Or

"Or" is the simplest of the logical rules. An Or-function situation states that if *any* of the inputs are true (or "on" or "1"), then the output will be true. Let's imagine a system with two inputs, A and B, and apply the Or function to it. If either input A *Or* input B is true, then the output will be true. If *neither* input A *Or* input B is true, then the output will be false (or "off" or "0"). This function is easier to understand through the use of a "truth table," showing all the possible conditions of a set of inputs, and their output value based on the function. Here is the truth table for the Or function:

Table 1.1   Or Truth Table

Input A	Input B	Output
False	False	False
False	True	True
True	False	True
True	True	True

Exclusive Or

A variation of the Or function is the "Exclusive" Or, where only one input will cause the output to be true. If all the inputs are true, the output will be false. Here is a truth table for the Exclusive Or function:

Table 1.2   Exclusive Or Truth Table

Input A	Input B	Output
False	False	False
False	True	True
True	False	True
True	True	False

And

In an "And" function, all of the inputs must be set to a true state for the output to be set to true. Let's use the And function as above with our two-input (A and B) system. If input A *And* input B are both true, then the output will be true. Any other condition will cause the output to be false. This is also expressed in a truth table:

Table 1.3   And Truth Table

Input A	Input B	Output
False	False	False
False	True	False
True	False	False
True	True	True

Not

A "Not" function "inverts" the state of any input. If the input is true, the output of the Not function will be false. If the input is false, the output is true. This Not or "negating" condition is often represented by a horizontal bar over a label, such as $\overline{A}$, or referred to as an "Inverting" input. Here's a truth table for the Not logical function.

Table 1.4   Not Truth Table

Input	Output
True	False
False	True

Logic Combinations

Complex systems are usually built up of combinations of various functions. Using the simple Not, Or, and And functions, highly sophisticated systems can be developed.

OPERATING SYSTEMS

Since so much of entertainment control today is based on computers, a few words about computer operating systems are useful here. A computer operating system, or "OS," is the low-level computer code that takes the inputs and outputs from the user and application programs, and interfaces them to the computer hardware, peripherals, and memory.

Real Time

In an office environment, if a background program is hogging processor resources, and it takes a few seconds longer than normal to load up a word processing document or a spreadsheet, the user might be inconvenienced. However, in the show environment, delaying the execution of a cue by a few seconds could be aesthetically disastrous or even dangerous. In entertainment, we are always concerned with "real time" issues.

Real time is, unfortunately, one of the most misunderstood and misused terms in the control and computer worlds. There is no single formal definition for what is and what is not "real time," but in general, a real-time system can execute a task as fast as it is needed, or in a predictable amount of time. The amount of time it takes a system to do something is often referred to as "latency." If the latency of a system or task is known, the system can be designed around it. If a system's latency is variable to a degree noticeable to the user or system, then it is not a real-time system.

Multitasking

At today's blindingly fast computer speeds, it is often easy to forget that at the lowest level, most processors can still only execute one instruction at a time. Since the machines are so fast, it is often possible for the computer to appear to the user or control system to be doing more than one thing at once, or "multitasking."

In a "cooperative" multitasking system, multiple tasks can be run, but there is no guarantee that a task that you consider important will be considered important by the operating system. For instance, the most important task you may require of a control program is to update the control signal output. However, the computer may start writing to a disk at some point and not release control over the processor until it is finished, seconds later. The control output would likely "burp" and drop out, and this is unacceptable for entertainment applications.

More advanced multitasking operating systems are capable of what is called "preemptive" multitasking. In such a system, the operating system is capable of prioritizing tasks according to a hierarchy established by the programmer. This structure is extremely useful for real-time entertainment applications. To fix the problem in our previous example of a control signal output dropping out while a processor attended to other tasks, a programmer could assign a higher priority to the control output task than the disk write. In this way, limited processor resources are allocated to the tasks most important to the programmer. Preemptive multitasking operating systems have tremendous advantages, but application software for these systems can be more complex to write.

Multithreading

Multithreading is slightly different than multitasking, but the distinctions are not easily explained (even by experts on the topic) without going into OS details beyond the scope of this book. However, in general, multithreaded operating systems have processes or tasks that are made up of or are assigned "threads" that share a common memory space. The multiple threads can share resources such as memory and are managed by the operating system.

2

Electrical Control System Basics

Now that we've covered some general control concepts, we can move on to the basics of control systems. The vast majority of entertainment control systems are operated and controlled electrically, so electrical systems are the focus of this chapter and much of this book.

SENSORS AND SWITCHES

Inputs to a control system can come either from another system's outputs or from sensors and switches,[1] which sense some condition in the environment and report that condition's status to the control system. A sensor or switch could be a button pressed on a control console by a human operator, a photoelectric beam crossed by an actor, or a proximity switch that senses when a metal machine part is near. There are many types of sensors and switches, and because they're common in a variety of entertainment control systems, we'll cover some basic types here.

---

[1]There are no hard and fast definitions of the difference between sensor and switch, but a good working definition for our purposes is that a switch involves something operated by a mechanical force, while a sensor can sense conditions in its environment in other ways. So a mechanical limit would be a "switch," but a temperature probe would be a "sensor."

Figure 2.1   Operator Controls (Courtesy Automationdirect.com)

Operator Controls

This category can include anything from an industrial push button actuated by a theme park employee to a "Go" key on a lighting console (see Figure 2.1). In any professional system, these controls should be only of the highest quality, and this means they will be expensive. But this is not a place you want to scrimp—do you really want your show to go down because a simple switch broke?

Wireless Remote Controls

Wireless (typically radio or infrared) remote controls are another form of operator control that is useful in many types of entertainment control systems, and they come in both handheld and mounted versions. The best handheld units for our market come from the security industry, where actuation reliability is taken seriously. These can be useful where a client or actor wants to trigger an effect discreetly, control a private entrance, and so forth, or, of course, in any situation where wires are not desirable.

Limit Switches

A limit switch is typically actuated by a machine part physically contacting the switch, indicating that a "limit" has been reached. These switches come in a variety of forms and designs (see Figure 2.2) and are useful in stage machinery and other applications.

Encoders

While "encoder" is a very general term, in entertainment control systems we usually use the term to refer to a device that takes positional information,

Figure 2.2 Limit Switches (Courtesy Automationdirect.com)

Figure 2.3 Rotary Shaft Encoder (Photo by Barbara Wohlsen)

and senses or "encodes" it. Encoders come in a wide variety, but most common are rotary shaft encoders (see Figure 2.3), which take a rotating motion and generate a digital signal to a control system. The control system can then decode this signal to determine a device's position, or the encoder can be a user interface, interpreted by the system. Linear and a huge variety of other types of encoders are also available.

Photoelectric Sensors

These sensors typically send an infrared beam of light directly or indirectly (via a reflector) to a receiver, which sends out a control signal when the beam is either interrupted or made, depending on the application (see Figure 2.4). "Light Operate" sensors turn on their outputs when light is detected; "Dark Operate" sensors turn on when the light beam is broken. "Retroreflective" sensors are those that use a beam bouncing off a reflector, and are so named because the reflector reflects light back at the same angle from which it arrived.[2] "Thru-Beam" photo sensors are those that send a beam from a transmitter to an active receiver. Photoelectric sensors are useful in entertainment when you want an actor or audience member to activate something by simply breaking an invisible beam.

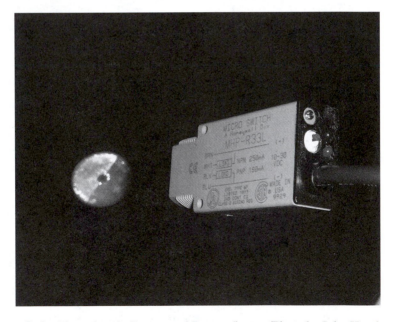

Figure 2.4 Photoelectric Sensor and Retroreflector (Photo by John Huntington)

---

[2] Retroreflectivity also is the reason stop signs reflect car headlights back to the driver from any angle.

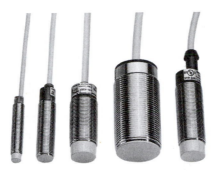

Figure 2.5   Proximity Switches (Courtesy Automationdirect.com)

Proximity Switches

Using no moving parts, proximity switches are able to detect the presence or absence of a proximate piece of metal. They are generally very reliable and durable, and have a wide variety of applications in machinery systems (see Figure 2.5).

Motion Detectors

While most of the sensors we've discussed so far are adapted from the world of industrial control and factory automation, motion detectors are adapted from the world of security and alarm systems. These devices either send an infrared light or microwave radio beam into a space; if someone walks through that space, they reflect the light or radio beam, and the motion can be detected from the change in reflections. These sensors can be useful for a variety of entertainment applications, from haunted houses to museums.

Other Sensors

Although this list of switches and sensors covers a wide variety of devices found in entertainment control systems, we've only scratched the surface in what's available. Sensors exist for nearly any physical characteristic you can imagine, including temperature, velocity, force, strain, position, flow, and so on.

CONTACT CLOSURES

One of the simplest ways to interface something electrically is to use a "Contact Closure," otherwise known as a "Dry Contact Closure" (DCC) or

"General Purpose Interface" (GPI). Because it is common to so many entertainment applications as a lowest-common-denominator interface, it is included in this chapter.

Dry Contact Closure/General Purpose Interface

A "Dry Contact Closure"[3] or "General Purpose Interface" both generally represent a nonstandardized "contact closure" like input or output. There may be in fact no physical contacts (see "Sourcing/Sinking Transistor Interfaces" below), but essentially the input accepts or outputs a small voltage or current to actuate a system. This type of interface is a lowest-common denominator way of connecting two systems, since only two states can be communicated—on or off. This makes things very simple and easy to understand, but since there are so many variations, successfully connecting two pieces of gear using such an interface often takes quite a bit of work by the system designer, and sometimes additional interface hardware.

Sourcing/Sinking Transistor Interfaces

Many Contact Closures or General Purpose Interfaces actually use transistors for interfacing instead of physical contacts. There are two configurations in which transistors are generally used for this purpose: "sourcing" or "sinking" (see Figure 2.6).

When a sourcing interface turns on, current flows through the transistor, out to the load, and then back into a ground often shared with the transistor. With a sinking interface, current flows from the power supply, through a load, into the transistor, and then to an internal ground. When interfacing to sourcing or sinking interfaces, care must be taken to get polarity and other characteristics configured correctly.

Open-Collector Transistor Interfaces

An "open-collector" transistor interface gets into electronics a little too deeply to be adequately covered here, but the basic concept is important to

---

[3] According to several people I have spoken with, "dry" contacts are those capable of working reliably with very low currents, and "wet" contacts need higher voltages and currents to work properly. Wet contacts are not commonly found today, and were generally made of inexpensive "base" metals such as copper, brass, or tin, which oxidize easily, unlike "precious" (and more expensive) metals such as silver and gold. The oxides that form on base metals are often nonconductive, so to keep the corrosion from affecting performance, telephone engineers "wetted the circuit" by running a constant DC voltage across the terminal, to ensure that the AC signal they were switching would work reliably.

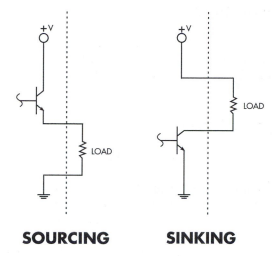

SOURCING   SINKING

Figure 2.6 Sourcing and Sinking Transistor Outputs

the system designer. In an open-collector interface, only one of the three transistor terminals is wired internally to the device. The other two are presented to the outside world, and the system designer must then usually supply an external power supply through the transistor terminals (see Figure 2.7). This output type is very flexible, but requires some lower-level engineering by the system designer, and, frequently, additional devices or components to complete the interface.

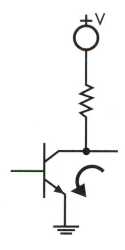

Figure 2.7 Open-Collector Transistor Output

CONTACT NOMENCLATURE

An important characteristic of sensors, switches, and contact closure interfaces is the contact arrangement. These range from simple, mechanical, relay contacts in single or multiple poles, to sophisticated transistor outputs.

Normally Open or Normally Closed

A switch or contact closure is typically either "normally open" or "normally closed." In a normally-open contact, the flow of current is interrupted when the switch is in its "off" state; current flows when the switch is in its "on" state. A standard light switch is normally open—in a "normal" state, the switch is off, the contacts are open, no current is flowing, and the light is off. A normally closed contact is exactly the opposite: In its "normal" state, current *is* flowing; when the switch is actuated, the flow of current is interrupted. This type of switch is very useful in control system applications where you want current to flow until a condition is met; one such case is an "Emergency Stop" button, where you want the system to work normally *until* the button is pressed. In other words, you want current to flow in the normal situation, and the flow to be broken in the emergency, or switch-actuated, state.

   In schematic drawings for industrial control systems, normally open and normally closed contacts are often depicted as shown in Figure 2.8. This type of schematic symbol is very useful for complex systems, as it allows the logical—rather than physical—flow to be depicted.

Contact Arrangements

Contacts on switches or sensors come in a wide variety of arrangements and can offer multiple, independent control circuits. These contact

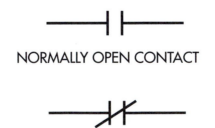

NORMALLY OPEN CONTACT

NORMALLY CLOSED CONTACT

Figure 2.8   Industrial Schematic Symbols

SINGLE POLE, DOUBLE THROW (SPDT)

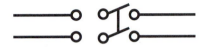

DOUBLE POLE, DOUBLE THROW (DPDT)

Figure 2.9 SPDT and DPDT Contact Arrangements

arrangements are typically known either by their "Form" schedule, or by a more intuitive nomenclature like SPDT. SPDT simply means Single Pole, Double Throw, and could be represented schematically as shown in Figure 2.9. In such an SPDT switch, one wire or circuit can be routed to either of two outputs, hence the nomenclature Single Pole (one wire), Double throw (two output positions). With a DPDT switch contact, two independent wires can be routed to two separate contacts, although the switch contacts for both circuits are linked together so that they change states at the same time. This nomenclature can represent nearly any type of switch contact; for instance, a 4PST (4-Pole, Single Throw) switch would have four wires on separate circuits, and only two possibilities: on or off for all four wires simultaneously.

GALVANIC AND OPTICAL ISOLATION

When you connect electrical devices or systems using wire, all sorts of nasty things can happen. For instance, the system could create a ground loop, where current flows from one point of a system to another through the grounds; this can cause data corruption (or hum in a sound system). Another possibility is damage—what happens if high-voltage, high-power electricity connects to a low-voltage input or output? Fire and smoke, typically!

The easiest way to overcome these problems is to electrically disconnect the two devices, or, in other words, to provide "galvanic," or DC (direct current), isolation. This can be achieved through several methods, with "optical isolators" being the most common for control systems (see Figure 2.10). In an optical isolator, an input signal turns on a light (typically an

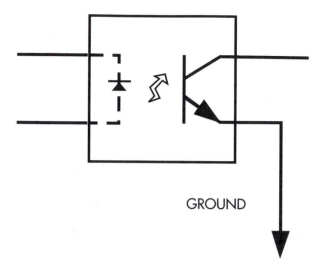

Figure 2.10 Optical Isolator Schematic

LED). A separate output circuit, incorporating a phototransistor, turns on when the input light is shining, and off when it is not. In this way, the only connection between the input and the output of the optical isolator is light, and electrical ground loops, surges, and other anomalies (within the electrical limits of the device) are blocked.

Numbering Systems

Before moving on to data communications and networks, we have to cover one more thing: numbering systems. These are not complex concepts, but you may not have encountered them since grade school.

BASE 10 (DECIMAL) NOTATION

Humans generally deal with quantities in "base 10," in which numerals represent quantities of ones, tens, hundreds, thousands, and so on.[1] Numbers in base 10 are represented with the Hindu-Arabic digits 0 through 9; the numeral 235 represents a quantity of two hundred and thirty-five units. Each position in 235 has a certain "weight." The least-significant (rightmost) digit has a weight of 1, or 10^0; the most-significant (leftmost) digit has a weight of 100, or 10^2 (see Figure 3.1).

Figure 3.1   Base 10 Weights

---

[1]Why base 10? Count your fingers.

So the numeral 235 would break down as follows (right to left, or least to most significant digit):

Symbol	Weight	Quantity		Total
5	$10^0 = 1$	5×1	$=$	5
3	$10^1 = 10$	3×10	$=$	30
2	$10^2 = 100$	2×100	$=$	200
				235

BASE 2 (BINARY) NOTATION

Digital machines deal with a universe consisting of only two states: on or off, electrical current flowing or not flowing; theirs is a "binary" or base 2 universe. We have ten potential states in our decimal world, so we have ten discrete digits (0-9); when base 2 is represented using Hindu-Arabic numerals, only the first two digits are used: 0 and 1.

In a digital system, each digit of a binary number is called a "bit," short for binary digit. A bit is simply an on or off state, referenced to a specific point in time. Since a single bit can represent only two possible quantities (none or one), bits are generally grouped into "words," typically in groups of eight called "bytes" or "octets"[2]; a part of a byte (usually 4 bits) is called a "nibble." The bits in an 8-bit byte are numbered 0-7 (right to left), with the bit position numbers corresponding to the digit's weight. An 8-bit byte can represent 256 different quantities (0-255). As in base 10, the least-significant (rightmost) binary digit represents units: in base 2 this digit can denote only 0 or 1. Weights of digits in base 10 are powers of 10; weights in binary

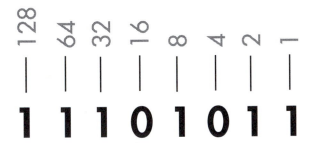

Figure 3.2   Base 2 Weights

---

[2]While the term byte is sometimes (and somewhat incorrectly) used to refer to a "word" of any number of bits, the term "octet" is more specific, and refers only to 8-bit words. For this reason, you will find it used in many network standards.

numbers are powers of 2, so the next digit to the left or the least-significant digit represents the quantity of 2s, the next the quantity of 4s, the next the quantity of 8s, and so on (see Figure 3.2).

The quantity of 235 units has a binary equivalent of 11101011, which breaks down as follows (right to left, or least to most significant digit):

Symbol	Weight	Quantity		Total
1	$2^0 = 1$	1×1	=	1
1	$2^1 = 2$	1×2	=	2
0	$2^2 = 4$	0×4	=	0
1	$2^3 = 8$	1×8	=	8
0	$2^4 = 16$	0×16	=	0
1	$2^5 = 32$	1×32	=	32
1	$2^6 = 64$	1×64	=	64
1	$2^7 = 128$	1×128	=	128
				235

BASE 16 (HEXADECIMAL) NOTATION

Since it is awkward for humans to think in terms of 8-bit bytes or octets, hexadecimal notation is often used, and "hex," as this notation is often called, is used extensively in this book. Hex is useful as an alternative way to represent 8-bit bytes because it is base 16 notation, and each binary nibble (4 bits) can range in value from 0 to 15 decimals. Since there are only ten symbols in the Hindu-Arabic number system, the letters A-F are used to represent digit positions 10-15, as shown in Table 3.1.

In hex, the least-significant digit represents—as with all the other bases—counts of 1 (16^0), the next representing counts of 16 (16^1), and so on (see Figure 3.3).

Figure 3.3 Base 16 Weights

Table 3.1   Decimal/Hex Digits

Decimal Digit	Hex Digit
0	0
1	1
2	2
3	3
4	4
5	5
6	6
7	7
8	8
9	9
10	A
11	B
12	C
13	D
14	E
15	F

The decimal quantity 235 is thus EB in hex and breaks down as follows:

Symbol	Weight	Quantity		Total
B	$16^0 = 1$	11 x 1	=	11
E	$16^1 = 16$	14 x 16	=	224
				235

I'm sure you're starting to get confused by now, so here are a few examples of some hex numbers:

Decimal	Hex
000	00
001	01
015	0F
016	10
127	7F
255	FF

Since 01 and 10 as shown above could be decimal, hex, or even binary, hex numbers are usually differentiated in some way. In this book, a small h is appended after hex numbers. So 01 in hex would be shown as 01h. In user's manuals, you may also see a notation like 0x01, where the 0x means the number following is in hex.[3] You may also see a capitol H instead of the lower case h, but they all mean the same thing: the number is hexadecimal.

BINARY-CODED DECIMAL NOTATION

In binary-coded decimal (BCD), 4-bit binary numbers represent base-10 *digits* (not values). For instance, the BCD representation of the decimal number 82 is 1000 0010, where the nibble 1000 represents 8, the original tens digit, and the second nibble 0010 represents 2, the units digit. (The higher possible binary values in each 4-bit nibble are not used, since they represent more than ten states.) While this notation is not very efficient since it leaves some bits unused, it is very useful in control system applications, where you want a few control lines to represent many possible combinations. For example, BCD switches use 8 control lines to represent up to 100 (0-99) different control combinations, and it's very easy to convert these signals from BCD into binary or decimal.

CONVERTING NUMBER BASES

Nowadays, it's easy to convert numbers from one format to another—many computers have built-in calculators that make doing this easy. But it's important to know how to convert from one base to another so that you understand it, and also in case you get stuck somewhere with no calculator.

Creating hex numbers from binary is quite simple: just determine the value represented by the least-significant nibble, and write the hex symbol denoting that value (0-Fh). Next, determine the value of the most-significant nibble and write that hex symbol to the left of the character you just wrote. For example, let's figure out the hex equivalent of the binary number 11101011. First break the byte into two nibbles:

Least-significant nibble: 1011

Most-significant nibble: 1110

The least-significant nibble, 1011, has a value of 1 ones, 1 twos, 0 fours, and 1 eights: $1 + 2 + 0 + 8 = 11$ (decimal). The symbol representing 11 in hex is B. Now let's analyze the most-significant nibble, 1110. It has a value of 0 +

---

[3]This 0x approach comes from the C programming language.

2 + 4 + 8 = 14, or E in hex. So the hex representation of 11101011 is EBh—our old friend 235.

What do we do if we want to convert hexadecimal numbers into binary? Let's find out by converting D4h. First, since we think in decimal, it's easiest to convert D4 to base 10. So, as shown before:

Symbol	Weight	Quantity		Total
4	$16^0 = 1$	4×1	=	4
D	$16^1 = 16$	13×16	=	208
				212 Decimal

Now, lets convert the decimal number 212 into binary. First, let's determine if an 8-bit byte can represent a number as big as 212. What is the biggest binary number we can represent with 8 bits (11111111)? Math tells us that it is 2^n-1, where *n* is the number of bits.[4] But let's look at that in a more intuitive way:

Symbol	Weight	Quantity		Total
1	$2^0 = 1$	1×1	=	1
1	$2^1 = 2$	1×2	=	2
1	$2^2 = 4$	1×4	=	4
1	$2^3 = 8$	1×8	=	8
1	$2^4 = 16$	1×16	=	16
1	$2^5 = 32$	1×32	=	32
1	$2^6 = 64$	1×64	=	64
1	$2^7 = 128$	1×128	=	128
				255

So an 8-bit byte can represent numbers up to 255, which is bigger than the 212 we're trying to convert. To make the conversion, we'll subtract out the biggest number possible, and proceed until there is nothing left from the subtraction.

First, let's determine the quantity represented by the most significant binary digit in our decimal number 212. In this case, we're dealing with an 8-bit byte, so the most significant digit has a weight of 128, and we can either

---

[4] We subtract 1 because 0 is a valid value. For example, 2^8 would be 256, so an 8-bit byte can represent 256 possible values. But since 0 is a valid value, the highest decimal value that can be represented by 8 bits is 256-1, or 255.

have 1 or 0 128s. Since 128 is less than 212, we'll subtract, and then progress through each binary digit.

$$212$$
$$\underline{-128}\ (2^7)$$
$$84$$

We now know that the most significant bit will be a 1, but we don't know the value of the other bits. So this gives us 1??????? and we can move on.

$$84$$
$$\underline{-64}\ (2^6)$$
$$20$$

This gives us 11??????. Now let's try the next most significant digit.

$$20$$
$$\underline{-32}\ (2^5)$$
$$??$$

Twenty, our remainder, is smaller than 32. So what quantity of 32s can we use to represent it? Zero. So this gives us 110?????, and now we can try the next most significant digit.

$$20$$
$$\underline{-16}\ (2^4)$$
$$4$$

Now we can subtract a quantity of one 16s, giving us a remainder of 4. So we now have 1101????, and we can move on to the next most significant digit.

$$4$$
$$\underline{-8}\ (2^3)$$
$$?$$

Eight is bigger than 4, so we get 0 eights, and we now have 11010???.

$$4$$
$$\underline{-4}\ (2^2)$$
$$0$$

With this subtraction of one 4s digit, we get 110101??. Since we have 0 left over, we don't need to do any more subtraction, and we can fill in the rest of the number with 0s, giving us 11010100.

So, we converted our hexadecimal number D4 into the decimal number 212, and that decimal number into the binary 11010100.

SAMPLE NUMBERS IN DIFFERENT FORMATS

Just to make sure you're not completely confused, Table 3.2 shows some examples of the same number represented using various schemes; a complete conversion list of numbers between 0 and 255 is included in Appendix A, "Useful Tables."

Table 3.2   Sample Numbers in Different Formats

Sample Numbers in Different Formats			
Decimal	*Binary*	*Hexadecimal*	*Binary-Coded Decimal*
231	11100111	E7	0010 0011 0001
137	10001001	89	0001 0011 0111
033	00100001	21	0000 0011 0011
085	01010101	55	0000 1000 0101
240	11110000	F0	0010 0100 0000
175	10101111	AF	0001 0111 0101
219	11011011	DB	0010 0001 1001
255	11111111	FF	0010 0101 0101
020	00010100	14	0000 0010 0000
070	01000110	46	0000 0111 0000

PART II

Data Communications

So far, we've discussed issues relating abstractly to control systems. Now we move on to digital data communications ("datacom") methods, which are fundamental building blocks of modern entertainment control systems. Other, larger industries have developed a huge number of datacom techniques and technologies, and so (as usual), the entertainment industry has adapted or adopted many of these for our purposes.

As of this writing, it is unfortunate that datacom concepts are rarely taught in traditional entertainment technology training programs. Although this situation is likely to change, many of these topics may be completely foreign to even accomplished entertainment industry technologists. If you haven't yet worked on a job site where Ethernet is ubiquitous, or had to control something via EIA-232, much of Part 2 may seem extraneous. But rest assured, if you stay in this industry, you will encounter datacom and networking technologies (if you haven't already), as more control systems—lighting, sound, scenery, pyrotechnics, show control—are networked every day.

If this is all new to you, please don't be intimidated. Some of the more difficult concepts presented in Part 2 may only make sense after you've absorbed later chapters and understood a particular datacom technology's application. (On the other hand, if you're already familiar with the topics discussed here, feel free to skip ahead.)

4

General Datacom Concepts

To attain data communication (the goal of much entertainment control), we need to move data from one point to another. By far the most common data communication technique is the transmission of electrical signals through wire; the use of other electromagnetic signals, such as light and radio, has also recently been on the rise. To get started, let's first cover some general concepts that apply to all datacom systems.

AMERICAN STANDARD CODE FOR INFORMATION INTERCHANGE (ASCII)

To allow systems to communicate, we must first agree on the way that machines model and represent the physical world. The digital control standards covered in this book describe how commands and data specific to entertainment applications are coded. For instance, in one standard, called MIDI Show Control (MSC), the following sequence of bytes in hex,

```
F0  7F  0A  02  10  01  32  37  F7
```

tells Device number 10 to execute a Sound Format Cue 27 "Go" Command. The meanings of these bytes were determined and agreed upon by the creators of the MIDI Show Control standard, and by the creators of MIDI, upon which MSC is based. The MSC standard committee also decided to use a computer-industry standard for representing the cue-number component of the message: the bytes that represent cue 27 (32h and 37h) are encoded using the American Standard Code for Information Interchange (ASCII).

ASCII is an assignment of numbers representing text characters and computer control signals. ASCII is basically a grown-up version of the game you may have played as a child: substituting numbers for letters of the alphabet so that you could send coded messages.

To send the text message "show control" in ASCII, the following hex numbers would be used:

```
73 68 6F 77 20 63 6F 6E 74 72 6F 6C
s  h  o  w     c  o  n  t  r  o  l
```

A listing of the ASCII character set, along with decimal, hex, and binary equivalents, is in Appendix A, "Useful Tables."

BANDWIDTH

Whatever the communications medium, there is always some limit as to how much data a single communications connection or "channel" can handle; this capacity is known as the channel's bandwidth. Since a full-color television broadcast signal contains more information and occupies more of the radio frequency spectrum than an audio-only radio signal, the TV channel is said to require more bandwidth. In data communications, since bandwidth usually limits how fast information can be sent, it determines how much information can be sent in a given period of time.

BITS PER SECOND

A digital data link carries a binary stream of 1s and 0s. The rate of transmission is known as the "data rate," which is measured in bits per second (bps or b/s) (see Figure 4.1).

You may encounter the term "Baud"[1] rate in the world of datacom. Baud actually refers to the number of "signaling units" per second, and since a signaling unit could consist of more than 1 bit, the Baud rate of a communication link could be different than the link's bps. For this reason, bps will be used throughout this book.

---

[1] Named after Maurice Emile Baudot, who invented a five-bit teletype code in *1874!*

1 Bit Period

Figure 4.1 Bits Per Second (100 bps Shown)

MULTIPLEXING

One way to get more information over a single channel is to "multiplex" the data. There are three primary forms of multiplexing: space division, time division, and frequency division.

Space Division

Space-division multiplexing is the way your local phone company connects many local lines to a single long-distance line. Since not every local line needs access to the long-distance circuit at all times, the phone company can have fewer long-distance lines and connect a local circuit to a long-distance channel only when required. The long-distance line space is thereby multiplexed.

Frequency Division

In frequency-division multiplexing, multiple channels of information, each modulated at a different frequency, are sent over a single communications link. For example, in the case of cable television: hundreds of channels are sent over a single coaxial cable from the central office to your home. Each channel is modulated at a different frequency, so the link is frequency-multiplexed.

Time Division

In time-division multiplexing, multiple communications channels are each chopped into time slices, which are sent sequentially over a single link and reassembled into discrete channels on the receiving end. In other words, each channel occupies the data link for some fraction of the total time available. For instance, four 300-bps channels could be sent over a single 1200-bps link if each channel occupied the multiplexed link a quarter of the time.[2] Obviously, the multiplexed data link must have a faster information-transfer rate than the sum of the individual channels.

POINT-TO-POINT OR MULTIPOINT/MULTIDROP

A "point-to-point" connection is one where devices are directly connected together. In "multipoint" or "multidrop" communications, multiple stations share a common connection, and communications can either be "broadcast," with one transmitter and many receivers, or multiple transmitters can be connected. In such a multitransmitter link, "contention" issues (who gets to speak when) must be resolved.

COMMUNICATIONS MODE

A communications link can be designed to operate in one or more modes, transmitting data in one direction only, one direction at a time, or both directions simultaneously.

Simplex

A simplex communications link allows a transmitter to send information in one direction and one direction only. The receiver can only listen and not reply. A cue light in a theatrical situation (described in the cueing section of Chapter 1) is an example of simplex communications: the stage manager who turns the cue light on can send a message (cue light on or off) using the cue light, but the operator has no way to respond.

Half-Duplex

In a half-duplex link, two parties can speak to each other over the same link, but only one party can speak at a time. A pair of handheld walkie-talkies works in half-duplex mode: you can talk to someone else on the radio, but you can't hear while you're talking. Conversely, you can't talk while you are listening.

Full-Duplex

Full-duplex means that two parties can both talk at the same time. A telephone uses a full-duplex link: while you are speaking, you can hear the other party, and vice-versa.

---

[2]Not counting communications overhead, of course.

BASEBAND OR BROADBAND

In a communications link, there are two basic ways of transmitting data down the line: "baseband" and "broadband." Using baseband communications, the data stream is transmitted directly on the transmission line, with the signal going on or off with each 0 or 1 being transmitted. For example, on an electrical link, this might mean that a voltage of 5 volts indicates a 1, while no voltage means 0.[3]

In broadband communications, the 1 or 0 "modulates" some other signal, which actually carries the data on the transmission link, and a link might carry multiple channels simultaneously. The receiver then "demodulates" the signal, recovering the original 1s and 0s of the data stream. A device capable of modulating and demodulating information is known as a "modem," short for modulator/demodulator.

TRANSMISSION/MODULATION METHODS

There are many schemes to transmit digital 1s and 0s from one system to another. A few you're likely to encounter in the entertainment industry are included here.

Non-Return to Zero

Non-Return to Zero (NRZ) is one of the most common communication methods, with two different voltages representing the 1 or 0 bits (see Figure 4.2). For instance, no volts could represent a 0 bit, and +5V could represent a 1 bit. More common in data communications interfaces is a scheme where a negative voltage represents a 1, and a positive voltage represents 0. If a long string of 1s or 0s is sent using NRZ encoding, the signal can remain at one voltage level for a period of time, and this will mean that the signal will have a direct current (DC) component. DC can cause problems for some transmission devices such as transformers (which can not pass DC). To solve this problem, other schemes have been developed.

Manchester

"Manchester" encoding solves this DC problem by guaranteeing that the voltage will swing back through 0 within a given period of time, and that

---

[3] In many practical datacom systems, a binary zero is represented by a positive voltage, with a binary one represented by zero or less volts. This often confuses beginners, however, so for clarity in this book (and many datacom books), a binary one is represented by a positive signal, and a binary zero by a zero or negative signal.

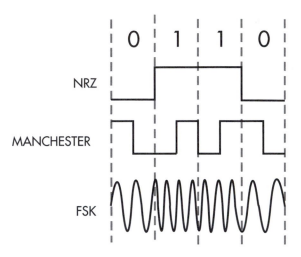

Figure 4.2   Some Common Data-Encoding Schemes Found in Entertainment Control

there is a signal transition in the middle of every bit period. While there is no single official standard for Manchester, in the implementation used in many networks, if that middle transition goes low to high, it represents a binary 1; a high-to-low transition indicates a binary 0 (see Figure 4.2). These transitions allow a receiver to synchronize to a transmitter, and they can also act as an additional error check—if there is no transition, the receiver will know something went wrong. Manchester encoding is the core of some implementations of Ethernet (described in detail in Chapter 24).

Bi-Phase

While Manchester encoding is a form of "bi-phase" modulation, there is another form used in the SMPTE Time Code standard (described in detail in Chapter 17 below) which uses a transition from high to low or low to high at the start (and because bits are trailed together, at the end) of every bit. A bit with no internal transitions is a 0; a transition within a bit time denotes a 1 (see Figure 17.2). In this bi-phase coding scheme, the polarity is irrelevant, and the signal can be read backwards as well as forwards.

Frequency Shift Keying

In Frequency Shift Keying (FSK), digital data is used to modulate the frequency of some analog carrier. For a bit with a value of 1, a particular frequency is transmitted; for a 0 bit, a different frequency is transmitted (see Figure 4.2). In entertainment control systems, this modulation method is often used to record digital data as an audio signal.

ERROR CORRECTION

No communications link is perfect; there is always some probability of error occurring in the transmission. Whether caused by noisy lighting dimmers or background radiation, errors can be corrected—or detected—in a number of ways.

Parity

In the simplest form of error correction, known as parity checking, the transmitter adds a bit to each byte, making the arithmetic total of the byte's bits either even or odd, depending on the parity type (which is determined by the system designer and configured into the system). The parity-containing byte is sent to the receiver, which sums the bits, checking to see if the sum is even or odd. If the sum is not what the receiver has been configured for, it can ask for retransmission or discard the byte; if the sum is correct, it assumes that the data was received intact. (Obviously, both receiver and transmitter must be set for the same operational mode for this approach to work properly.)

This technique will be easier to understand if we look at an example. The arithmetic sum of the bits in the byte 10111001 is 5, an odd number. If the transmitter is set for even parity, it would add a parity bit with a value of 1 to this byte: 10111001**1**. This brings the sum of the bits to 6, an even number. If the data traveled over the communications link intact, the receiver (previously set for even parity) would sum its received byte, determine that the total was even, and accept the byte as valid. If the transmitter were set for odd parity, it would add a parity bit of 0 to this same byte, leaving the sum odd: 10111001**0**.

Neither even nor odd parity has an inherent performance advantage, although the internal workings of some systems make it easier to use one type of parity or the other. Parity, no matter which type, adds 1 bit of overhead to every 8-bit byte, and this will occupy 12 percent of the transmitted signal's bandwidth.

Parity is simple to implement, but at a cost: parity checking can detect only an odd number of bit errors. To see why, assume that the byte shown above is transmitted using odd parity and a single bit gets corrupted along the way. Here 1 bit (which is *italicized*) is corrupted: 10*0*110010. The receiver catches this single bit error because the sum of the received byte is 4, an even total; since the receiver is configured for odd parity, it was expecting an odd total. Here's the same byte with 2 bit errors: 1001110. When the receiver adds the bits in the corrupted byte, it gets an odd sum, 5, so it assumes that the data has been correctly transmitted, which is not the case. It can be proven that parity-based error correction is incapable of detecting any even number of corrupted bits. However, parity is still useful since it is simple to implement and should catch at least 50 percent of errors. If a system designer has reason to believe that data corruption is highly unlikely to occur, and if the consequences of a receiver acting incorrectly on corrupted data are not severe (i.e., an LED sign in a retail store), then parity error correction is useful.

Checksum

A more complicated, but more effective, error-correction scheme is the "checksum." With this approach, the transmitter sums a block of data bytes and sends the checksum total along with the data:

```
 10010100
 11110111
 01101000
111110011  Checksum
```

The receiver adds the value of the received block of bytes (not including the transmitted checksum) and compares the checksum it has calculated with the sum transmitted along with the block. If the two numbers agree, the receiver assumes that the transmission of the block was good. If the checksum does not agree, then the receiver can alert the transmitter or ignore the corrupt data.

While a checksum approach is more effective than parity schemes, checksums still can't catch all errors. For instance, if these same 3 data bytes somehow arrived at the receiver out of order, the checksum would still come out the same. Also, if there were 2 single-bit errors in the same bit in 2 bytes, the checksum would remain the same:

```
 10010110  Error
 11110101  Error
 01101000
111110011  Checksum still the same, although 2 bytes
           in the block are different
```

Another drawback of checksums is that they can be larger than any of the data bytes (as in our examples above, where the checksum was 9 bits long). Such a checksum would either have to be transmitted over several bytes, or bits would have to be discarded, compromising the checksum's accuracy.

Cyclic Redundancy Check

The Cyclic Redundancy Check (CRC) is an extremely effective error-detection method, with nearly 100 percent accuracy. While the concept of CRC error correction is fairly simple, the theories explaining its efficacy involve complex mathematical proofs well beyond the scope of this book.

CRC codes are somewhat similar to checksums, except that the data to be checked is treated as a continuous block of bits instead of a series of digital words to be summed. This data block is divided by a "generator" value, which produces a quotient and a remainder; the remainder is the check value. Because of the properties of the specially selected divisor, the remainder for any given block is one of a huge number of possible check values; the probability that both pure and corrupted data would generate the same checksum is extremely low. This is what gives CRC its nearly 100 percent accuracy for single-bit errors (slightly less for multi-bit errors).

CRC has other advantages besides accuracy. In CRC division, the remainder is always shorter than the divisor, so the size of the check value is predictable; this is a major advantage in the rigidly structured datacom world. In addition, the CRC code can be calculated for huge blocks of data, rather than only a single byte at a time, so it is very efficient.

FLOW CONTROL

In a data link, the transmitter might not be able to blindly send data forever, because the receiver may have limited processing capacity and can "overflow," causing data to be lost. For this reason, the receiver should be able to signal the transmitter when to stop and start transmission—a process known as flow control.

There are two types of flow control: hardware and software. In hardware flow control, additional control lines are run between the receiver and transmitter; when the receiver's buffer starts filling up, it signals the transmitter to halt transmission. Once the receiver is ready to accept data again, it signals the transmitter to restart. In software flow control, specially designated characters act as start and stop signals. One common approach to software flow control, known as XON/XOFF, uses the ASCII control character DC3 (13h) to instruct the transmitter to stop sending and DC1 (11h) to instruct it to start again. For reasons of data-link efficiency, however, hardware flow control is generally preferable.

Today, flow control is less critical for many applications than it was in the past. Modern devices are often equipped with large data input "buffers," which store excess incoming data until the receiver's processor can deal with it. Data rates today are also generally fast in comparison to the amount of data typically sent and slow in comparison to typical processing horsepower. But a system designer should still be careful and not make casual assumptions about whether or not flow control is required.

5

Physical Communications Media

Many types of physical media are used for the purposes of communicating data, and each has advantages and disadvantages for a particular application. Electrical signals can be used to send data signals over wire, light can be used to send signals through the air or through fiber-optic cables, and radio waves can transmit information through the ether. Increasingly, control protocols and procedures operate independently from the "physical" transmission (as we'll see in subsequent chapters).

ELECTRICITY

The most common physical communications method is the transmission of a voltage or a current over a wire, with the state of the voltage or current representing the data signal. This approach is cheap, reliable, well understood, and easy to install and troubleshoot. Two general schemes are used to transmit the electrical signals: voltage loop and current loop.

Voltage Loop or Current Loop

To indicate a particular state to a receiver, a transmitter uses either the presence or absence of voltage or the flow of current. "Voltage-loop" interfaces—where a certain voltage indicates a particular state—are common and well defined. In order to ensure successful data transmission (and to avoid equipment damage), the voltage, polarity, and other characteristics of a voltage loop interface must be agreed upon, and there are a number of internationally recognized voltage-loop standards (see the EIA standards in Chapter 6). Voltage loops are the most common way to send data electrically over a wire.

"Current-loop" interfaces have not been as formally standardized, although there is an informal standard: a flowing current of 20 milliamps (mA) equals a logical 1; the absence of current equals a logical 0. Since current can't exist without voltage (and vice versa), voltage is of course present on current loops, but the precise voltage is only important in that it allows the proper current to be delivered. Current loops have some advantages over voltage loops: they interface easily with opto-isolated equipment and are highly immune to Electro-Magnetic Interference (EMI), since the currents induced by EMI are very low relative to the signaling levels.

Single-Ended or Differential

There are two primary voltage loop transmission schemes: single-ended or differential (see Figure 5.1). In single-ended transmission, all lines in the

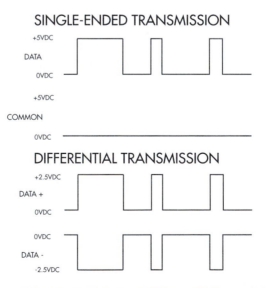

Figure 5.1   Single-Ended and Differential Transmission

communications link, both data and control, share a common ground, to which all signals are referenced. If EMI induces voltage on a line, this noise is simply summed into the data stream, and this can confuse the circuitry in the receiver.

In differential transmission, the signal is sent in opposite polarity over a pair of wires, and the receiver looks at the *difference* in potential (hence differential) between the two wires, irrespective of ground. Differential lines are also known (particularly in audio) as "balanced," while single-ended lines are called "unbalanced." Differential transmission lines are more robust, but they cost more (two pieces of wire are required for every line) and require more transmitting and receiving components.

Wire and Cable Types

We've talked so far about how electrical signals are transmitted; we'll move on now to the media over which those signals travel: wire (a single conductor) and cable (an assembly of wires). Selecting an appropriate cable is a seemingly simple task, but is something that system designers often spend a considerable amount of time doing, especially when dealing with the transmission of unfamiliar signals. Cable cost is a factor, but a bigger factor—particularly in a permanent installation—is labor, and installing or running the wrong cable can lead to system problems and costly mistakes and re-pulls. Quality cable manufacturers offer application support, and you should use it; cable manufacturers design their products with specific applications in mind, and you should be sure to choose a cable carefully. Entire books have been written on the subject of wire and cable (see the Bibliography), and we can only cover the basics here.

The simplest type of cable consists of cheap, unshielded, untwisted wires, as you might find connecting a doorbell. However, since this type of cable is very susceptible to EMI, and since the signals used in data transmission are relatively small, this type of cable should not be used for data transmission. Twisted-pair cable, made of two pieces of wire twisted tightly together, is more appropriate for datacom, because it is immune to magnetically induced currents. Twisted-pair cable is, however, susceptible to "common-mode" voltages—those induced equally on both conductors. Common-mode voltages however, can be effectively rejected by well-designed differential communications, so twisted pair cable works well for differential communications—and is cheap, effective, and easy to install. This type of twisted-pair cable, without a shield, is called Unshielded Twisted Pair, or UTP.

Adding a shield—such as metal foil or a braid of tiny conductors—makes twisted pair cable less vulnerable to noise; the shield conducts EMI-induced voltages straight to ground. This type of cable is known as Shielded Twisted Pair, or STP.

Coaxial cable, or "coax," consists of a center conductor surrounded by a coaxial shield and is very robust. Capable of very high bandwidth operation, it has been the choice for everything from cable TV systems to local area networks. Because it is difficult to manufacture, coax is relatively expensive, and the coaxial structure makes the cable more difficult to terminate. For these reasons, engineers in recent years have developed ways to push phenomenal amounts of data through simple twisted pair cable, and the use of coax for networking and datacom applications has been declining.

TIA/EIA Cable Categories

In recent years, much of the wire and cable industry's focus has shifted to the explosion of networking equipment, and the TIA and EIA have standardized cable types into "Categories" 1-5.

Category 1 is unshielded twisted pair cable for "Plain Old Telephone Service" or POTS. The cable impedance is not standardized, and data rates are typically up to 20kbps. These days, this type is primarily found in "legacy," or previously installed, applications.

Category 2 is UTP cable at any impedance, up to 4Mbps.

Category 3 is either UTP or STP, a standardized impedance of 100Ω, and data rates up to 10Mbps.

Category 4 is either UTP or STP, impedance of 100Ω, and data rates up to 16Mbps.

Category 5 is the standard cable run in countless networking installations and systems today, and is the most common cable type used for Ethernet. "Cat 5" cable comes in both UTP and STP varieties, has an impedance of 100Ω, was specified to run up to 100Mbps, and is made up of four twisted pairs. In addition to the specifications of cable, Category 5 also has standardized installation practices. All hardware used must be rated for Cat 5; the maximum length of wire that can be untwisted is specified, as is the bend radius; and many other criteria. Installing a critical Cat 5 cable system is not something that a casual user should attempt; there are many contractors who have experience with it, and good contractors also have the test equipment needed to certify the installation.

RJ-45 Connectors

We'll discuss the connectors used by each type of standard as we cover it, but there is a series of connectors that is becoming so ubiquitous today that it warrants mention here: the RJ-45 (see Figure 5.2).

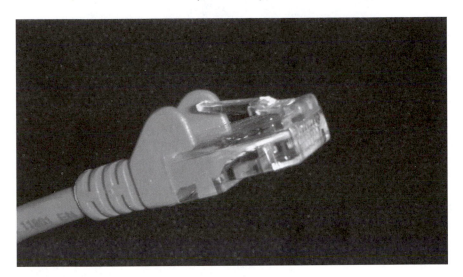

Figure 5.2   RJ-45 Connector on Category 5 Cable (Photo by Charles Scott)

RJ stands for "registered jack." The RJ series connector was developed by the telecommunications industry, and it is now used to carry everything from low- and high-speed data to plain old telephone services. The RJ-45 has eight pins and can carry four pairs of wire, and it is a slightly bigger version of the "modular" phone connectors (RJ-11) used on home telephones. They are made of easily-shattered plastic and are not well suited to the backstage environment. However, they are extremely cheap and can be easily installed in a few seconds with "crimping" tools. Some available varieties of these connectors have small ramps on either side of the release tab (see Figure 5.2), protecting them when a cable is pulled through a tangle. These are highly recommended for entertainment applications, as the release tab can easily break off.

TIA/EIA-568A Cabling Standard

TIA/EIA-568A specifies a "structured" layout of network wiring in a building. TIA/EIA-568 has been recommended by the Control Protocol Working Group of the Entertainment Services and Technology Association (ESTA) for entertainment networking installations. This standard is very complex, but, basically, 568 takes a typical multistory office building and breaks its cable runs into "vertical" and "horizontal" lines. Vertical cables are high-bandwidth "backbones" that connect, through network distribution systems, to a floor's individual "horizontal" lines. The horizontal cables are sometimes run through air handling plenums, so a type of cable for this application is often called "plenum" cable. The vertical cables often run through cable risers in buildings, and because they run vertically, "riser" cable must have a high fire-resistance rating. Further details of the 568 standard are outside the scope of this book, but you should investigate the details if you are installing networking cables into your facility.

LIGHT

Instead of sending electrons over wire to send data, it is possible to send a beam of light either through the air or over a piece of glass or plastic fiber. Light is turned on or off to represent the data being transmitted.

Fiber Optics

While sending light through the air is often useful (as in infrared remote controllers), it is typically more useful in control system applications to send light through a glass or plastic cable known as "fiber optic." Light travels down a length of fiber-optic cable by bouncing back and forth off the boundary edge between the center glass or plastic and the air, or between the center and a jacket known as the cladding or buffer (see Figure 5.3). Fiber comes in two types: multimode and single mode. Multimode allows multiple "modes" or pathways for the light to bounce. Single mode

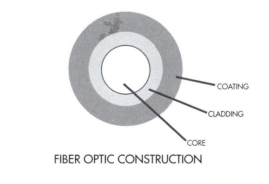

FIBER OPTIC CONSTRUCTION

MULTI-MODE LIGHT TRANSMISSION

Figure 5.3   Fiber-Optic Construction and Multimode Light Transmission

allows fewer possible pathways for the light beam, which leads to less bounces, which in turn leads to less loss. These characteristics allow extremely high bandwidth, but single-mode fiber is much more difficult to terminate, needs more accurate end alignment, and is, therefore, more expensive to use.

Because fiber transmits light, fiber-optic data links are completely immune to all forms of electrical interference. Potential bandwidth in fiber is extremely high, but this high bandwidth and noise immunity comes at a price: compared to wire, fiber-optic cable is expensive and difficult to terminate. In recent years, fiber has become more common, and easier to terminate, but, as of this writing, it is typically installed only when high bandwidth or extreme noise immunity is required.

RADIO

In recent years, data transmission via radio, something once only done by high-end users like the military, has become common even in the entertainment industry. "Radio modems," which accept digital data and retransmit it over radio waves, are now commonly available and can be used to connect a variety of computers. Radio modems using "Spread Spectrum" technologies take a single data stream and spread it across many possible radio transmission paths. This approach makes it much more robust and resistant to interference, and since backstage is typically a hostile environment for RF (radio frequency) signals (with wireless mics, handheld radios, multiple RF noise sources, etc.), this type of transmission works well in entertainment data applications. However, because of radio interference, no RF link is as robust as wire or fiber-optic links.

6

Point-to-Point Interfaces

Now that we've covered all the basics, we can finally get into the details of some real data communications standards and start talking about ways to actually interface machines. I've broken down data communications in this book into two groups: point-to-point and network. The lines between the two get blurry in some instances, but generally, point-to-point interfaces are meant for connecting two, or a few, devices together in a point-to-point fashion. Networks (covered later in Part 5) are more generic connection methods used to connect two through a large number (or almost infinite number with the Internet) of stations.

INTERFACE TYPES

There are two basic ways to send data over a communications link: parallel and serial.

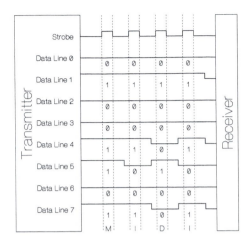

Figure 6.1 Parallel Data Transmission

Parallel

The simplest way to connect two digital devices is through a group of wires—one for each bit transmitted across the interface. An additional wire, known as a strobe line, indicates to the receiver when the transmitter is ready to have its data read. When data is sent using this technique, transmission is said to be in "parallel." Figure 6.1 shows the ASCII text "MIDI" being transmitted across an 8-bit parallel interface.

Parallel communications are fast and efficient. However, parallel transmission requires a large number of wires, which is expensive when data must be sent over significant distances. For this reason, parallel interfaces are used primarily for short-haul communications, such as connecting a computer and printer.

One older interface for parallel printer communications is the "Centronics" interface, which uses bidirectional, twisted pairs to send each of the 8 bits. See Figure 6.2 for a pin out of this interface.

Another common parallel interface is the 25-pin female "D" connector used on IBM PCs and compatibles. This common parallel interface is actually available in several varieties. The original Standard Parallel Port (SPP) version was based on the Centronics interface. The PS/2 type port (PS/2 was an IBM series of PCs) added bidirectional capabilities. The Enhanced Parallel Port, or EPP, is a faster version of the PS/2 type of port, able to work very quickly, at the speed of the PC's Industry Standard Architecture (ISA) bus. The most recent version, the Extended Capabilities Port (ECP), has built-in hardware buffers and data compression. Most newer ports are backwards compatible and can emulate older interfaces. See Figure 6.3 for the control signals.

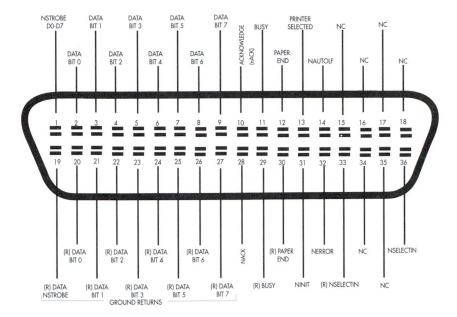

Figure 6.2 Centronics Parallel Interface Signals Commonly Used for PCs (Male Connector Shown)

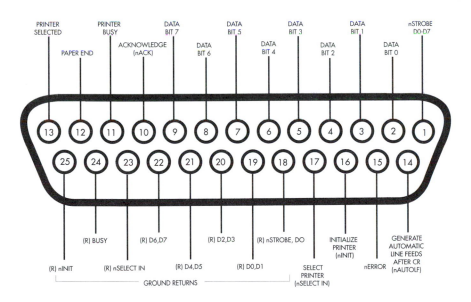

Figure 6.3 IBM PC and Compatible Parallel Interface Signals (Female Connector Shown)

Serial

Instead of sending all the bits simultaneously in parallel over a group of wires, it is also possible to send bits "serially," one after the other, over a single communications line. Serial communications are ideal for longer-haul applications, or any application for which a large number of wires is not practical. While parallel interfaces have a strobe line to indicate when the receiver should read the data, serial interfaces instead require that the transmitter and receiver agree on a timing, or synchronization, scheme.

The simplest form of serial communication is the synchronous serial link, where the clocks of both the receiver and the transmitter are locked precisely in sync. Figure 6.4 shows the synchronous transmission of the ASCII text "Ren."

The easiest way to lock the clocks of the transmitter and receiver together is to run additional synchronization lines from the transmitter to the receiver, delivering clock pulses between the two. But doing so defeats one of the primary advantages of serial communications, because additional wires are required. A synchronous link is indeed possible without external clock lines: if the data is sent according to certain conditions agreed on by both the transmitter and the receiver, the receiver can actually derive its bit-timing clock from the incoming data stream itself. However, both ends of the link must have a certain amount of sophistication, which can be costly and complicated to implement. Another solution is to run the link "asynchronously."

In asynchronous communications, the receiver's clock essentially starts and stops (in other words, "resyncs" itself) at the beginning of each and every byte. To enable the receiver to detect the beginning of a byte, the transmitter adds a 0 "start" bit to the beginning of each data byte, and a 1 "stop" bit to the end of each byte. Figure 6.5 depicts a typical asynchronous link sending the text "Ren," encoded using ASCII.

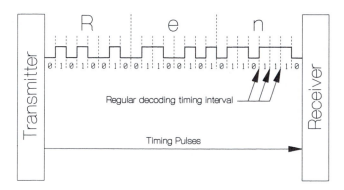

Figure 6.4 Synchronous Serial Data Transmission

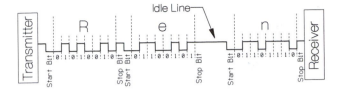

Figure 6.5 Asynchronous Serial Data Transmission

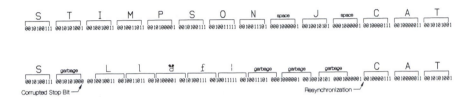

Figure 6.6 Asynchronous Resynchronization after Single-Bit Corruption

The receiver can synchronize itself to this "asynchronous" signal because the start/stop-bit structure *guarantees* a transition from 1 to 0 at the beginning of every byte, even if data bytes contain all 1s or all 0s. This is true because at the end of each byte, the stop bit returns the line to the "mark," or 1, condition—the state in which most asynchronous serial links idle.

Of course, this scheme works only if both the transmitter and receiver are set for exactly the same parameters: bps, parity, start-bit enabled, and the correct number of stop bits. Anyone who has ever fooled around with a modem has certainly seen the result of improperly configured asynchronous serial communications (a continuous stream of secret Martian instructions).

The start- and stop-bit scheme also allows the link to resync itself if the data is corrupted, since the receiver doesn't pass on data unless a stop bit (typically a binary 1) validates the byte (see Figure 6.6).[1]

The first line in Figure 6.6 shows a clean transmission; the second line shows what happens when noise corrupts the second byte's stop bit. The second byte is discarded, since it is missing a stop bit. The system starts counting bits after the next one-zero transition (falling edge of the start bit) and incorrectly decodes the third byte as an "L." This continues with several apparently valid characters, and then the system discards 3 apparent bytes in a row, because, coincidentally, they seem to be lacking valid stop bits. Finally, after the second "Space" character, the system locks back in sync, and "CAT" is correctly decoded. An asynchronous link will eventually

---

[1] In most systems, the most-significant bit is sent first, but this drawing depicts the least significant bit first for clarity.

resync itself, but how long it takes depends on the random placement of the bits. More stop bits generally allow faster resynchronization.

TIA/EIA SERIAL STANDARDS

Some of the most widely used computer interface standards are the Telecommunications Industry Association (TIA) and Electronics Industry Association (EIA) standards for serial communications. There are a huge number of incompatible implementations of these standards, because there are varying levels of implementation sophistication: just because two pieces of gear have "standard" serial ports in no way means that the machines will be able to communicate, at least not without some interfacing work and possibly even additional hardware.

These standards describe only the electrical connections between equipment; they do not dictate the number of bits in a word, the method of error correction, how many start/stop bits, or other parameters critical to successful communication. As a result, the interfaces are extremely flexible; but with this flexibility comes confusion.

DTE and DCE

This group of EIA standards was designed, years before the advent of the PC, to connect Data Terminal Equipment (DTE), such as "dumb" computer terminals, with Data Circuit-terminating Equipment (DCE), such as modems. These acronyms, while brilliantly designed to be as confusing as possible, are important to understand, since the standards are designed only to allow DTE devices to communicate with DCE devices, and vice versa.

EIA-232

The EIA-232 standard is by far the most prevalent point-to-point serial standard in use today, and is officially titled, "Interface Between Data Terminal Equipment and Data Circuit-Terminating Equipment Employing Serial Binary Data Interchange (ANSI/TIA/EIA-232-F-1997)." As of this writing, the standard has been revised six times, hence the F. EIA-232 is a single-ended, voltage-loop interface, and is limited in application to systems with data rates less than 20,000 bps (20 kbps). While the cable length is not defined in the standard, a typical maximum length is 50 feet or less. The standard was originally developed in 1962, and up through the "C" version was known (and is still known by many) as "Recommended Standard" or

"RS" 232. Now, the standard is officially known as EIA/TIA-232. For the sake of simplicity, in this book EIA-232 will be used.

In EIA-232, the voltage polarities are the opposite of what you might expect. A logical one, called a "mark" value, is any negative voltage between –3 and –25 V with respect to ground. Logical zero, called a space, is any positive voltage between +3 and +25 V. When the line is idle, it is held in the mark, or negative voltage, state. Just to confuse things even more, control lines are inverse in sense to data lines: a control line's true condition is any voltage from +3 to +25 V; control false is any voltage from –3 to –25 V.

There are 25 lines designated in EIA-232, and a D-shaped, 25-pin connector is widely used. According to the specifications, DTE uses male connectors and DCE uses female. The control signals of a 25-pin connector are shown in Figure 6.7.

EIA-232 allows for synchronous communications (through the timing lines) and a wide variety of flow-control options. For asynchronous connections, a subset of the 25 lines is generally sufficient. This subset was implemented by IBM on its AT (for mode number) computers in a 9-pin connector; Figure 6.8 shows the control signals.

These 9 pins (or less) really form the heart of EIA-232 for asynchronous applications. Transmitted Data (TD or TX) is the line on which the DTE sends data to the DCE; Received Data (RD or RX) is the line used by the

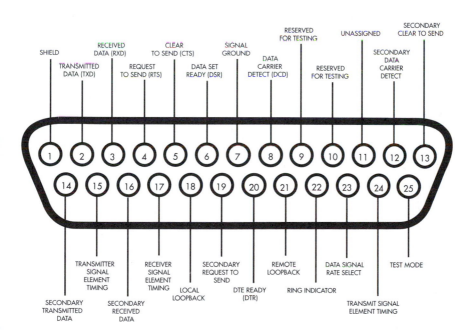

Figure 6.7 Interface Signals of 25-Pin Implementation of EIA-232 (Male Connector Shown)

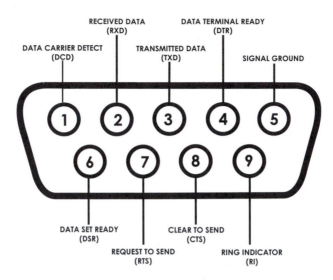

Figure 6.8 Interface Signals of 9-Pin Implementation of EIA-232 (Male Connector Shown)

DCE to send data back to the DTE. Signal Ground is the common point for all the data and control lines in this single-ended link. DCE Ready indicates to the DTE that the DCE is powered up and ready; DTE Ready indicates to the DCE that the DTE is ready. Request to Send (RTS) is used by the DTE to indicate to the DCE that it would like to send some data; Clear To Send (CTS) is the DCE's response.[2]

EIA-423

The most notable drawbacks of EIA-232 are its limited link distance and, perhaps most important for entertainment control applications, its inability to connect more than one receiver to a single transmitter. Another EIA standard, TIA/EIA-423-B, titled, "Electrical Characteristics of Unbalanced Voltage Digital Interface Circuits (ANSI/TIA/EIA-423-B-96)," deals with some of these problems. Older Apple Macintosh® computers are one place an entertainment technician is likely to encounter this interface, but new machines no longer have this port.

Like EIA-232, EIA-423 is a single-ended system, but can interface easily with differential receivers, since unlike 232, 423 can broadcast its data to up

---

[2]I know all this DTE/DCE nonsense is confusing, but you might as well get used to it. This is not the last time you will encounter these acronyms in this book and especially in the real world!

to ten receivers and uses voltages of –3.6 to –6 V for mark and +3.6 to +6 V for space. The data line can typically run about 4000 feet, depending on the data rate, cable, and so on. Due to the fact that EIA-423 uses lower voltages than 232 but runs at the same slew rate,[3] 423 can be used to send data at rates up to 100 kbps. EIA-423 has some disadvantages for industrial communications; chief among these is its single-ended nature, which makes it more susceptible to noise. The EIA recognized this limitation and created two differential serial interfaces: EIA-422 and EIA-485.

EIA-422

In EIA-422-B, "Electrical Characteristics of Balanced Voltage Digital Interface Circuits (ANSI/TIA/EIA-422-B-94)," a binary 0 is between +2 and +6 V; binary 1 is between –2 and –6 V. However, EIA-422 is a differential standard, with two "balanced" wires for each data line. Like 423, EIA-422 has a typical working length of about 4000 feet (as usual, limited by data rate, cable type, etc.) and can broadcast to up to ten receivers. However, because the differential structure offers better noise immunity and common-mode rejection, 422 can be used for data rates up to 10 million bps (10 Mbps). Connectors are not standardized in 422.

EIA-485

TIA/EIA-485-A, "Electrical Characteristic of Generators and Receivers for Use in Balanced Digital Multipoint System," has many of the same specifications as EIA-422, with one key difference: EIA-485 allows 32 transmitters and 32 receivers. EIA-485 uses lower voltages than any of the other general-purpose EIA serial standards: voltages between +1.5 and +6 V is 0 (space), and from –1.5 to –6 V is binary 1 (mark). But EIA-485 has the same maximum data rate as EIA-422: 10 Mbps. EIA-485 is the foundation for a number of the standards in this book, including DMX512, SMX, and others. As in 422, connectors are not standardized in 485.

Comparison of EIA Recommended Standards

Each of the general-purpose EIA Recommended Standards is suited to different applications, and each has strengths and weaknesses. The determining factors include cost, noise immunity, and data transmission rate. Table 6.1 summarizes the features of each standard.

---

[3] Slew Rate is the rate of change in an electrical signal (usually in volts per ms).

Table 6.1 Comparison of EIA Standards[4]

	EIA-232	*EIA-423*	*EIA-422*	*EIA-485*
Mode	Single-Ended	Single-Ended	Differential	Differential
Drivers	1	1	1	32
Receivers	1	10	10	32
Typical Maximum Link Distance	50	4000	4000	4000
Data Rate	20kbps	100kbps	10Mbps	10Mbps
Mark (1) Voltage	–3 to –25	–3.6 to –6	–2 to –6	–1.5 to –6
Space (0) Voltage	+3 to +25	+3.6 to +6	+2 to +6	+1.5 to +6

[4]Basic table structure borrowed from *Data Communications*, William Schweber, McGraw-Hill, 1988.

Connecting DTE to DTE (Null Modem)

Although this series of standards was designed for connecting DTE devices to DCE devices, today, the lines between those two categories is fuzzy. For example, we often want to connect two computers together, and computers typically have DTE ports. For devices to communicate properly, the data transmit and receive lines, and, possibly, some other control lines, have to be swapped. An adaptor that does this is called a "null modem." See Figure

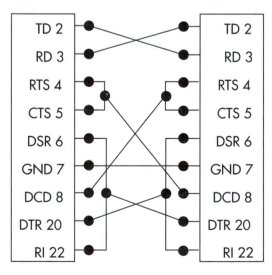

Figure 6.9 Connecting Two 25-Pin DTE Devices Using a Null Modem

6.9 for a schematic of a typical 25-pin null modem. Nine-pin null modems don't swap as many flow control lines; bare minimum null modems swap only transmit and receive lines.

UART

You may come across this acronym, which stands for "Universal Asynchronous Receiver-Transmitter." A UART is the chip used in computers (or any device with a serial port) to take the serial data and turn it into electrical signals, and vice versa.

PART III

Production Element Control

Now that we've covered the basics, we can move on to actual entertainment applications of control systems. Part 3 covers basic production element control; networks are covered later. In the future, this whole book may be about nothing but networking systems, but for years to come, the basic systems developed for each production element will persist, and, in any case, they serve as a good foundation for understanding networks.

7

Lighting

Control of light in the entertainment industry has come a long way in the last hundred years or so. Gaslights offered the first centrally controllable luminaires; they were dimmed using mechanical valves—less gas produced less light. Today, lighting fixtures are powered by electricity and controlled by electronic, solid-state valves known as "dimmers." Modern dimmers are easily computer-controllable, and in the last few decades, computer control of lighting has become widespread—even the smallest theatre or club can now afford computerized or computer-assisted lighting controllers.

Early dimmers were operated manually: a handle on the dimmer was directly coupled to the wiper on a resistance plate or autotransformer. The advent of electronically controlled dimmers allowed remote, centralized control to become a reality. Early remote controllers mimicked the positions of the manual handles on dimmers: a row of sliders would be set as a "scene" or "preset"; the operator would then manually "cross-fade" between the presets. Early computer-based controllers mimicked this preset operation, where each scene would have to be meticulously entered into the system and recorded. In more recent consoles, only the changes to each scene need to be entered; these consoles are known as "tracking" consoles.

LIGHTING CONTROL EQUIPMENT

There are generally two parts to a modern lighting control system: a control "console" and the controlled devices such as dimmers, color scrollers, or moving lights.

Figure 7.1 Two-Scene Preset Lighting Controller and 6-Channel Dimmer Pack (Courtesy Leprecon/CAE)

Lighting Consoles

Lighting control consoles today fall into four basic categories (of course, like anything else, the lines between the categories are often blurry): two-scene preset, submaster-based rock-and-roll/club consoles, fully computerized systems, and moving-light controllers.

In simple terms, two-scene preset consoles allow one scene to be preset while another is controlling the lights onstage. At the cue-go point, the live scene is cross-faded to the preset scene. Recent two-scene consoles also incorporate some programmability (see Figure 7.1).

Like two-scene consoles, rock-and-roll/club consoles still allow individual control of each individual dimmer, but instead of using preset cues, the show can be run from "submasters," which allow individual "looks" to be recorded or patched (see Figure 7.2). This approach allows the designer quick, spontaneous access to different looks, which can be selected randomly. Most recent higher-end rock-and-roll consoles are able to operate in cue-based as well as manual modes.

Fully computerized consoles allow "Go-button" operation for shows of a well-defined, sequential nature, such as theatrical productions or corporate events. Each preset look is recorded, along with the transition time to the next look, as a cue. In this way, the show lighting can be performed (theoretically, at least) exactly the same way each night, provided the operator and stage manager execute the cues at the appropriate points. Such

Figure 7.2 Rock-and-Roll Lighting Console (Courtesy Celco)

Figure 7.3 Computerized Tracking Lighting Console (Courtesy Electronic Theatre Controls)

consoles still generally retain some manual fading functions, so that talented operators can match lighting fades to onstage action; submasters are also generally provided for a variety of uses (see Figure 7.3).

In recent years, a new type of console has appeared along with a new type of luminaire: the moving light. Moving lights have many more control parameters than conventional luminaires; controlled parameters on a moving light might include intensity, color, multiple axis positions, gobo,[1] shutter, iris, focus, or even framing shutters. While some traditional consoles offer moving light functionality for a limited number of units, for bigger shows, consoles designed specifically for the application are typically used (see Figure 7.4).

---

[1]A gobo, or "template," is a stencil-like metal piece used to create an image for projection by a luminaire.

Figure 7.4 Moving-Light Console (Courtesy High End Systems)

For permanent installations, the cost and space requirements of a large console can be prohibitive, and having so many physical controls available to an untrained user can cause confusion and unneeded service calls. To solve this problem, many manufacturers have developed rack-mount versions of their systems with limited user controls, and some have even gone so far as to put all the

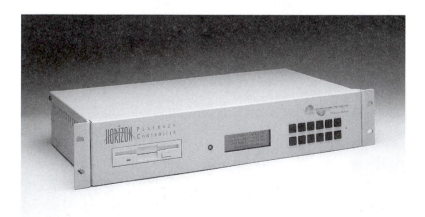

Figure 7.5 Rack-Mounted Lighting Controller (Courtesy Rosco/Entertainment Technology)

intelligence of a typical lighting console into the software of a standard personal computer. With these standard computer-based systems, the show can generally either be run from the computers directly, or show information can be downloaded into a rack-mount unit for playback (see Figure 7.5).

Patching

In the early days of electronic dimmer control, it was desirable to have the largest dimmer possible. Load circuits from the individual luminaires were "patched" into the dimmer's output through telephone operator-style patch cords hanging from a panel, or a series of sliders over a matrix of copper bus bars. As dimmer prices began dropping in the late 1970s and computer control became widespread, it became cost-effective to have many small dimmers—one for each light—rather than a few large dimmers, with many lights patched in.

With "dimmer-per-circuit" systems, patching is done on the control side (rather than the load side) of the dimmer. In modern computerized consoles, this "soft-patching" is accomplished totally within the realm of the controller. With these systems, designers and operators do not directly control dimmers; they deal with virtual "channels," to which any number of physical dimmers (see Figure 7.6) can be electronically patched.

Figure 7.6 Dimmer-per-Circuit Dimmer Rack (Courtesy Strand Lighting)

Dimmers

In modern electronic dimmers, the alternating current (AC) waveform is "chopped" to vary the overall average voltage output. Little of the AC waveform passes through a dimmer set to a low level; all of the waveform passes through a dimmer set to full. Almost all modern dimmers use a pair of silicon controlled rectifiers (SCRs) to switch the power line—one SCR for each half of the AC waveform. The SCR is turned on at some point in the half cycle via a control signal on its gate; the SCR, by its nature, turns itself off at the AC waveform's zero-crossing. By varying when the SCR is turned on, a controller can vary the light's output level. This control method is known as forward-phase control (FPC) (see Figure 7.7).

Turning on the SCR in the middle of the AC half-cycle generates a big spike, which makes noise, both mechanical (filament "sing") and electrical (Radio Frequency Interference [RFI]/Electromagnetic Interference [EMI]). To counteract such noise, a toroidal inductor, or "choke," is wired in series with the output of the SCR to soften the dimmer's turn-on transition. The time it takes for the current to start flowing, known as the dimmer's "rise time," is proportional to the size of the choke.

Forward-phase control is cheap to implement and has proven very reliable, but it has a few disadvantages: the choke adds weight and size to the dimmer module, and even good dimmers are never silent. In addition, the rise time is load dependent, and regulation of the dimmer's output can be no better than one half-cycle delayed—once the SCR is turned on, only the absence of flowing current (an AC zero-crossing) can turn it off.

Recently, some manufacturers started implementing reverse-phase control (RPC) in their dimmers. Through the use of power devices such as insulated-gate bipolar transistors (IGBTs) or metal-oxide silicon field-effect transistors (MOSFETs), the waveform can actually be turned off in a controlled fashion at any point during the half-cycle (see Figure 7.8).

RPC lets the waveform ramp up in its normal sinusoidal fashion starting at the zero-crossing; the power device is then turned off at the appro-

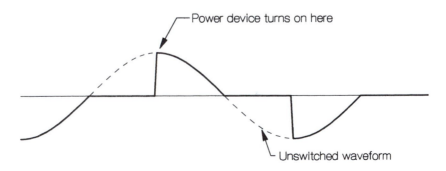

Figure 7.7 Forward-Phase Control

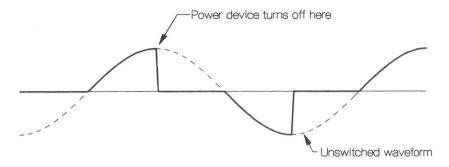

Figure 7.8 Reverse-Phase Control

priate point in the half-cycle. This approach has a number of advantages. Since there is no sharp turn-on spike, RPC virtually eliminates both electrical and physical noise, as well as the need for the bulky, heavy choke used to smooth out the waveform. RPC dimmers can actively sample the dimmer's output and shut off at any point; this allows dimmers to be designed that are virtually immune to short circuits and overloads, since regulation occurs within every half-cycle.

The advent of chokeless dimmers enabled manufacturers to offer viable distributed dimming systems (see Figure 7.9). Conventional dimmers are generally centrally located in racks, with large power feeds and individual load cables run to each light in the system (see Figure 7.6). In distributed systems, bars of small numbers of dimmers can be distributed throughout the lighting rig, each with a small power and control feed. Since the dimmers themselves generate so little noise, they can be placed in audience or stage areas.

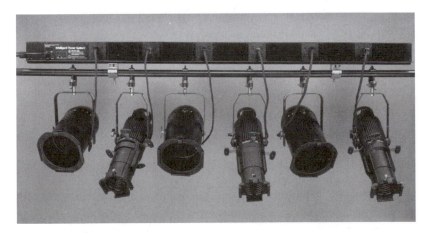

Figure 7.9 Distributed Dimming Bar (Courtesy Rosco/Entertainment Technology)

Moving Lights

In recent years, the moving light has had a huge impact on the lighting industry. With these automated luminaires, parameters such as pan, tilt, focus, gobo, color, and others are all remote-controllable. Some of the earliest commercially successful units were made for lease only, but an enormous variety of moving luminaires is now available for purchase. Control approaches for moving lights are sometimes proprietary (i.e., Vari*Lite and Icon), but there are some open approaches, detailed below.

Other Lighting Equipment

As detailed later in this chapter, the development of control standards in the lighting industry has led to a huge explosion of new types of lighting devices, all of which need control. Some examples are LED fixtures, which mix three colors of LEDs to create colored light; gobo rotators, which take a projected cut-out image and rotate it; and color scrollers (see Figure 7.11), which move a scroll of colored gel in front of a light.

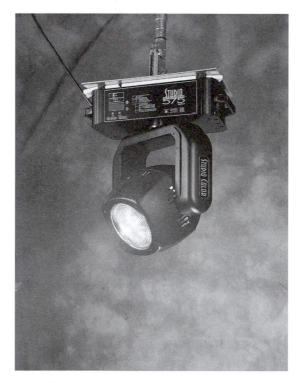

Figure 7.10 Moving Light (Courtesy High End Systems)

Figure 7.11   Color Scroller (Courtesy Wybron)

ANALOG (0-10V) CONTROL

Along with the advent of easily remote-controllable dimmers came the first de facto dimmer control "standards": analog direct current (DC) voltage control. The concept is quite simple: one wire is run from the console to each controlled dimmer, and a DC voltage corresponding to the level of the dimmer is sent down the wire. Zero volts represents an off condition; 10 volts (generally) represents a dimmer output of 100 percent or full on. In analog-controlled dimmers, this control voltage is received by trigger circuitry, which generates SCR firing pulses at the proper times to achieve the desired light output. While digital control (discussed in the DMX section below) is used in most professional installations today, analog control is still used in systems for low-budget venues such as clubs, discos, and small theatres, so coverage is warranted here.

In North American analog systems, this DC dimmer control voltage was often sent over "Jones" connectors, named for their manufacturer, Cinch-Jones. Although an effort within the United States Institute for Theatre Technology (USITT) to standardize Jones connections failed in 1991, a de facto standard was used by the majority of manufacturers and rental shops. Table 7.1[2] shows the control signals of this and other "standard" implementations,[3] in alphabetical order by connector type.

---

[2]This information was gathered by the ESTA Control Protocol Working Group's E1.3 Task Group.

[3]The mess you see in this table is the best possible argument one could put forth for tight, well-enforced standards!

Table 7.1 Common 0-10V Connectors and Pin-Outs

Connector	Typical Channels	Pin-Outs	Signal
Champ (Centronics)	32	1-32	Channels 1-32
		33-34	Not Used
		35-36	Signal Common
Cinch Jones, 8-Pin	6	1-6	Channels 1-6
		7	Power Supply (or fan relay)
		8	Signal Common
Cinch Jones, 10-Pin	6	1-6	Channels 1-6
		7	Power Supply
		8	Signal Common
		9	Power Supply (+15V)
		10	Power Supply (–15 V)
Cinch Jones, 10-Pin	6	1-6	Channels 1-6
		7	Not used (or signal common)
		8	Signal Common (sometimes tied to pin 7)
		9	Not Used
		10	Not Used
Cinch Jones, 15-Pin	12	1-12	Channels 1-12
		13	24 V to dimmer for fan relay
		14	Power Supply
		15	Signal Common
CPC-28 (Amp)	8	1-8	Channels 1-8
		25	Power Supply (+15V)
		26	Power Supply (–15 V)
		28	Signal Common
DA-15 (DB-15)	12	1-12	Channels 1-12
		13-14	Power Supply
		15	Signal Common
DA-15, Strand (DB-15)	12	1-12	Channels 1-12
		13-14	Signal Common
		15	Not Used
DB-9 (Rosco/ET)	6	1-6	Channels 1-6
		7-9	Signal Common
DB-25	24	1-24	Channels 1-24
		25	Signal Common
DD-50 (DB-50)	48	1-48	Channels 1-48
		49-50	Signal Common

(continued)

Table 7.1 *(continued)*

Connector	Typical Channels	Pin-Outs	Signal
DIN 8-Pin (Used by Pulsar and Others)	6	1	Power Supply
		2	Signal Common
		3-8	Channels 1-6
DIN, 5-Pin (180°) (Used by NJD, Anytronics, and Others)	4	1	Channel 1
		2	Signal Common
		3	Channel 4
		4	Channel 2
		5	Channel 3
DIN, 7-Pin (180°) (Used by NJD, Anytronics, and Others)	4	1	Channel 1
		2	Signal Common
		3	Channel 4
		4	Channel 2
		5	Channel 3
		6	Power Supply (+15V)
		7	Power Supply (+15V)
DIN, 8-Pin (Used by Zero 88 and Others)	6	1-6	Channels 1-6
		7	Power Supply
		8	Signal Common
Socapex 337P	30	1-30	Channels 1-30
		31-34	Not Used
		35-37	Signal Common
SRC-16 (Cannon)	12	1-11	Channels 1-11
		12	Power Supply (+15V)
		13	Power Supply (–15 V)
		14	Not Used
		15	Signal Common
		16	Channel 12
XLR, 5-Pin	4	1-4	Channels 1-4
		5	Power Supply (+15V)
		Shell	Signal Common
XLR, 7-Pin	6	1-6	Channels 1-4
		7	Power Supply
		Shell	Signal Common

As of this writing, a task group inside ESTA's Control Protocol Working Group is in the final stages of developing a document titled "E1.3, 0 to 10V Analog Control Specifications" to tighten up some of the vagaries of this control approach. Unfortunately, the mess of connectors is so well established that it is here to stay.

AMX192

In large systems, it is expensive and troublesome to have one wire control only one dimmer—in a 1000-dimmer system, you would need a control cable from the console to the dimmers with more than 1000 wires. To reduce the number of wires, the AMX192 standard was developed. AMX192 has now largely fallen out of favor (replaced in nearly all modern installations by DMX512; see below), because, among other things, its unbalanced signal and low voltages make it highly subject to ground loops and other noise problems. It is included here only because you may encounter it in older "legacy" installations.

"AMX192 Analog Multiplex Data Transmission Standard for Dimmers and Controllers" was standardized through the United States Institute for Theatre Technology in 1986. As often happens, this standard had its roots in one company's approach; in this case, AMX is based on Strand Lighting's CD 80® protocol, which was first used in Strand's LightPalette® control consoles in the early 1980s. The CD 80 system was originally designed for use within Strand consoles, but Strand engineers eventually transformed it into an external interconnection standard. Many aspects of the system are not desirable for use outside a console, but CD 80 gained acceptance because of Strand's market position at the time. AMX192 became a USITT standard in 1986, primarily through the efforts of Brad Rodriguez, then a Strand engineer.

The AMX192 standard derives its name from "Analog MultipleXing," in which some number of analog control signals, up to 192, are time-multiplexed and sent down four wires. The four wires carry two types of signals: multiplexed single-ended analog-level data, and differential clock-synchronization pulses. The analog level varies between 0 and +5 V DC, with +5 V DC representing 100 percent (full intensity) and 0 V DC representing 0 percent (off). The low-voltage and nondifferential nature of this signal makes it quite susceptible to noise and ground loops. The maximum number of receivers per line can range from 4 to 16, depending on the type of receiver circuit.

Physical Connections

AMX specifies the type of cable to be used: two unshielded 18 AWG (American Wire Gauge) twisted pairs. The maximum length given in the standard is 1000 feet, although in practice, runs more than 400 feet are not recommended.

AMX192 is sent over either 4-pin XLR-type connectors, or mini "TY4" model connectors, made by Switchcraft. With XLRs, male connectors are used on controllers and female connectors on dimmers (see Figure 7.12). With mini plugs, all equipment has female connectors and all cables are male-male.

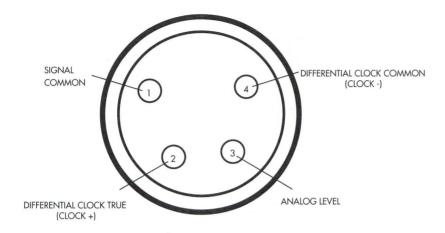

Figure 7.12 AMX 4-Pin XLR Output Signals (Male Connector Shown)

While USITT AMX defines standard pin-outs, others have existed. The original mini connectors, much hated by rental houses due to their small size and lack of durability, were replaced in many cases with full-size, 4-pin XLRs, with the pin-out transferred pin for pin.

Timing Characteristics

The timing relationship between the analog line and the sync line is one of the most critical aspects of AMX. Each dimmer's analog level pulse should be sent before the leading edge of the synchronization pulse, and should last at least 50 μs. The refresh cycle—the time it takes for an entire group of dimmers' information to be sent—varies with the number of dimmers. The minimum acceptable refresh value is 10 ms, the maximum is 500 ms, and a typical time is 50 ms. The dimmer frame duration, by specification, has to be at least 50 μs (see Figure 7.13).

Like everything else today, lighting control is mostly going digital, and the next standard we will cover is far more prevalent.

DMX512

The "DMX512 Digital Data Transmission Standard for Dimmers and Controllers" started humbly, but today it is the most successful and widely used entertainment lighting control standard in the world. DMX stands for Digital MultipleXing; 512 is the number of control channels in the standard.

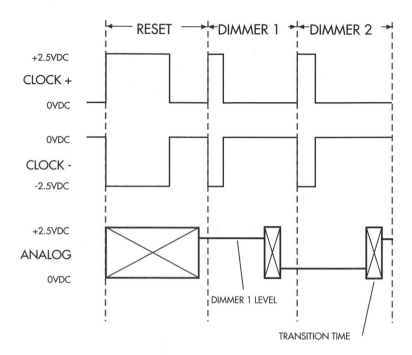

Figure 7.13 AMX Timing Diagram

DMX was developed within the USITT at the prodding of a number of individuals in the entertainment lighting industry, particularly Steve Terry of the rental house Production Arts Lighting, and Mitch Hefter, then of Strand Lighting. At that time, several competing multiplexing protocols were in the marketplace. Colortran had its proprietary digital multiplexing protocol, known as CMX, which had been developed by Fred Foster.[4] Lighting Methods Incorporated (LMI) had developed the Micro 2 protocol to connect the then-dominant Kliegl Performer control console to LMI dimmer racks. Kliegl had its own K96 protocol; Strand had CD 80 (later to become AMX); and Electro Controls and Avab also had systems. At a session at the 1986 USITT conference in Oakland, California, panelists from all the major lighting companies of the time discussed the possibility of creating an open, digital, multiplexed lighting-control standard. Remarkably, by the end of the session, the basics of the standard had been worked out, and the compromise was to use the CMX data format running at a Micro 2–like data rate.[5]

---

[4] Owner of Electronic Theatre Controls, which acquired LMI.

[5] CMX ran at about 150 kbps, while Micro 2 was a 250-kbps, 7-bit protocol that used a full byte of eight 1s (FFh) for reset. Micro 2, developed in the early 80s to control LMI's RD2000 series of dimmer racks, had two completely redundant data links; a third link back to the console carried error-correction and link-status information.

DMX512 was first published by the USITT in August 1986, and in 1998, maintenance of the standard was transferred to ESTA's Control Protocol Working Group.

The originators of the DMX512 standard by no means thought they were creating a lighting-control panacea; in fact, they readily acknowledged that the standard was aimed at lowest-common-denominator applications, and especially at the needs of lighting rental houses. At the same time, however, the standard's simplicity and ease of implementation are certainly reasons that it has gained such broad acceptance; DMX is now used to run moving lights, color scrollers, LED luminaires, and devices that weren't even invented when the standard was written.

Physical Connections

DMX512 is electrically based on the differential EIA-485 standard, meaning that a link can accommodate up to 32 receiver device loads. The DMX standard specifies that connectors, if used, should be 5-pin XLR type, with receiving devices using male XLRs, and transmitters using females. The standard specifies that only shielded, twisted-pair, low-capacitance data communications cable designed for use with EIA-485 should be used. Three of the 5 pins are used for a single DMX link; the other pair of pins was designed for a second, reverse DMX link, which might be used, for example, to send dimmer rack over-temperature or other information back to a console (see below). Figure 7.14 details the control signals.

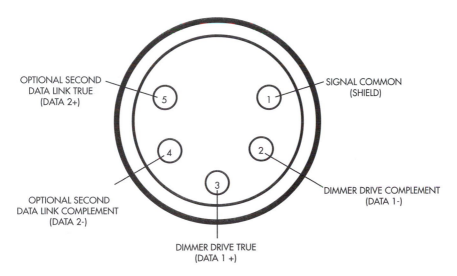

Figure 7.14 DMX512 Output Signals (Female Connector Shown)

Data Specs

DMX transmits 8-bit level data asynchronously, in a serial format, at a rate of 250 kbps with no parity and 2 stop bits. The data for dimmer 1 is sent first, then data bytes are sent sequentially for any number of dimmers, up to the maximum of 512. Installations with more than 512 dimmers simply use multiple DMX "universes," with the other links representing dimmers 513-1024, 1025-1536, and so on. A table in Appendix A, "Useful Tables," shows various DMX universes.

Packet Makeup

In its idle state, the DMX line is held at a "Mark" level with the data line in a high condition (see Figure 7.15). When a DMX "Packet" is to start, a "Break" signal is sent, dropping the line to a low level for at least 88 μs (equivalent to two frame times). Following the Break is a short pulse known as the Mark After Break (MAB) signal; this is the general sync pulse for the start of the data portion of the DMX packet, which warns the receiver that the next transition from high to low will be the start of data. Next, a "Start Code" is sent, and a "Null" Start Code of eight 0s indicates to the receiver that valid dimmer information is to follow. While other start codes are allowed by the standard (see below), dimmer receivers should not update dimmers unless they receive a Null (00h) Start Code. After the start code, the actual data bytes are sent using 8-bit words, each with 2 stop bits. Any number of data bytes from 1 to 512 can be sent. While 8 bits means a range of 0-255, the standard does not specify how to map the 256 possible levels onto a typical lighting scale of 0 to 100 percent.[6]

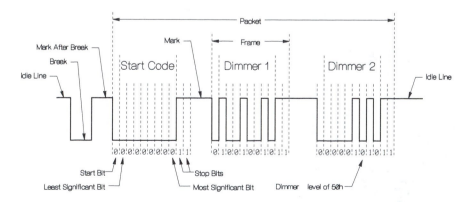

Figure 7.15   DMX512 Timing Diagram

[6]This relationship is covered in the USITT ASCII Light Cues standard, which is outside the scope of this book (it's an off-line system).

The number of times a dimmer level is updated in 1 second is the "refresh rate," in Hertz. Because any number of dimmers from 24 to 512 can be sent, the refresh rate varies with the number of dimmers; sending data for fewer dimmers allows a faster refresh rate. Keep in mind that the refresh rate here pertains only to the update rate of the DMX signal itself, not the rate at which the console updates the DMX data, or how fast the receiving device can act on it. This is an important distinction: for rock-and-roll style "chases," (sequentially lit circuits) a console and data update rate less than 20 Hz is considered unacceptable. A refresh rate of 44 Hz (nearly one update per AC cycle) is generally considered adequate for most applications, and the maximum update rate for a full packet of 512 bytes, with typical values as given in the standard, would be 11 times per second.

DMX512/1990

The 1986 DMX512 specification left some technical areas open to interpretation; some of these ambiguities were ironed out in 1990, and an update, DMX512/1990, was published. The original 1986 standard specified that the Mark After Break portion of the DMX packet be no less than 4 µs; however, some dimmer receivers, which counted the duration of the MAB signal to determine when the start-code frame begins, needed longer than 4 µs to recover. No one really noticed this problem in 1986, since microprocessor-based consoles were then rarely capable of putting out DMX at those lightning-fast speeds. However, some discrete-component (non-microprocessor) consoles designed later were generating DMX approaching the standard's limit, and some dimmer receivers were not able to handle it. DMX512/1990 specified that the MAB signal must be no less than 8µS, and that dimmer receivers must be able to take even the fastest possible DMX512/1990, even if the receiver doesn't update the dimmers as fast as the incoming signal.

DMX512/200n?

As of this writing, the DMX standard is being revised within ESTA's Control Protocol Working Group. Some want to take the current mess of conforming and nonconforming DMX implementations and standardize them; many others want to simply tighten and clean up the specification, include a few well-designed additions, and get on with new technologies such as ESTA ACN (see ACN section in Chapter 25). We can only hope that this situation is resolved and a new standard can be issued soon.[7]

---

[7] I was actually holding the second edition of the book for this new DMX standard, but I finally had to give up. I hope it will be covered in detail in the third edition.

Addressing

DMX broadcasts its data to all receiving devices connected to a particular link, and each device on that link must be configured in some way to read data starting at a user-configured "address." For example, let's say you have two 6-channel dimmer packs and one 12-channel pack, all connected to the same DMX link, and you want to address them from your console as dimmers 1-24. You configure the first 6-dimmer rack to listen to DMX channels 1-6, the second to 7-12, and the 12-channel pack to 13-24 (see Figure 7.16). Single-channel color scrollers and moving lights are addressed in a similar fashion.

Some manufacturers have the user set the actual starting DMX dimmer number as the address, and with this approach, the first dimmer rack would be set to address 1, the second rack would be set to 7, and the last rack would be set to 13. Other manufacturers think it easier to have the user set a "rack," "device," or "unit" number. With this approach, the dimmer packs above would be set so that the first is unit 1; the second, unit 2; and so on. This approach makes things easier in small systems, but can get confusing for larger systems, and especially for multi-universe systems.

Each manufacturer decides how this information will be configured into their products. Some use buttons and an electronic display that displays the address; others use "thumbwheel" switches that mechanically display the setting. Some manufacturers opt for the cheapest and most confusing way: "DIP[8]" switches. This small bank of switches allows the user to set a number in (typically) 8-bit binary. Confusion comes in that some manufacturers use the binary settings to deal with a range of 0-255, while others use 1-256. In addition, an 8-bit DIP switch can only represent 256 possible combinations, so to be able to listen to any of the 512 possible control channels, another switch must be used.

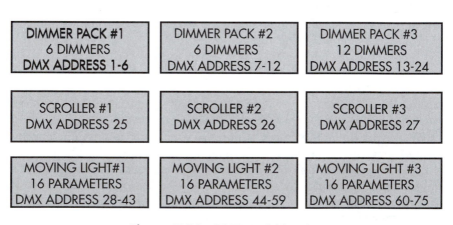

Figure 7.16 DMX512 Addressing

---

[8]DIP is an electronics term standing for Dual Inline Package.

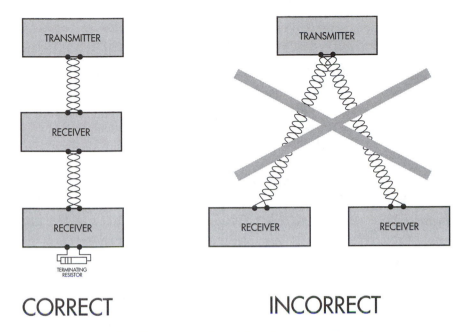

CORRECT   INCORRECT

Figure 7.17 DMX512 Signal Distribution and Termination

DMX Distribution and Termination

Since DMX runs at a fairly high data rate, precautions must be taken to ensure that the data is transmitted and received properly. For electrical reasons, cables run to receivers on a DMX link should only be "daisy chained" sequentially through each receiver, and never "two-ferred" (see Figure 7.17). Also, the last physical device in any DMX link, whether it connects 1 device or 20, should be "terminated," typically with a 100 Ω resistor. This termination is often provided in good equipment designs with a switch that can switch the resistor across the line. Running the DMX signal properly ensures good data integrity, as unterminated lines tend to "reflect" the DMX signal back down the line, possibly corrupting the data. "Stubs" off the data transmission line, as would be found in a two-fer, tend to act like antennas and adversely affect the impedance of the transmission line.

Optical Isolation

DMX is a balanced, differential electrical signal, and connects very high-power devices (such as dimmer racks) to delicate, low-power, electronic devices (such as consoles). If a high-voltage failure occurs in a dimmer rack, it is quite possible for the voltage to travel back up the DMX line and blow up the console; it is

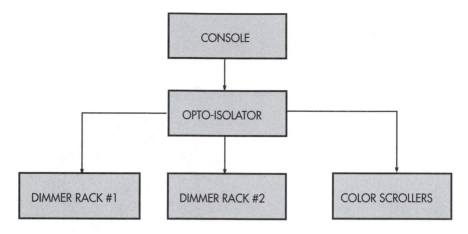

Figure 7.18   Opto-Isolated DMX512 Signal Distribution

also possible for a failure in one dimmer rack to damage the control electronics of another. For this reason, DMX links should, if at all possible, be optically (or galvanically) isolated (see Figure 7.18). With an opto-isolated approach, there is no electrical connection between the input and the output, and high-voltage or other electrical failures are isolated from delicate control electronics.

Three-Pin Connectors and Mic Cable (Don't Use Them!)

Since 2 pins in the 5-pin XLR connector defined by DMX were designated for "Optional Second Data Link" purposes, some manufacturers (especially moving-light manufacturers) ignored the specification of 5-pin connectors and instead used 3-pin XLR connectors. This created a nightmare for rental houses and end users, who have to mix and match such equipment with standard DMX equipment. Either a separate inventory of 3-pin XLR cable must be maintained, or 5-to-3-pin adapters must be used with every such moving light or other device. The more reputable moving-light manufacturers have, in recent years, finally abandoned this practice, or are at least including both 3- and 5-pin XLR connectors on their equipment.

The standard specifies that shielded, twisted-pair, low-capacitance data communications cable designed for use with EIA-485 should be used. This is the ONLY type of cable you should consider using. Microphone cable, for example, was never intended to carry high-frequency square waves as are found in DMX. And while you may be able to successfully run a DMX link on a piece of microphone cable, without test equipment you have no way of knowing what is actually going on in the data link, and you may be running on the edge of failure. It may work today, but adding one more device, or changing the layout of the system slightly, might cause the data corruption to rise to the point that the whole system fails. Is your whole show worth the few dollars you might save using substandard cables?

DMX Over Category 5 Cable

As of this writing, various methods of sending the DMX signal over Cat 5 cable are being investigated by a number of manufacturers. Cat 5 cable and its associated patching, termination, and distribution equipment is much cheaper and more widely used than typical DMX cables. No standards currently exist on the use of Cat 5 for DMX, but some manufacturers and system integrators are currently using Cat 5 cable in their permanent installations.

DMX Patching/Merging/Processing/Test Equipment

One of the primary advantages of standardization is that the market for all products using the standard typically expands dramatically, and it then becomes economically possible for new types of devices to be created. Patching, merging, routing, and processing equipment (see Figure 7.19) can do whatever you want done to a DMX signal. It can reroute the DMX

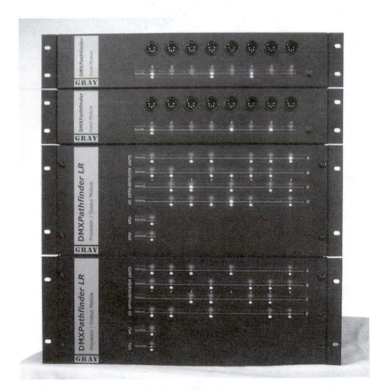

Figure 7.19 DMX512 Signal Routing Equipment (Courtesy Gray Interfaces)

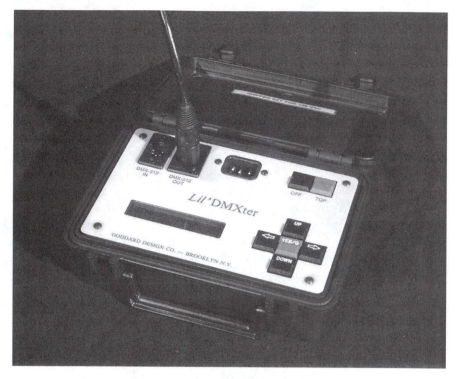

Figure 7.20   DMX512 Test Set (Photo by Charles Scott)

data to multiple points throughout a facility, remove or add dimmers to a data stream, merge the outputs of multiple consoles, and so on.

Digital (DMX)-to-Analog Converters (DACs) interface modern consoles with older equipment, or vice versa. Opto-isolators distribute DMX and protect the electronics in the system from catastrophic failures or ground loops. DMX adaptors for personal computers are used in computer-only lighting consoles and other special devices. DMX test-sets greatly simplify DMX troubleshooting, allowing a user to measure and analyze the DMX signal, and quickly find and troubleshoot problems (see Figure 7.20).

Moving Lights and DMX

DMX was not designed for moving-light control, and is, in fact, poorly suited to the task. The 8-bit byte used to represent data in standard DMX can only represent 256 possible levels, and this means that for a moving light a single DMX channel couldn't even achieve control of 1-degree resolution in a 360-degree axis. More bits are needed to give higher resolution to some axes, while, on the other hand, some parameters might need only 1 bit—on or off. DMX allows only 8-bit words to be sent, and must send out its data over and over, while a moving light might only want some types of data now, and some later. For these reasons, some manufacturers developed proprietary schemes to control their own fixtures from their own controllers.

However, the market power of standardization has been shown once again; most purchasable moving lights today use DMX for control, and many moving-light consoles today output only DMX. But the DMX standard includes no provisions for moving-light data, so each manufacturer has developed its own way of mapping the DMX signal for its purposes. Many manufacturers use more than 1 DMX byte for control of high-precision moving-light functions. Going from 1 8-bit byte to 2 (giving 16 bits total) increases the resolution from 256 steps to 65536. But because there are no standards, one manufacturer may assign its first 2 bytes to pan, another might use those same bytes for tilt.

There are nearly as many DMX moving-light implementations as there are brands and models of moving lights. To give you an idea of how a manufacturer might use DMX for its fixture, let's look at one commonly available fixture—in this case, the High End Systems Studio Spot™ 575.[9] *Each such fixture on a link uses 24 DMX control channels.* The first channel (based on the configured address) is used for "coarse" pan adjust; the second channel is for "fine" pan adjustment. Tilt is controlled by channels 3 and 4 in a similar way. Those parameters map out fairly directly, but after that, things get much more complicated, as functions like Color Wheel, Litho Wheel, Frost, Focus, Iris, Shutter, Dimmer, Speed, Macros, and Lamp On/Off are assigned various control channels. It would be simplest to assign each of these functions as many DMX channels as necessary, but with such a design, it would be easy to eat up the 512 channels available on a DMX link very quickly with only a few fixtures. In addition, many of these functions—even the simple ones—do not map neatly to simple 0-255 levels. To show you how complicated this can get, Table 7.2 shows the implementation for one *single* DMX channel for this fixture's iris.[10] The iris channel is the 18th channel after the fixture address (if the unit was set to DMX address 1, this parameter would be address 19).

When this DMX control channel is set inside a range of various levels, the iris will do certain things. Clearly, this is not a very elegant control scheme, but DMX is such a prevalent standard that manufacturers feel it worthwhile to work around the limitations, and DMX is the most prevalent form of moving light control today. Every manufacturer uses their own scheme for control, and, thankfully, modern moving-light consoles keep all

---

[9] I picked this fixture because it is popular and the company had a well-organized Web site that made it easy to find this information.

[10] An iris is a circular mask of variable size that can change the apparent beam diameter.

Table 7.2   Iris Channel for Studio Spot 575

DMX	Function	Parameter	Decimal	Percent	Hex
19	Iris	**Variable Iris**			
		Closed	0	0	0
		Variable	1-127	1-49	1-7F
		Open	128-143	50-55	80-8F
		Iris Effects (Variable Ranges)			
		Periodic strobe	144-159	56-62	90-9F
		Random strobe	160-175	63-68	A0-AF
		Ramp open/ snap shut	176-191	69-74	B0-BE
		Snap open/ ramp shut	192-207	75-80	BF-CF
		Random ramp/ snap	208-223	81-87	DD-DC
		Random snap/ ramp	224-239	88-93	E0-EF
		Open	240-255	94-100	F0-FF

this configuration information in "fixture libraries" or "personality files" so you don't have to keep track of it. If you do need it, check the manufacturer's Web site; the good ones have the information easily accessible.

Alternate Start Codes

Dimmer data is always sent with a start code of 00h, but the creators of the DMX standard left room for expansion and other types of data transmission through the use of an "alternate" start code, and a number of manufacturers have taken advantage of these codes to use DMX to transmit nondimmer data. No start-code registration procedure was defined in the original standard, although an informal start-code registry has been maintained by both USITT and ESTA.

OTHER LIGHTING CONTROL STANDARDS

DMX is ruling the world of entertainment lighting control. However, there are a number of other standards in existence, some of which are new, and some of which are being phased out.

Rosco/Entertainment Technology Talkback

While we've talked so far in this chapter about ways for a controller to control various types of lighting equipment, it is often desirable for a controlled device to "talk back" to the controller. For example, it would be useful for a dimmer to report its current temperature, attached load, and other status information. To send this kind of information, Entertainment Technology (now Rosco/ET) developed a "talkback" scheme in conjunction with its Intelligent Power System (IPS®) technology. Rosco/ET will license this technology to any company who wants to use it for $1 (Wybron and others have adopted it). Because it was developed for use with the IPS system (see Figure 7.9), this talkback scheme is sometimes referred to as "IPS talkback."

The Rosco/ET talkback scheme uses the "Optional Second Data Link" lines defined by DMX512, which are transmitted on pins 4 and 5 of the XLR connector (see Figure 7.14). Instead of carrying data out *from* the controller to the controlled devices, these lines carry data back from the controlled devices *to* the controller. While a typical DMX line uses one transmitter (console) and several or many receivers (dimmers, color scrollers, etc.), the Rosco/ET talkback scheme can have several transmitters and one receiver. This is allowable since the standard is based on DMX, which is in turn based on EIA-485.

Three types of devices can exist on the talkback link: "transmitter," "responder," and "monitor." The transmitter is the device that sends the normal DMX control data; this would typically be a lighting control console. A responder is a device that sends talkback data; this would typically be an "intelligent" dimming system, color scroller, or other device. Finally, the monitor is a device that receives, processes, and displays the talkback data for the user. This could either be a stand-alone system monitor unit, or a function incorporated into a control console.

Under the talkback scheme, the 512 DMX data bytes are broken into 171 possible 3-byte groups. Each time a responder sees a DMX data value in the first group that matches its address setting, it sends some data back up the line. For example, if a 6-channel dimmer pack was set to address 13 (and therefore occupied address space 13-18), it would send 1 talkback byte back to the monitor sometime after receiving the start of the 13th DMX data byte and before the end of the 15th data byte (see Figure 7.21). With this scheme, the monitor, by also monitoring the transmitted data, can easily tell to which group of DMX addresses a particular status data refers.

During each DMX packet, the responder sends 1 byte of a group of talkback data. Over successive DMX refresh cycles, a reasonable amount of data can be sent back up the line to the monitor. Compared to the torrent of DMX data from the controller, 1 byte from each responder device per DMX update isn't very fast, but the type of data this link is designed for

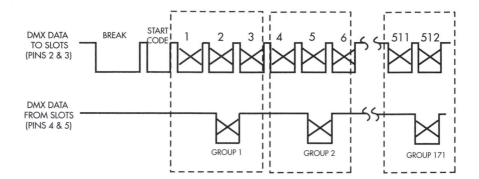

Figure 7.21 Rosco/Entertainment Technology Talkback Synchronization

isn't typically time-critical; it wouldn't be a problem if it takes a few seconds for a dimmer to tell a controller its operating temperature.

Talkback data is sent at the DMX data rate of 250kbps, using 8-bit words, each with 1 start bit, 1 "flag" bit, and 1 stop bit. If the flag bit is set to 1, the monitor can tell that this byte is a "Response Start ID." The Response Start ID, which is registered with Rosco/ET, indicates to the monitor the start of a talkback data cycle from a particular device, and also indicates the format of the data.

Any manufacturer who registers a Response Start ID with Rosco/ET can send whatever data they like using the system. Rosco/ET uses the talkback scheme in their IPS product line for each dimmer in the system to return information such as dimmer output voltage, nondim status, overload shutdown, temperature shutdown, dimmer capacity, and various diagnostic signals.

While the Rosco/ET talkback scheme is closely compliant with the DMX512 standard, not all DMX distribution or processing equipment carries through the optional data lines used for talkback. Most good-quality temporary or permanent installations of DMX have implemented and cabled both data pairs, but it would only take one broken link to cause problems for this talkback scheme. Care must be taken when setting up a distribution system that will use the talkback scheme to make sure all components are capable of transporting or accepting the data. But this is a small price to pay for greatly enhanced functionality.

Strand Lighting SMX

Strand Lighting developed an interconnection protocol known as SMX, which it offered as an open standard in 1990. SMX does fill in some of DMX512's gaps (such as its lack of error correction); however, the improvements come at a cost of increased complexity and, therefore, expense. As of this writing, SMX is still being used by Strand for configuration purposes and device status monitoring, but for many other applications, it is being replaced by either DMX, or Strand's ShowNet Ethernet implementation.

The lowest layer of SMX is its physical layer, which, like DMX512, consists of an EIA-485 interface over the same standard 5-pin XLR connectors and cable types as DMX. SMX messages actually contain 11 bits: 1 start bit, an 8-bit data byte, a framing bit, and a stop bit. The data byte is sent with its least-significant bit first.

SMX has two types of operation, known in the spec as Class 0 and Class 1. Class 0 operates much like DMX: it is unidirectional, has no error correction, and can be sent to a large number of stations simultaneously. Class 1 contains error correction and can send messages between stations with any of 32,767 individual addresses. Messages can be up to 255 bytes long, and bad bytes are retransmitted. There are two types of stations in SMX: master and slave. In Class 0 (unidirectional) operation, neither master nor slave retransmits anything; in Class 1 operation, the slave acknowledges successful data reception.

The highest layer and the real meat of SMX is the applications layer. There are two types of application messages: dimmer level and dimmer supervisory. The dimmer-level application type was issued in January 1992, with an application type code of 09h. Dimmer-level application-request messages contain a 2-byte base dimmer field, which is the first dimmer in a sequence to be addressed; this gives a range of 1-65,535. Following the base dimmer field are the actual 8-bit dimmer levels. In Class 0 operation, only 249 dimmers can be addressed, due to structural limitations. Presumably in Class 1 operation, close to 65,000 dimmer values could be sent.

The dimmer-supervisory application type is used in Strand's EC 90/CD 90 dimming products. It allows external supervisory equipment to monitor and control the operation of a dimming system, which is made up of racks, crates (subassemblies of racks), and dimmers. A rack is a physical rack that contains some number of crates, which contain some number of dimmers. In an SMX system, each crate maintains databases, which contain information about every entity in the system.

Strand Lighting D54 Protocol

In 1983, Strand Lighting placed into the public domain a lighting control protocol known as Dimmer Multiplex Standard "D54." The "D" designates a Strand company standard or practice; this was the 54th such document, hence D54. Like AMX192, D54 uses analog multiplexing techniques; in D54, however, level information for up to 384 dimmers can be sent over a single cable and return. The standard was originally used in the "M24" console, and has now been phased out for new products by Strand. You are not likely to encounter it today except in "legacy" installations.

D54 differs from AMX in one major way: in D54, both analog level information and synchronization clock signals are sent over a single conductor and shield (or "screen" in U.K. parlance). Dimmer-level information is sent over a line known as "DMX" (nothing to do with the digital DMX512 standard), which looks electronically similar to a video signal, and which is received differentially between the conductor and shield.

At the head of each group of dimmer levels, the DMX line drops to a –5V "sync" level for at least 35 µs, denoting the "End of Frame" marker. At the end of this pulse, the line returns to 0V, then another, shorter negative pulse (maximum 10 µs) is sent to denote that the next positive voltage on the line will be the control level for the first dimmer. This control voltage ranges from 0V to +5V, sent proportionately to dimmer level. For instance, a dimmer set to 50 percent would be represented by a control voltage of +2.5V.

The standard specifies that D54 be sent over good-quality mic cable, with a wire diameter of at least .5mm², capacitance less than 300pF/m, and nominal impedance of 75Ω. Three-pin XLR-type connectors are used (when connectors are necessary); female connectors are used on the outputs of consoles, while dimmer inputs are male. Pin 1 of the connector is 0V reference, Pin 2 is the FMX signal, and Pin 3 is the DMX signal. Strand says D54 can be transmitted 1000m, although larger cable is required for distances over 500m.

AVAB Protocol

Another older protocol found primarily in Europe is Swedish lighting manufacturer Avab's protocol, which digitally transmits data for up to 256 dimmers. The open Avab protocol is similar in many ways to today's DMX512 standard, but was introduced in 1982 before the advent of DMX. Avab's protocol is based on the EIA-485 serial data communications standard with a data rate of 153.6 kbps, with 8 data bits, 2 stop bits, and no parity. The system is elegantly simple: two FFh bytes are sent first as sync bytes, then the hex value of each of the subsequent dimmer levels is sent. Allowable dimmer level values are from 00-FEh (0-254 decimal). This gives a dimming range of 255 steps (1 less than DMX512), which is far more than is necessary for conventional dimmer control, since consoles (and human users) generally work in a 0-to-100-percent scale.

Low capacitance cable rated for EIA-485 use should be used to transmit the protocol; 8-pin DIN connectors were used. As with most DIN connections, female connectors are used on equipment, with male-to-male cables used for connections. The + and –12 volts on the line is provided by the console, in order to switch on and off peripheral systems.

MIDI

Some manufacturers, especially those in the musical instrument market, have used the Musical Instrument Digital Interface (MIDI—covered in Chapter 9) to control dimmers directly in small systems, with each dimmer using one of the 16 MIDI channels. Since it is easy to exceed the bandwidth of MIDI with this configuration, only very small systems, such as those found in clubs, can effectively use MIDI to control dimmers directly. Where direct MIDI control of a lighting system is desired, it is vastly superior, although certainly more expensive, to interface with the dimmers through a MIDI-capable lighting controller.

NETWORKS FOR LIGHTING CONTROL

As more and more lighting control intelligence is distributed around a performance facility, the need for data and control networking is ever increasing. Networks used for lighting, such as Ethernet, are covered in Part 5, since they share so much in common with networking systems for other disciplines.

8

Lasers

Many kinds of productions, from big-budget corporate spectaculars to small theatre productions, use laser systems to provide spectacular effects. These effects are typically provided as a service by laser companies. Traditionally, these supply companies have custom-built or modified their own systems. However, in recent years, de facto and actual standards have been emerging, and these can be covered here.

LASER SYSTEM COMPONENTS

The basic concept behind a laser light show is very simple. Using one or more colored beams of light, a picture is drawn very rapidly—so fast, in fact, that it's hard for the eye to see the dot as it draws the picture. Laser systems generally break down into some standard components. First, of course, there is the laser light source, which produces a powerful, colli- mated beam; modern lasers for light shows are often "white" lasers, which produce multiple colors simultaneously. Next in the system is typically a very sophisticated, color-splitting and blanking device, which acts as a sort of remotely-controlled electric prism. This device, typically a polychro- matic acousto-optic modulator (PCAOM), allows only a certain color to pass at any given instant, with all the remaining light sent out a "waste"

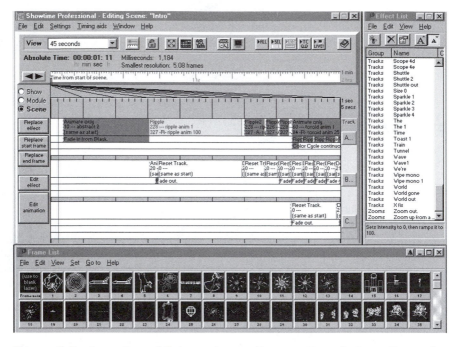

Figure 8.1 Laser Control Software Screen (Courtesy Pangolin Laser Systems)

beam. Under sophisticated computer control, and with no moving parts, these devices work at blindingly fast speeds, allowing the subsequent components of the laser system to deal only with a particular color at any given fraction of a second. The last part of a typical laser projector is the part that "scans" the beam, typically using two "galvanometers," one for the X axis and one for the Y. These "scanners" typically use high-speed DC servo-control electronics, while the PCAOMs use custom controllers to generate their high-frequency control signals.

So far, we've only talked about hardware; a crucial part of a laser system, of course, is the software which takes a graphic image from the mind of the designer and turns it into raw control signals to control the projector components. One of the most widely used control software packages these days is "Lasershow Designer," made by a company called Pangolin (see Figure 8.1).

This software can either control a laser projector directly, or signals from the software can be recorded on a digital multitrack tape recorder such as an Alesis ADAT. Often the computer is used during the design phases of the project, and once the project is completed, the show data is transferred, along with associated music tracks, to the digital recorder. Playback is then as simple as pressing "Play."

ILDA STANDARDS

The International Laser Display Association (ILDA) has in recent years been standardizing various aspects of laser systems. They have developed "The ILDA Standard Projector," which standardizes things like scanner tuning (ILDA also provides some standard test patterns), connector and pin-out specifications, DMX512 effects control, and ADAT tape track assignments.

Projector Interface

The ILDA standard connector pin-out for a 25-pin connector is shown in Figure 8.2.

DMX512 Channel Assignments

The continuous nature of DMX makes it well suited to some aspects of laser control, although it is neither precise nor fast enough to control devices like scan heads directly. However, the ILDA has standardized 32 channels of DMX control for auxiliary (nonscanning) functions, and these channel assignments are shown in Table 8.1.

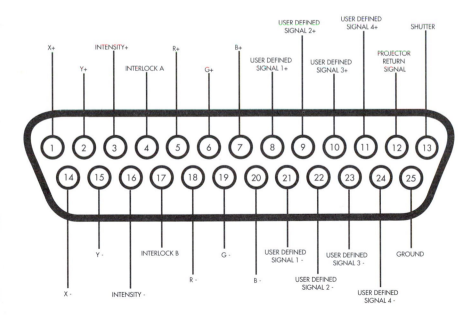

Figure 8.2 ILDA Connector Control Signals (Male Connector Shown)

Table 8.1 ILDA Standard DMX Channel Assignments

Channel	Assigned Effect
1	Effects fader (controls beams and nonscan through effects)
2	Effect/beam red fader
3	Effect/beam green fader
4	Effect/beam blue fader
5	Lumia fader
6	Lumia speed
7	Scan through effect #1 engage, diffraction grating
8	Scan through effect #1 coarse speed control
9	Scan through effect #1 fine speed control
10	Scan through effect #2 engage, fuzz
11	Scan through effect #2 coarse speed control
12	Scan through effect #2 fine speed control
13	House lights
14	Fog
15	Strobe
16	Laser control (start or current up)
17	User 1
18	User 2
19	User 3
20	User 4
21	Beam diffraction effect 1
22	Beam diffraction effect 2
23	Beam actuator 1
24	Beam actuator 2
25	Beam actuator 3
26	Beam actuator 4
27	Beam actuator 5
28	Beam actuator 6
29	Beam actuator 7
30	Beam actuator 8
31	Beam actuator 9
32	Beam actuator 10
33-66	Reserved for future ILDA assignment

Table 8.2 ILDA ADAT Track Assignments

ADAT Track	Signal Assignment
1	X axis
2	Y axis
3	Red
4	Green
5	Blue
6	SMPTE time code and/or DMX projector control
7	Left Audio
8	Right Audio

ADAT Track Assignments

The ILDA also has set up some standard track assignments for multitrack digital recorders. With this standard, tapes from different companies can be exchanged and still share some common functionality. Table 8.2 shows these track assignments.

SMPTE TIME CODE, MIDI

Many laser systems can accept or generate various show-control signals such as MIDI or SMPTE (see Chapter 9 and Part 4 for detailed explanations of each), as can commonly used digital multitrack tape decks such as ADAT. Safety considerations, of course, are always paramount when dealing with lasers, and especially when interfacing a laser system with another controller.

9

Sound

Performance sound systems traditionally break down into two basic types: reinforcement and playback. Reinforcement systems use microphones, mixers, amplifiers, and speakers to bring live music, singing, speech, or other sounds to a larger audience than would be possible acoustically. These systems are used in musical or other live productions—everything from rock and roll to Broadway theatre. Playback systems take prerecorded music, dialogue, or effects, and present those sounds to an audience, such as those found in legitimate and corporate theatre productions, special events, theme parks, product launches, and even rock-and-roll concerts (although the audience may not know it). With the explosion of digital technology for sound, more and more productions are using hybrid reinforcement/playback systems: the (human) reinforcement mixer for a Broadway show is now able to press a single button and initiate complete sound-effects sequences. Conversely, a playback operator on a corporate presentation could also control a few channels of microphones.

CENTRALIZATION

In the world of lighting, there are an increasing number of intelligent devices distributed throughout a performance facility, each of which needs control communications. In audio, however, the opposite is happening—with the advent of inexpensive yet high-power Digital Signal Processing (DSP) technologies, self-powered loudspeakers, and other innovations, more functionality is being put into less physical boxes, and it is now possible to have an extremely sophisticated performance audio system with very few components.

SOUND CONTROL EQUIPMENT

A wide variety of audio devices is capable of being controlled, and a few types are covered here. Devices capable of control break down into audio playback devices, mixers/matrices, processors, amps, and self-powered speakers.

Audio Playback Devices

For many years, the primary machine for professional audio playback was the reel-to-reel analog tape deck, which offered acceptable fidelity, "editability," and simple and automatic cuing using leader tape and a photo-detector. "Cart" (from "cartridge") machines operated similarly, but housed analog tape in an endless-loop cassette. Today, however, you are extremely unlikely to see an analog tape deck in even the smallest professional performance audio system; slowly but surely, analog playback machines of all sorts have been replaced by a number of digital playback devices: MiniDisc players, digital audiotape (DAT) machines, samplers, EPROM[1] players, PC Card units, hard-disk based systems, CD players, and even DVD players.

MiniDisk and DAT machines, originally designed for the consumer market, have flourished in the professional and semiprofessional markets. While DAT machines offer excellent sound quality, standard models are difficult to cue consistently, and models capable of time-code operation are very expensive. Until very recently, MiniDisk players capable of remote control were very expensive, but there are now a few low-cost professional units. Samplers, originally designed to offer musicians quick, musical access to digital sound "samples," offer excellent sound quality and instant cue access because the sound is stored in memory. A similar device for long-term applications (as in theme parks) is the EPROM or PC Card playback unit, in which the sound is stored in programmable memory or PC Cards.

With the prices of sophisticated computers and storage media dropping all the time, computer hard-disk-based playback and editing systems are becoming more and more popular. They offer nearly instant, random access playback capabilities, with cue durations limited only by the amount of disk space. Some of these computer-based units act as virtual samplers, while

---

[1] Erasable, programmable, read-only memory.

Figure 9.1 Hard-Disk-Based Audio Player (Courtesy Akai Musical Instrument Corp.)

others incorporate level, routing, and cueing functions for performance applications. Other units use dedicated processors to play back sounds from hard drives (see Figure 9.1).

The price of writable CD media and CD "burners" has plummeted in recent years, and it is now possible for nearly anyone to make their own CD. Finding a CD player that can easily be interfaced into a control system, however, is sometimes a difficult task—often the only units capable of professional remote operation are broadcast-quality CD or DVD players.

Mixers and Matrices

The core of any traditional sound system is the "mixer," often called the "console" or "desk," which routes, distributes, and manipulates audio in various ways. Traditional performance audio mixers come in two basic flavors: "front of house" (FOH), or "monitor." Performance-oriented FOH consoles (see Figure 9.2) typically combine a large number of inputs into a smaller number of outputs; monitor consoles typically route a smaller number of inputs to a large number of outputs. Of course, like everything else these days, the lines between these two types are getting blurry, and many mixers are now available that are designed to do both tasks.

While the majority of performance consoles today are still analog, there are an ever-increasing number of digital systems that offer sophisticated automation and recall capabilities. Some even move the mixing functions into a rack that can be located backstage, while the human operator mixes on a remote, all-digital "control surface" (see Figure 9.3).

Other digital mixing systems do away with the control surface altogether and use software "front ends." These systems are generally not designed for seat-of-the-pants live operation, but often work in a "live assist" capacity on complex live shows, or completely automate "canned" shows. These systems are really less like a traditional mixer and more like a digital

Figure 9.2 Large Performance Audio Mixer (Courtesy Cadac)

Figure 9.3 Large Digital Audio Mixer for Live Performance (Courtesy Yamaha)

"matrix" (named for the schematic appearance of the unit's signal flow), which allows any or many inputs to be routed (sometimes proportionately) to a number of outputs. Some of these units (see Figures 9.4 and 9.5) are designed specifically for show applications, are cue-based, are capable of sophisticated timed and triggered transitions between programmed presets, and can be controlled in real time.

Figure 9.4 Show-Oriented Audio Matrix System (Courtesy Level Control Systems)

Figure 9.5 Show-Oriented Audio Matrix System (Courtesy Richmond Sound Design)

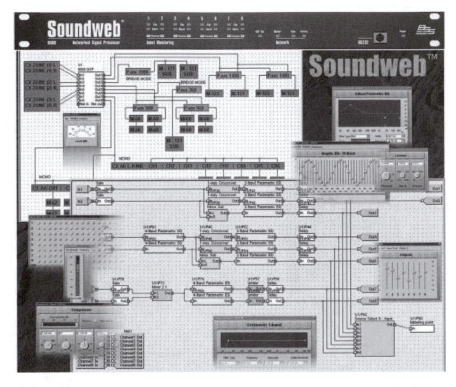

Figure 9.6 Installation-Oriented Audio Matrix System (Courtesy BSS Audio)

Other matrix systems are designed primarily for the permanent installation market and are more flexible in their configuration, but less flexible in their transitional and cueing ability. They are, therefore, generally cheaper (see Figure 9.6).

Audio Processors

Using audio "processors" such as equalizers, signal delays, crossovers, reverberation and effect units, designers can control many aspects of audio signals. Many of these processors are now capable of interfacing in a wide range of ways with control systems, or even come with sophisticated software that runs on an external PC for control or configuration.

Amplifiers

Amplifiers (see Figure 9.7) are the workhorses of audio (equivalent to lighting dimmers in many ways), taking the small signals from mixers or processors

Figure 9.7 Audio Amplifer (Courtesy Crown International)

and increasing those signals in magnitude to drive loudspeakers. In the past, amps were generally set to one level using local manual controls; any gain manipulations were done by varying the level of the input signal. Amplifiers today, however, are increasingly capable of remote-controlled operations; many manufacturers have proprietary systems that allow centralized control of nearly any amplifier parameter, no matter where in a performance facility an amp is located.

Self-Powered Speakers

Self-powered speakers (see Figure 9.8) combine equalization, crossover, protection, and amplification functions directly into the speaker cabinet,

Figure 9.8 Self-Powered Loudspeaker (Courtesy Meyer Sound Laboratories)

minimizing complex signal connections and adjustments, and length-limiting high-power speaker-cable runs. While many manufacturers have used this approach for performance audio systems over the years, one manufacturer—Meyer Sound Labs—has in recent years successfully pushed the concept into our industry. With so much intelligence in every speaker, and speakers distributed all over a performance facility, remote control and monitoring become even more important.

INFRARED

Many audio devices have infrared (IR) interfaces for handheld remote controls. Some control systems can sample the data sent from these handheld units (typically simple serial strings), and play them back either through the air or over a piece of plastic fiber, the end of which is kludged somehow to the front of the audio device.

These consumer interfaces are generally not suitable for professional applications, except as a means of absolute last resort. The world of IR is a highly nonstandardized and undocumented quagmire; some handheld remote controls don't even spit out the same data when the same button is pressed twice! There are many other disadvantages: there is typically no way to address multiple, identical units using the simple coding schemes; the IR path through the air can be blocked by a person or object; or, someone could knock out of alignment the fiber-optic cables used to pipe the commands to a specific unit. IR may be the only way to interface to some pieces of equipment, but this gear is typically suited for home theatres, not professional applications.

CONTACT CLOSURES

Playback and other kinds of audio devices often offer simple GPI or Contact Closure interfaces (see Chapter 2 for more information). These give the designer a crude way to interface with the device—and many times a crude interface is better than none at all, or is all that is needed. These interfaces rarely can do more than simple "Play" and "Stop" kinds of commands; trying to tell a unit to cue up to a certain sound or to "back up three cues" might be difficult, depending on how the manufacturer has implemented the interface. Serial interfaces offer much more powerful control.

EIA SERIAL STANDARDS

Many devices in audio, particularly those that have roots in the broadcast market (which is much larger than the live market), can be controlled using serial commands over an EIA serial link such as 232 or 422.

EIA and ASCII Commands

PC card, CD/DVD, and MiniDisc players and other devices often have EIA-232 or 422 ports and can be triggered by simple ASCII commands, with each manufacturer making up their own command set. For example, a playback device might be designed to start playing when it receives the ASCII characters "PL⇐" (where ⇐ means carriage return). While this means that each device may have a different command set, the fact that the manufacturer put a serial port on the device at least gives a system designer a fairly straightforward and powerful way to interface with it, and control can be quite sophisticated with a well-designed unit. Since every manufacturer designs their own control language, there are few standards, but some of these units follow de facto video control approaches such as the Sony "9-Pin" protocol, which is covered in Chapter 10, "Video."

AES-15/PA-422

In 1991, the Audio Engineering Society (AES) developed the "PA-422" remote-control standard for audio equipment, the official title of which is AES-15. The standard was based on a control protocol developed by audio manufacturer IED and originally implemented in 1981. Because of the protocol's limitations, it never really caught on, but you might encounter it in an older installation, so an introduction is warranted here. Full details, of course, are available from the AES.

PA-422, as you might expect, is based on the EIA-422 differential serial-data interface standard, and is therefore designed for communications between DCE and DTE components. PA-422 is a master/slave system, implemented with a single master control computer and a number of slave devices. Actual commands sent over the link are defined by the manufacturer of a controlled device, but a general device control language is laid out in the standard for informational purposes. PA-422 uses 1 start bit, 8 data bits, an even parity bit, and 1 stop bit. The data transmission rate is 19.2 kbps, although higher rates are allowed if all devices on the link can operate at higher speeds. PA-422 specifies shielded, twisted-pair cable, and sub-miniature DB-9-type connectors, with female connectors for data output (DTE) and male connectors for input (DCE).

In PA-422, the control computer (DTE) initiates transmission by sending an 8-bit equipment-address code on the transmit circuit. The receiving device, which must be set to one of the 250 valid addresses, receives these bytes and sets the link's Data Set Ready (DSR) line on. The control computer then sets the Data Terminal Ready (DTR) line to an on condition. Once the DCE has detected this signal, it returns 2 bytes of data to the DTE: a device-type code and a manufacturer's ID code. The device-type code tells the controller what

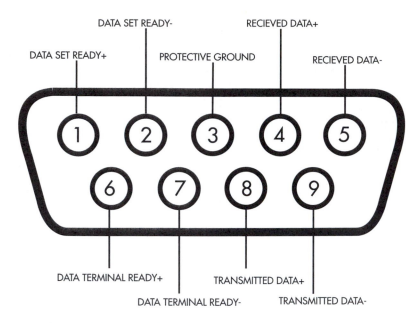

Figure 9.9 PA-422 Interface Signals (Male Connector Shown)

kind of device has replied, and some general device codes are specified in the standard, such as programmable equalizers, signal delays, gain/level controls, signal routers, and so on. Once the control computer has received the device and manufacturer data from the DCE, it sends a command followed by the appropriate data. When the operation is complete, the controlled device (DCE) returns a communications status (comstat) code and then resets its DTR line. The comstat code is used to indicate if the transmission proceeded properly. If a proper comstat code is not received, the controlling computer (DTE) times out (generally the time-out is 250 ms) and returns the DTR line to its idle state. The controlling software on the master controller should report a fault to the (human) operator if the device sends no response, an invalid response, or any non-00h comstat-error code.

MUSICAL INSTRUMENT DIGITAL INTERFACE (MIDI)

The Musical Instrument Digital Interface (MIDI) was originally designed for synthesizer interconnection and is now used in many parts of the entertainment industry. MIDI's core commands relate more closely to sound control than any other performance media, so the basics will be covered in this chapter. Other branches of MIDI, such as MIDI Show Control, are important for many entertainment applications and are covered separately in subsequent chapters.

MIDI's roots are in the early 1980s, when, with the explosive growth of sophisticated keyboard synthesizers, musicians began to want their keyboards linked to simplify complex studio and live-performance setups. Several manufacturers had developed proprietary interfaces to connect their own equipment, but these systems would not work with gear from other manufacturers. In 1981, engineers at Sequential Circuits, a major manufacturer at the time, began talks with their counterparts at Roland and Yamaha in order to standardize inter-synthesizer connections. These talks eventually resulted in the formation of the MIDI Manufacturer's Association (MMA) and the release of the official MIDI specification in 1983.

Basic Structure

In its most basic configuration, MIDI allows instruments to be connected in a simple master/slave relationship (see Figure 9.10).

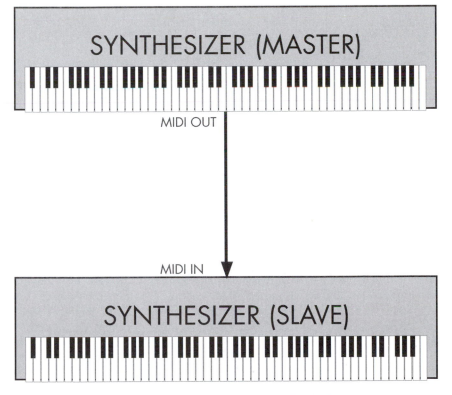

Figure 9.10   Simple MIDI System Block Diagram

No audio is transmitted over a MIDI line; control information representing musical events is all that is sent. So, if the MIDI output from synthesizer 1 is connected to synthesizer 2's MIDI input, pressing the third "A" note key on synthesizer 1 simultaneously creates the electronic equivalent of an $A3^2$ key-press on "synth" 2. Synthesizer sound program changes and other commands are transmitted in a similar fashion: if a program is selected on synth 1, the same program will also be selected on synth 2. MIDI is unidirectional and open loop; so in the configuration shown in Figure 9.10, nothing you do on synth 2 will have any effect on synth 1; in fact, synth 1 has no way of knowing whether synth 2 is connected, powered up, or even exists.

Physical Connections

MIDI runs asynchronously at 31.25 kbps. It is, by specification, opto-isolated: the inputs of a MIDI receiver connect directly to an opto-isolator chip. The interface circuit is relatively simple, and data transmission is accomplished using common and inexpensive universal asynchronous receiver-transmitter (UART) chips. The circuit is a current-loop type; a current-on state is logical zero. Since MIDI was designed for low-cost synthesizer interconnection, the maximum standard cable length is 50 feet. However, many MIDI devices can drive significantly longer cables, and a number of devices have been developed to send MIDI over nearly unlimited distances.

MIDI transmits its data over standard, shielded, twisted pair cable, and uses DIN 180° 5-pin connectors. Female connectors are used on equipment, with the shield connected only at the MIDI Out port. All cables are male-to-male, with the shield connected at both ends. The MIDI DIN connector has the control signals shown in Figure 9.11.

Since the standard is unidirectional, a MIDI instrument usually has both a receiver (MIDI In), a transmitter (MIDI Out), and sometimes a pass-through connector (MIDI Thru)—an opto-isolated copy of the data on the MIDI In port. This Thru port is invaluable for daisy-chaining devices.

MIDI Messages

MIDI's data is transmitted in a 10-bit word, composed of a start bit, an 8-bit data byte, and a stop bit. Musical data is broken down into "messages," each composed of a "status" byte followed by 0 or more "data" bytes. A status byte always has its most-significant bit set to 1 (i.e., 1xxxxxxx); a data byte has its most-significant bit reset to 0 (i.e., 0xxxxxxx).

---

[2]This may look like hex, but it's musical terminology that means the A in the third octave.

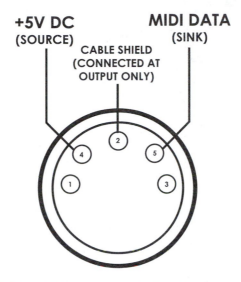

+5V DC
(SOURCE)

MIDI DATA
(SINK)

CABLE SHIELD
(CONNECTED AT
OUTPUT ONLY)

Figure 9.11   MIDI Output Signals (Female Connector Shown)

Pressing a key on a MIDI keyboard generates a message in hex such a 90 24 3F, which breaks down as follows:

90	Status Byte	9 means Note On; 0 means channel 1
24	Data Byte 1	Note C2 (second C note from the left)
3F	Data Byte 2	Velocity[3] of 63 (decimal)

Releasing the second C key on the keyboard generates the hex message 80 24 3F, or Channel 1 Note Off, C2, Velocity of 63.[4]

There are two primary types of MIDI messages: "channel" and "system."

Channel Messages

Four bits of Channel message status bytes are used to denote the message's channel, and one controller can separately address, on a message-by-message basis, different devices. Four bits give us 16 discrete control channels; each receiving device is configured to listen to one or more of the channels. MIDI is a broadcast standard, so all messages are simply sent out to all devices on a given MIDI link; each receiver is responsible for

---

[3]Velocity indicates how quickly—that is, how hard—a key was pressed. Synthesizers and samplers can use this information to create different sounds for differing key-press intensities.

[4]In many cases, the receiver ignores the release velocity, or uses a Note On with a velocity of zero to trigger an "off" event.

Table 9.1 MIDI Channel Voice Messages

Function	Status Byte		Data Byte(s)	Where
	Binary	*Hex*		
Note Off	1000cccc	8c	0nnnnnnn 0vvvvvvv	c or cccc = Channel Number, 1-16 (0-Fh) nnnnnnn = Note Number, 0-127 (00-7Fh)
Note On (Velocity of 0 equals Note Off)	1001cccc	9c	0nnnnnnn 0vvvvvvv	vvvvvvv = Velocity, 0-127 (00-7Fh)
Poly Key Pressure	1010cccc	Ac	0nnnnnnn 0rrrrrrr	rrrrrrr = Pressure, 0-127 (00-7Fh)
Control Change	1011cccc	Bc	0xxxxxxx 0yyyyyyy	xxxxxxx = Control Number, 0-120 (00-78h) (78-7F Reserved, see next table) yyyyyyy = Control Value, 0-127 (00-7Fh)
Program Change	1100cccc	Cc	0ppppppp	ppppppp = Program Number, 0-127 (00-7Fh)
Channel Pressure	1101cccc	Dc	0xxxxxxx	xxxxxxx = Pressure Value, 0-127 (00-7Fh)
Pitch Bend Change	1110cccc	Ec	01111111 0mmmmmmm	lllllll = Least Significant Pitch Byte mmmmmmm = Most Significant Pitch Byte (both bytes must be sent)

determining, based on its configuration, whether it should act on a particular message.

Within the channel classification there are voice messages, which control the instrument's voices, and mode messages, which determine how the synthesizer will deal with the voice messages. These days, one physical MIDI-controllable synthesizer may have many "virtual" synths, each operating on a different channel. The Channel Voice messages are shown in Table 9.1.

I'm including all standard MIDI messages here for reference, but in entertainment control applications, you are most likely to encounter only the Note On, Note Off, Program Change, and Control Change messages. The Control Change message was defined as a sort of configurable generic control message, and there are a number of standardized controller types for the Control Change messages in the MIDI spec, for musical parameters like "breath Controller," "portamento time," and so forth. The control numbers 78-7Fh were reserved and make up the "Channel Mode" messages in Table 9.2.

These messages are very closely related to synthesizer operation and are not often found in general entertainment (nonmusical) operations.

System Messages

The other general category of messages is the channel-less group of "System" messages. Within System Messages, there are three subcategories: "System Common" messages, which are intended for all devices connected to the system; "Real-Time" messages, used for timing and other functions; and "System Exclusive" messages, designed so that manufacturers could send any kind of data over the MIDI line. System common messages are shown in Table 9.3.

MIDI Time Code will be covered in subsequent chapters. "Song Position Pointer" and "Song Select" are part of a MIDI sync system (see below) used primarily in musical sequencers. "Tune Request" is used with an analog synthesizer to request that the synthesizer tune all its internal oscillators.

System-real-time messages are shown in Table 9.4. These messages have no data bytes.

The "Timing Clock" message, used for MIDI sync applications, is sent out at a rate of 24 messages per quarter note. "Start" messages are sent when a play button is pressed on a master sequencer; "Continue" continues after a sequence has been stopped; "Stop" is the equivalent of pressing the stop button on a sequencer. See below for description of "Active Sensing." "System Reset," as you might expect, resets the entire system to an initial power-up state.

Table 9.2 MIDI Channel Mode Messages

Function	Status Byte		Data Byte(s)		Where
	Binary	Hex	Binary	Hex	
All Sound Off	1011cccc	Bc	01111000 00000000	78 00	c or cccc = Channel Number, 1-16 (0-Fh)
Reset All Controllers	1011cccc	Bc	01111001 00000000	79 00	
Local Control Off	1011cccc	Bc	01111010 00000000	7A 00	
Local Control On	1011cccc	Bc	01111010 01111111	7A 7F	
All Notes Off	1011cccc	Bc	01111011 00000000	7B 00	
Omni Mode Off	1011cccc	Bc	01111100 00000000	7C 00	
Omni Mode On	1011cccc	Bc	01111101 00000000	7D 00	
Mono Mode On (Poly Mode Off)	1011cccc	Bc	01111110 0nnnnnnn	7E	nnnnnnn = Number of Channels
Poly Mode On (Mono Mode Off)	1011cccc	Bc	01111111 00000000	7F 00	

Table 9.3 MIDI System Common Messages

Function	Status Byte		Data Byte(s)	Where
	Binary	Hex		
MIDI Time-Code Quarter Frame	11110001	F1	0nnndddd	nnn = Message Type dddd = Values
Song Position Pointer	11110010	F2	01111111 0mmmmmmm	1111111 = Least Significant Byte mmmmmmm = Most Significant Byte
Song Select	11110011	F3	0sssssss	sssssss = Song Number
Undefined	11110100	F4		
Undefined	11110101	F5		
Tune Request	11110110	F6		

Table 9.4 MIDI System Real-Time Messages

Function	Status Byte	
	Binary	*Hex*
Timing Clock	11111000	F8
Undefined	11111001	F9
Start	11111010	FA
Continue	11111011	FB
Stop	11111100	FC
Undefined	11111101	FD
Active Sensing	11111110	FE
System Reset	11111111	FF

Active Sensing

For complex sequencer-based systems, MIDI has a mode called "Active Sensing," and this mode sometimes causes confusion among entertainment system designers. In this mode, if a device is not sending out MIDI data, it will send an FEh Active Sensing byte (a System Real-Time Message) every 300ms. If a receiver does not receive either a standard MIDI or Active Sensing message every 300 ms, it can assume that a problem has occurred upstream, and it will shut down all open voices and wait for the problem to be resolved. When entertainment system engineers are looking at raw MIDI data, they may see this byte flooding their capture buffers; many musical devices have this feature enabled.

MIDI Sync

A MIDI Note On message is relative; it contains no information about where in a musical composition that note belongs. A system based on Song Position Pointers (SPPs) was implemented in the original MIDI spec to communicate this information for sequencing and tape-sync applications. For most entertainment control applications, the SPP scheme has been replaced by MIDI Time Code, but here is a brief introduction.

The SPP is a count of the number of 16th notes that have elapsed since the beginning of the song or since a tape deck's start button was pressed. If the MIDI system is locked to a tape deck and the deck is fast-forwarded, the system sends SPP messages only before and after shuttling (fast-forwarding or rewinding). When the tape is playing, the sync device maintains its own SPP count, which is incremented every 6 Timing Clock messages, which are sent out at a rate of 24 per quarter note. The timing clock is based on tempo, not real time, so its frequency varies with the tempo of the song.

System-Exclusive Messages

The MIDI specs set aside two status bytes—Start of System Exclusive (SysEx) and End of System Exclusive (EOX)—to allow manufacturers to send any kind of data down the MIDI line, and to leave room for future expansion (a very wise move). System-exclusive messages are not channel-specific; any device that receives the SysEx messages can act on them, assuming they are configured to do so. The structure of these messages is shown in Table 9.5.

In a System Exclusive message, the F0h SysEx header byte is sent first, then a manufacturer's ID number, and then a number of 7-bit data bytes, whose meaning is determined by the manufacturer. When complete, an EOX message is sent to return the system to normal operation.

Any manufacturer can register for a Manufacturer's ID number with the MMA, and if they make a product and publish the data within one year, the ID number becomes permanent. Enough manufacturers around the world registered numbers that the MMA had to expand the ID number from 1 to 3 bytes, but still keep the "legacy" numbers active. So they chose the unassigned 00h ID for expansion; if a receiver sees the 00h ID number, it should treat the next 2 bytes as an extension to the ID number, instead of as data.

Three of the 127 possible manufacturer's ID numbers are set aside for some special types of messages. 7Dh is for research or academic development, and devices using this ID are not to be released to the public; 7Eh is used for "non-real-time" messages; and 7Fh is used for "real-time" system-exclusive messages, very useful for our industry, as we will see later. The overall structure of messages using these special ID numbers is F0 7Fh (or 7D or 7E), the "device ID," indicating to which device the message is

Table 9.5 MIDI System Exclusive Messages

| Function | Status Byte | | Data Byte(s) | Where |
	Binary	Hex		
Start of System Exclusive	11110000	F0	0iiiiiii	iiiiiii = ID Number of 0-124 (00-7Ch) (125-127, 7D-7Fh reserved, see text). If first byte is zero, the next 2 bytes are extensions to the ID number.
Data			0xxxxxxx ...	xxxxxxx = 7-bit data (or extended ID) any number of bytes
End of System Exclusive	11110111	F7		End of System Exclusive

addressed, then 2 sub-ID bytes, the data bytes, and then the F7h EOX status byte to close out the message:

```
FO 7F [Device ID] [Sub-ID #1] [Sub-ID #2] [Data]…[Data] F7
```

Since MIDI is a simple point-to-point interface, no priority levels can be assigned to particular messages. But the "real-time" and "non-real-time" categories do, theoretically, allow a receiver to deal with them in different ways. The non-real-time messages are shown in Table 9.6.

Table 9.6 MIDI Universal Non-Real-Time System Exclusive (7Eh) ID Numbers

Function	Sub-ID #1	Sub-ID #2
Unused	00	
Sample Dump Header	01	
Sample Data Packet	02	
Sample Dump Request	03	
MTC Special	04	00
MTC Punch- In Points		01
MTC Punch- Out Points		02
MTC Delete Punch- In Point		03
MTC Delete Punch- Out Point		04
MTC Event- Start Point		05
MTC Event- Stop Point		06
MTC Event- Start Point with Additional Information		07
MTC Event Stop- Point with Additional Information		08
MTC Delete Event- Start Point		09
MTC Delete Event- Stop Point		0A
MTC Cue Points		0B
MTC Cue Points with Additional Information		0C
MTC Delete Cue Point		0D
MTC Event Name in Additional Information		0E
Sample Dump Multiple Loop Points	05	01
Sample Dump Loop Points Request		02
General Information Identity Request	06	01
General Information Identity Reply		02
File Dump Header	07	01
File Dump Data Packet		02
File Dump Request		03
MIDI Tuning Standard Bulk Dump Request	08	00
MIDI Tuning Standard Request		01
General MIDI System On	09	00
General MIDI System Off		01
End of File	7B	
Wait	7C	
Cancel	7D	
NAK	7E	
ACK	7F	

Table 9.7 MIDI Universal Real-Time System Exclusive (7Fh) ID Numbers

Function	Sub-ID#1 (Hhex)	Sub-ID #2 (Hhex)
Unused	00	
MIDI Time- Code Full Message	01	01
MIDI Time- Code User Bits		02
MIDI Show Control	02	
Notation-Bar Number	03	01
Notation-Time Signature (Immediate)		02
Notation-Time Signature (Delayed)		42
Device Control-Master Volume	04	01
Device Control-Master Balance		02
MIDI Time- Code Real- Time Cueing	05	
MIDI Machine Control Command	06	
MIDI Machine Control Response	07	
MIDI Tuning Standard	08	

Many of these non-real-time messages are found primarily in musical MIDI applications, but several are worth mentioning here. The Sample Dump commands are all part of a standard way to interchange sound files between digital samplers; General MIDI is discussed later in this chapter; Wait, Cancel, NAK, and ACK are all part of the Sample Dump standard. Many of the MIDI Time-Code commands listed here are part of the MIDI Set-Up commands used to position sequencers and other devices in musical synchronization systems.

In addition to the non-real-time messages we've covered, there are also a number of globally defined, "real-time" SysEx messages, as listed in Table 9.7.

MIDI Show Control, MIDI Time Code, and MIDI Machine Control

MIDI Show Control, MIDI Time Code, and MIDI Machine Control, are all "Universal Real-Time System Exclusive Messages." MIDI Show Control is a MIDI-based show control standard. MIDI Time Code is a method of sending SMPTE Time Code over a MIDI line. MIDI Machine Control is designed for the control of time-based, transport-oriented equipment such as audio tape decks. All three of these standards are important for us and have applications broader than just sound control, so they are covered completely in their own chapters later in this book.

MIDI Running Status

With extremely complex, multichannel musical compositions, the bandwidth limits of MIDI can sometimes be approached, and this can cause slight musical mistimings. To allow as much musical data to be sent down the line using the fewest messages, the developers of MIDI developed a feature called "Running Status." Running Status allows 1 MIDI status byte to be sent, followed by a group of data bytes. The data bytes in the group will then each be treated as the same type of message until another status byte is received.

For instance, to trigger and release a chord of three notes using standard MIDI, we would need to send six messages total, consisting of three Note On messages, and three Note Off messages:

```
90  3C  7F
90  27  62
90  43  80
80  3C  00
80  27  00
80  43  00
```

Using MIDI running status, and using Note On, velocity 00 messages instead of separate Note Offs, we would only have to send the following bytes:

```
90  3C  7F
    27  62
    43  80
    3C  00
    27  00
    43  00
```

After the first 90h status byte, the receiver enters Note On running status, and all subsequent data bytes are treated as note information. Running Status is cancelled as soon as another valid Status Byte is received. With this approach, 5 less bytes need to be sent, and this would allow two more note messages to be sent in the same period of time. In a simple application, this wouldn't count for much, but in complex MIDI streams, any bandwidth saved is useful.

General MIDI

In some ways, "General MIDI" is a misnomer; it really doesn't affect MIDI at all—it specifies a standard way of *implementing* MIDI in synthesizers for simple musical applications. Nonetheless, it deserves a brief mention here.

Musicians, individualistic lot that they are, set up their systems in a way that is comfortable for them: channel 1 for this keyboard, channel 2 for that tone module, channel 10 for a drum machine, and so on. Each synthesizer, in turn, uses different program numbers (triggered by MIDI Program Changes) for each of its possible sounds. General MIDI standardizes these setups so that you can build a song on one synthesizer, transport it to another system, play it back, and hear some semblance of what you created on the original system. This has become increasingly important with PC MIDI cards with onboard synthesizers.

The highlights of General MIDI are as follows:

- Middle C is MIDI Note 60 (3Ch).
- All voices must respond to velocity information.
- All synthesizers should have a minimum of 24-voice polyphony.
- All synthesizers must be capable of responding to all 16 MIDI channels.
- Percussion is on MIDI channel 10.
- The 128 program changes are standardized.
- Percussion sounds are mapped to specific notes and specific program changes.
- Each channel must respond to several continuous controllers in a specific way.

MIDI Processors/Routers/Interfaces

Because of the large musical market, there is a wide array of sophisticated MIDI processors, routers, and interfaces that allow MIDI to be converted, changed, interfaced, and transposed in a nearly infinite number of ways.

For electrical reasons, MIDI cannot be "two-ferred"—a "Y" cable cannot be used. Instead, a splitter or "Thru" box is used, which takes an input and buffers and repeats the received data for a number of outputs. MIDI splitters are very useful when a single MIDI device must connect to or drive a number of other devices (see Figure 9.12).

A MIDI merger merges two MIDI signals, for cases when two outputs must be combined to drive one input. These devices buffer each MIDI stream to be merged and combine the data streams. The combined stream is then sent to the output.

MIDI patch bays are generally combinations of mergers and splitters, with user-configurable patching capabilities.

A useful device for interfacing purposes is the MIDI-to-contact-closure interface. These devices can take a contact closure input and send out a preprogrammed MIDI message, or vice versa (close a contact based on an incoming message) (see Figure 9.13).

One interesting MIDI device is the pitch-to-MIDI converter, which translates audio pitch information into MIDI notes. In entertainment control, pitch-to-MIDI converters can be used for triggering devices from an audio signal; for instance, a gunshot could (with some MIDI filtering) trig-

Figure 9.12 MIDI Splitter/Thru (Courtesy MIDIMan)

Figure 9.13 MIDI to Contact-Closure Interface (Courtesy MIDI Solutions)

ger a lighting effect. Other conversion devices are available to allow MIDI systems to generate ASCII messages on EIA-232/422 ports; the ASCII strings are constructed using SysEx messages.

When we enter the realm of the personal computer, another world of MIDI processing capability opens. There are a multitude of sequencing pro-

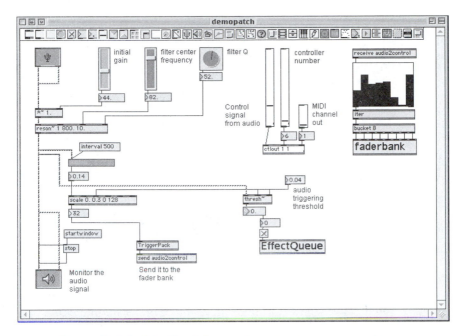

Figure 9.14 Max Patch Screen (Max Patch by Gregory Taylor)

grams, some of which include extensive MIDI processing capabilities. A unique program takes MIDI processing capability to the extreme: Max (see Figure 9.14).

Described as "an interactive graphic programming environment," with nearly infinite uses and applications, Max allows objects on the screen to represent various MIDI parameters and ports; connecting objects is as easy as drawing a line. This simple approach allows easy development of tremendously sophisticated systems. Because of the huge market created by the MIDI standard, there is a virtually infinite number of MIDI interfacing possibilities.

Recommended MIDI Topologies

In many musical MIDI installations, the control signal is simply daisy-chained from the Thru of one device to the In of the next. However, since MIDI devices are active repeaters, they need power at all times to pass data. With a single loop, a break in the physical connections or a power failure in a device can cause all downstream devices on the network to lose data. A better approach for critical entertainment control applications is a star, or home-run, topology (see Figure 9.15).

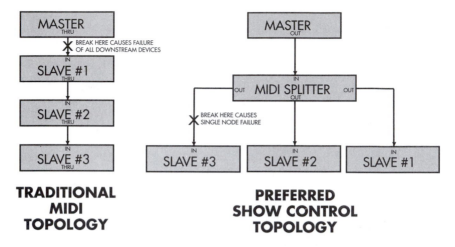

Figure 9.15   Preferred MIDI Network Topology

By using a MIDI splitter or patch bay, and running an individual line from the splitter to each device in the network, single failures between nodes on the network are isolated from other systems. Of course, if the central splitter goes down, messages will not be passed to any down-stream device.

Common MIDI Problems

MIDI is an amazingly powerful system, but it was designed for musical applications and not live entertainment control. For this reason, two maddening problems often surface when working with MIDI.

The first is the "Octave Problem." An octave is a doubling in frequency, or in typical western music scales, 12 half steps, which correspond to 12 MIDI note numbers. Often, one company will implement their device so that the octave containing middle C starts at some note number, and another company will implement their system in a different octave. This should have all been cleared up by General MIDI (middle C is note 60, or 3Ch), but a lot of non-General MIDI gear is out there, and many manufacturers simply misunderstand the numbering scheme. If you run across this problem, try adding or subtracting 12 from the Note number—one of the systems may be off by an octave.

The other common MIDI problem is the "Off by One" problem. This occurs because two companies have implemented a control range differently in their equipment: One company sets up their gear to work on program changes 0-127, and the other company designs their system to respond to 1-128. This problem can also manifest itself with channel numbers as 0-15 or 1-16. If you can't get two systems to talk, try adding or subtracting one from the parameter—you may be suffering the infamous off-by-one problem. In either of these cases, the best way to look at the data is in hex—there is no ambiguity there.

MANUFACTURER-SPECIFIC CONTROL SYSTEMS

A number of manufacturers, especially amplifier companies, have developed sound control systems to operate their own equipment. Most of these systems are designed for permanent installations, where amplifier rooms may be distributed throughout a large facility. Using one of these systems, a user can control and monitor many functions in any amplifier in the system from a central PC, usually running Windows software.

None of these systems interoperate, and each is developed and maintained by a particular company. However, to give you an idea of what's out there in the market, here's a brief introduction to several selected companies, listed alphabetically.

Apogee AmpNET™ Amplifier Control System

AmpNET™ is a relatively recent entry into the world of amplifier control systems by a well-established manufacturer—Apogee Sound (which recently

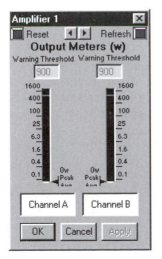 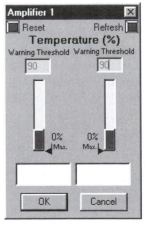

Figure 9.16   AmpNET™ System Screen (Courtesy Apogee Sound)

became a part of Bogen). Apogee has been known for many years for their loudspeakers, and in recent years has been manufacturing amplifiers as well. Apogee's AmpNET™ system offers a number of remote monitoring functions for Apogee amplifiers, such as level, mute, phase, on-off and breaker status, and reset. Each of these functions can be monitored or controlled with a few mouse clicks through Apogee's graphical user interface (see Figure 9.16), which runs under Windows.

AmpNET™ is based on the 32-bit Echelon LonWorks LNS network (see the Echelon section in Chapter 25), and operates over any twisted-pair cable. Apogee uses 2-pin "Euro-blok" connectors and, due to the structure of LNS, the polarity on the control link is irrelevant. The system can have up to 63 nodes before a repeater is necessary, and the system can span about 1500 meters.

Crest NexSys® Amplifier Control System

In 1990, Crest Audio introduced the NexSys system for control of its amplifier range. Through a graphical interface, NexSys lets a user control and monitor amplifier parameters such as gain, muting, polarity, temperature, and so on. Through standard hardware the system can generate or respond to contact closure or serial events, or, through the use of an optional MIDI interface, NexSys can control or be controlled by MIDI devices. In addition, with optional Load Monitor electronics, frequency-based load measurements of amp outputs can be taken. NexSys is also capable of storing user-defined system-operating thresholds; if these thresholds are exceeded, the program can log the events in a standard text file for later viewing.

NexSys has a Windows-based user interface (see Figure 9.17), allowing icons for each device in the system to be superimposed over graphic images, such as a stage layout. Clicking on an item with the mouse in this screen brings up virtual controls for that device. This Windows application can also be used to capture "snapshots" of control settings, which, in conjunction with the MIDI interface, allows scene-based control to be implemented.

NexSys operates over an optically-isolated EIA-485 data line, running at a rate of 120 kbps, with hardware-based error correction. A PC is used to control the entire system, interfaced through a "bus server" peripheral card. Standard twisted-pair cables connect the PC bus server to the other NexSys devices, such as Supervisors (which interface to the amplifiers), MIDI Interfaces, or Load Monitors. All NexSys devices in the system are run in a daisy-chain, with the last device terminated with a 120Ω resistor. Connections are through 3-pin "Euro-blok" connectors.

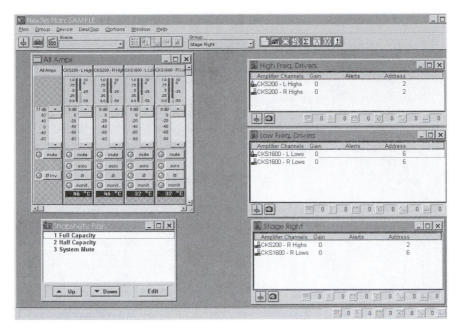

Figure 9.17 NexSys System Screen (Courtesy Crest Audio)

Crown IQ® Amplifier Control System

In the late 1980s, amplifier and microphone manufacturer Crown developed the IQ System to control their amplifier products from a graphical user interface (see Figure 9.18) running on a centralized computer. One of the early leaders of this technology, Crown, recently acquired by Harman International, has a large number of installed systems, allowing remote control of a variety of amplifier or DSP functions throughout a facility.

The control computer connects via an EIA 232/422 signal to a Host Computer Interface, which can connect to up to 8 system "loops," each of which can connect to 250 devices. IQ communications take place over a 20mA serial current loop operating at 38.4kbps. Since each unit is addressed by loop number, device type, and address, two devices of the same type cannot have the same address on the same loop. They can, however, have the same address on different loops, and using this feature, one loop might be used to control amps for the left speaker stack and another loop for the right. With this configuration, amps on both sides of the stage can be set to the same addresses (since they're on different loops), making the system easy to control.

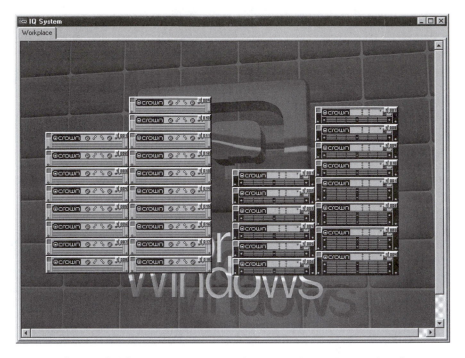

Figure 9.18 IQ System Screen (Courtesy Crown International)

For each device in the IQ System, data input connectors are different from data output connectors; this approach minimizes misconnections. Inputs to IQ devices were originally locking 5-pin female DIN connectors, with the output connectors as locking 4-pin female DIN connectors. More recent implementations use the ubiquitous RJ-45. The use of low-capacitance cable can greatly extend the effective range of the system, which is normally up to about 1000 feet. Longer links need to be repeated using IQ System repeaters; the signal can be repeated up to 57 times, allowing IQ networks to be spread over about 11 miles. For longer or supercritical applications, fiber-optic interfaces are also available.

Many IQ devices include a feature that greatly expands system-interfacing capabilities: the Auxiliary Control Port, which can be used for any electrically controllable device. The port itself is a 3-pin male mini-XLR connector, which outputs +15 V DC at 15mA on pin 3 (referenced to pin 1) when turned on from the master control computer. This port can be used to control external cooling fans for amp racks, or virtually anything that operates in a simple on/off fashion.

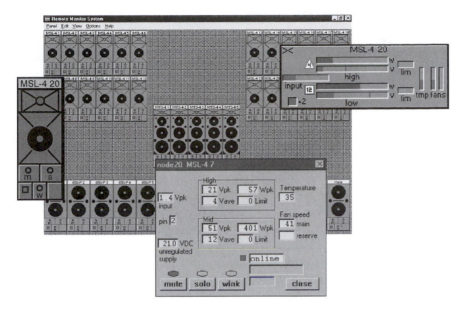

Figure 9.19 RMS System Screen (Courtesy Meyer Sound Laboratories)

Meyer Sound Labs RMS™ Self Powered Speaker Monitoring System

With the introduction of a line of self-powered speakers (see Figure 9.8), Meyer Sound Labs needed to develop a remote control and monitoring system as well, and the result was the Remote Monitoring System (RMS™). The system, similar to some of the commercially available amplifier control systems, allows a user to monitor parameters such as voltage, limiting activity, power output, temperature fan, and drive status for each speaker in the system. Access to the data is provided through a user-configured graphical user interface, with simple point-and-click access (see Figure 9.19).

The system is based on Echelon LonWorks technology, and allows up to 62 self-powered speakers to be connected. Using a "Free" topology (nodes can be connected in any way), a system can span about 1640 feet, and this range can be extended through heavier cable and a bus topology. Each speaker has two 2-pole "Euro-blok" connectors to allow for easy daisy chaining.

QSC QSControl™ Amplifier Control System

Amplifier manufacturer QSC was another one of the earlier pioneers into the amplifier control market,[5] and now has a product line based on TCP/IP

---

[5] QSC based their original system on MediaLink, but changed to Ethernet in recent years.

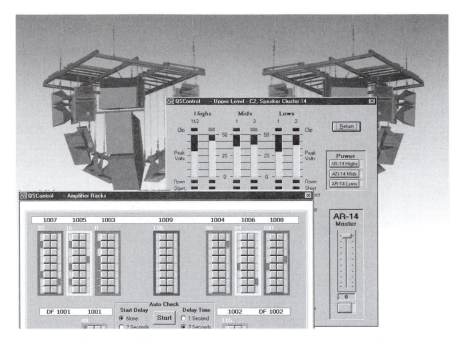

Figure 9.20   QSControl System Screen (Courtesy QSC)

and Ethernet (see Chapter 24). The system offers users either a standard or custom-programmed graphical user interface (see Figure 9.20) running on a Windows PC, which allows access to control and monitoring functions like channel power-on status, channel-protect status, clipping, input level, output level, thermal status, and so on, for any connected amplifier. Through custom-developed software on the PC, a user could also interface with standards such as MIDI.

The control computer connects to a MultiSignal processor via a standard Ethernet network, and the MultiSignal processor then connects to each controlled amplifier through a standard VGA cable. In this way, the interfaces are connected directly to the Ethernet network, but the amplifiers are not. Up to eight 2-channel amplifiers can be connected to and controlled by each interface. No audio is sent over the Ethernet link, but using associated QSC Rave products (which are based on Peak Audio's CobraNet, see below) and a switched Ethernet system, audio and control could be sent over the same Category 5 or other cabling.

Renkus-Heinz R-Control™ Amplifier Control System

R-Control™ was introduced in 1998 by Renkus-Heinz. The R-Control system offers remote monitoring and control functions such as scene store/recall,

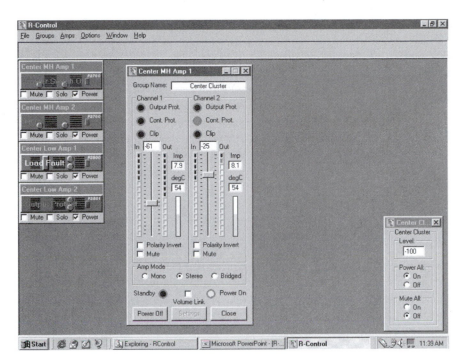

Figure 9.21 R-Control System Screen (Courtesy Renkus-Heinz)

event scheduler, fault logging, power on/off, channel level, "Solo" function, polarity inversion, level, mute, and loudspeaker-specific processor module status. Each of these functions can be monitored or controlled with a few mouse clicks through the R-Control graphical user interface (see Figure 9.21), which runs under Windows.

R-Control is based on the 32-bit Echelon LonWorks LNS network (see the Echelon section in Chapter 25), and operates over any twisted pair cable. Renkus-Heinz uses "Euro-Barrier" style connectors. The system can connect 64 amplifier nodes before a repeater is necessary, and a nonrepeater system can span about 2700 meters. Each R-H amplifier is manufactured with a unique ID number, so no addressing by the user is necessary.

AUDIO ENGINEERING SOCIETY AES-24

When the first edition of this book was released, work was under way on a radically new sound communications network standard—Audio Engineering Society (AES) 24. This was a very ambitious project, since the group was attempting to design an object-oriented and network-independent system from the ground up—not standardize or modify existing systems. After many years of on-and-off-again work, AES-24-1-1999, Part One of the proposed standard, was published in the April 1999 issue of the *Journal of the Audio Engineering Society.* While this part of the standard has been reviewed and issued, it is unlikely that the remaining (and key) pieces of the puzzle will ever be completed, and so, sadly, the standard is basically dead.

Two primary factors led to the failure of this standard effort. The first is that no clear market demand or commercial pressure ever developed for the creation of a unified audio control standard, so key manufacturers, many of whom had proprietary systems already on the market, supported the group's efforts only in token and not substantive ways. The second factor is that with the growth and power of modern DSP technologies, audio systems are becoming increasingly centralized, with more power housed in less physical devices, so there are less devices and types of devices that need to be connected and controlled.

SC-10, the AES standards committee that developed AES-24, has not stopped work, however; the group is, as of this writing, headed by Michael Karagosian of MKPE Consulting (Karagosian was formerly head of an SC-10 subcommittee). SC-10 is now acting as AES liaison with other groups developing related control technologies (such as ESTA), and is working to standardize approaches to software and networking "component" technologies. Audio systems today often feature control systems from multiple manufacturers, and component technologies should offer standardized tools to allow system integrators to create single control screens that combine control objects from many manufacturers, while the individual control networks remain segregated.

So, while it is unfortunate that AES-24 failed, the effort was not wasted. The list of those involved reads like a "who's who" of the industry, and those people have incorporated what they learned and developed into many products and systems on the market today.

NETWORKS FOR AUDIO DATA DISTRIBUTION AND CONTROL

With less equipment doing more in audio, the need for a unified control standard is less apparent, but the need for digital audio *data* distribution is increasingly clear. Since it's easy to "piggyback" control data onto digital audio, the two are often combined. Peak Audio has been a market leader in professional audio data distribution using Ethernet, and their CobraNet system is covered later in Chapter 24.

10

Video

With the ever-dropping prices and increasing sophistication of video and presentation technology, video images are finding their way into more live productions. Sophisticated control is allowing these images to move from the crudely cued applications of the past, to full integration into very live and even spontaneous productions.

VIDEO EQUIPMENT

As in audio, many video system components switch, route, or process the video signal itself, and many of those components are operated manually and locally. So in this chapter we'll focus our discussion on the control of video devices that can be controlled remotely.

Videotape Recorders

The oldest and most well established video medium is videotape, and since videotape is inexpensive and straightforward to work with, it is the medium of choice for "one-off" (one or a small number of performances) live events, or lower-budget, longer running shows. Because of the nature of tape, image quality degrades with repeated play of analog tapes, and even digital videotape will eventually wear out. Because videotape also has the disadvantage of being a linear format, it is slow to cue in comparison with other source devices.

Digital Disk Players

"Videodiscs" contain optically recorded video signals and (generally) four digital audio tracks. Videodiscs were, until recent years, the medium of choice for long-term and random-access playback applications. The discs do not degrade with multiple plays, and videodisc players can quickly and randomly access tracks anywhere on the disk, and cue either to a "chapter" or down to a single frame.

"Digital Video Disk" or "Digital Versatile Disk" (DVD) players are doing well in the consumer market, and are a modern replacement for videodiscs in the entertainment industry. DVDs use Moving Picture Experts Group "MPEG-2" technology to compress video; audio can be encoded in a variety of ways, at different quality levels with different numbers of tracks. While the MPEG coding scheme does not use traditional "frames," professional DVD players are generally able to cue to a specific frame. Industrial DVD players (see Figure 10.1) can be remotely controlled using serial commands, and recordable DVD players are also beginning to appear on the scene.

CRV Players

CRV Players are an older form of recordable, disk-based video player/ recorder made by Sony. They are no longer manufactured, but may be

Figure 10.1   Industrial DVD Player (Courtesy Pioneer New Media Technologies)

found in older installations. They recorded video on what looks like a giant floppy disk, and can be cued either to frame number (when controlled using Sony laser disc commands) or time (using the Sony "9-Pin" protocol; see later in this chapter).

Video Servers

"Video servers" take some sort of compressed video file, and play it back from a hard disk. These systems are usually either based on standard PCs, hard disks, and video cards, or are purpose-built machines (see Figure 10.2). Some of the servers can emulate other machines for easy control integration.

Video Routers/Switchers

Video switchers, like audio mixers, are generally used to switch the outputs of multiple video sources—cameras, videotape recorders, effects generators—into a smaller number of program outputs. Switchers are becoming increasingly automated, and external control is generally available on professional models.

A "routing matrix" or "crosspoint matrix" is essentially a fancy switcher; but unlike a switcher, which blends many inputs into a few outputs, a routing matrix can patch many inputs to many outputs simultaneously and independently. A number of audio/video routing matrices—capable of switching both audio and video—are remote-controllable and have many applications in the show environment.

Figure 10.2 Video Server (Courtesy Fast Forward Video)

Monitors, Projectors, and Video Walls

We've talked about video sources and video routing equipment, and now we move on to devices that take the video signals and display them to a group. The most common presentation device is the cathode-ray tube (CRT) monitor, or television. Professional monitors are generally capable of external control, if only for simple things like power on/off and input selection.

Video walls combine a number of images to create one large image, or use different signals (or parts of signals) to drive different monitors in the wall. Control of such systems is generally implemented using proprietary video-wall controllers, many of which can either act as a master controller for stand-alone applications, or act as a slave device in a larger system.

Video projectors have been improving dramatically in recent years, and most professional machines can accept a wide variety of input sources. Professional machines are also capable of external control, for power and lamp on/off, input selection, and many other parameters.

Video Sync Issues

In video studios, video frames from all equipment must lock together exactly in time; in other words, all the frames must be exactly in phase. For this reason, a separate video "sync" signal is often distributed around a studio or installation to synchronize all the video gear. This signal is often called "house" or master sync, and equipment that is synched in this way is often referred to as being "gen-locked" ("gen" for generator).

SMPTE TIME CODE

SMPTE Time Code's roots are in video editing, and its applications are well defined. SMPTE has now gone well beyond its original functions and become ubiquitous for a variety of time-based entertainment applications—everything from synchronizing tape decks to controlling huge time-based live shows. For these reasons, SMPTE Time Code is covered in detail in Chapter 17.

INFRARED

Many video devices, especially "prosumer" (professional/consumer) models, have infrared (IR) interfaces for handheld remote controls. Some control systems can sample the data sent from these handheld units (typically, simple serial strings) and play them back either through the air or over a piece of plastic fiber, the end of which is somehow kludged to the front of the video device.

These consumer interfaces are generally not suitable for professional applications, except as a means of absolute last resort. The world of IR is a highly non-standardized and undocumented quagmire; some handheld remote controls don't even spit out the same data when the same button is pressed twice! There are many other disadvantages: there is typically no way to address multiple, identical units using the simple coding schemes; the IR path through the air can be blocked by a person or object; or someone could knock out of alignment one of the fiber-optic cables used to pipe the commands to a specific unit. IR may be the only way to interface to some pieces of equipment, but this gear is typically suited for home theatres, not professional applications.

CONTACT CLOSURES/GENERAL PURPOSE INTERFACES

Playback and other kinds of video devices often offer General Purpose Interface (GPI) or Contact Closure interfaces (see Chapter 2). These give the system designer a crude way to interface with the device, and many times a crude interface is better than none at all, or is all that is needed. These interfaces rarely can do more than simple "Play" and "Stop" kinds of commands; trying to tell a unit to cue up to a certain piece of video or to "move forward 100 frames" would likely be complicated to implement. Serial interfaces offer much more powerful control.

EIA SERIAL STANDARDS

Many devices in video, particularly those that have roots in the broadcast market (which is much larger than the live market), can be controlled using serial commands over an EIA serial link such as 232 or 422. Each manufacturer has its own implementation and data control codes. A few of these implementations have become de facto standards, as detailed in the following sections.

PIONEER LDP/DVD CONTROL PROTOCOL

Pioneer® makes a line of popular industrial DVD players and was one of the dominant manufacturers of industrial videodisc players. Their command set for these devices has been used by many other companies in a variety of devices, so it can now be considered a de facto standard. To demonstrate how this class of protocols operates, a few basic commands are included here; contact Pioneer if you need more details, or if you need the complete command set.

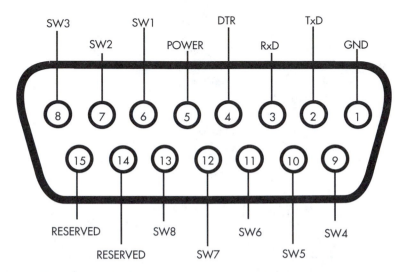

Figure 10.3   Pioneer DVD Control Interface Signals (Female Connector Shown)

Physical Connections/Data Specs

The system is based on EIA-232 and uses transmit (TxD), receive (RxD), Data Terminal Ready (DTR), and ground. The DVD-V7200, the most recent version of the DVD as of this writing, uses a 15-pin connector (see Figure 10.3). Data is sent in 8-bit words with no start bits, 1 stop bit, and no parity at either 4800bps or 9600bps, which is configurable in the DVD.

Command Structure

The command protocol is simple and straightforward, and therefore very easy to use and reliable. ASCII characters are sent from a controller to the unit over a bidirectional serial link. To tell the player to play, for example, the controller would send the ASCII characters "P" and "L," followed by a carriage return. The player would then acknowledge successful completion of this command by returning an "R" and a carriage return. If an error occurs, or if the target device doesn't understand a command received, it returns an error code. This simple approach is very powerful and allows very sophisticated operation. The fact that it is standard EIA-232 and ASCII means that a wide variety of computers or entertainment controllers can be used to send the commands.

Commands

Here are some of the more commonly used commands. The symbol ⇐ means Carriage Return (ASCII character 0Dh), and anything in <> brackets is optional.

Start

```
SA⇐
```

Starts disc rotation. Good for "spinning up" the disk at the beginning of the day.

Search

```
<FR>  nn  SE  ⇐
<TM>  nn  SE  ⇐
<CH>  nn  SE  ⇐
```

Causes the unit to search to an address specified in nn. The address can be a frame number, time, chapter, or a variety of other search points, depending either on the mode set in the unit, or the <optional> prefix added to this command. For example, FR3928SE⇐ searches the unit to frame 3928. Typically, when the unit reaches the specified address, it enters Pause mode.

Play

```
<Address>  PL⇐
```

Causes a disk to play. Putting an optional address in front of the play command will cause the unit to play until that address (frame, chapter, etc., depending on which mode is set) is reached, at which point an "auto stop" occurs.

Pause

```
PA⇐
```

The disk stops temporarily, and the image may or may not stay on the screen, depending on other mode settings of the player.

Still

```
ST⇐
```

The disk stops and the image freezes on whatever was on screen when the command was received.

Scan

```
NF⇐
NR⇐
NS⇐
```

Like fast forward or reverse, with the image displayed as the scan takes place. NF causes forward scan, NR causes reverse, while NS returns the unit to normal playback.

Reject

RJ⇐

Stops disc rotation; good for shutting down things at the end of the night.

Chapter Request

?C⇐

It is often useful for a controlled device to "poll" a target device in order to find out its current status. The Chapter Request command asks the player its current chapter, and the player returns 2 ASCII characters representing a 2-digit chapter number.

Frame Number Request

?F⇐

Frame Number Request asks the player to return its current frame number. The player responds with 7 ASCII characters, representing the frame number value.

Time-Code Request

?T⇐

Time-Code Request asks the player to return its current frame number. The player responds with 5 ASCII characters, the first 3 representing the number of minutes, and the last 2 representing seconds. Other numbering schemes are used for discs other than DVD.

P-Block Number Request

?A⇐

The P-Block Number Request polls all of the following at once: title number, chapter number, current minutes, and current seconds. The player responds with 10 ASCII characters, the first 2 for title number, the second 2 for chapter number, the next 4 for minutes, and the last 2 for seconds. Other numbering schemes are used for discs other than DVD.

SONY "9-PIN" PROTOCOL

Sony® is one of the largest corporations in the world, and it is a major manufacturer of broadcast and professional video equipment. Sony developed a serial control protocol for use in their equipment, which has become a de facto standard commonly referred to as "Sony 9-Pin." Because Sony never formally issued this protocol as a standard, finding accurate information is difficult; relevant commands for a particular type of equipment are typically contained in the manual for that piece of gear.

Physical Connections/Data Specs

The "9-Pin" implementation uses EIA-422 on a 9-Pin connector (see Figure 10.4). Data is sent at 38.4kbps in 8-bit words with 1 start bit, 1 stop bit, and an odd parity bit.

Command Structure

The command protocol is fairly complex for a serial, point-to-point connection method—it includes length information and a checksum. While these features require the transmitter and receiver to have added intelligence, they also make the standard very robust.

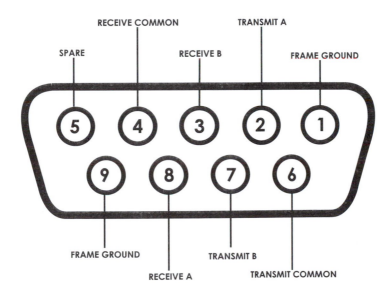

Figure 10.4 9-Pin EIA-422 Video Control Interface Signals (Female Connector Shown)

Each message consists of from 3 to 18 bytes in this order:

Command1/DataCount	4 Bits of Command, 4 Bits of Byte Count
Command2	Command
<Data>	Optional Data
Checksum	Checksum of previous bytes

The first byte is laid out ccccbbbb, where cccc is the Command Group, and bbbb is a 4-bit count of the number of data bytes in that message, ranging from 0-15 (0000-1111). If the data byte count is 0, that message has no data bytes; any number from 1 to 15 (1-Fh) indicates that the command has that number of data bytes, located between the Command2 byte and the Checksum.

The cccc nibble of the Command1 byte indicates the function of that message as follows:

Command1	Function	Message Direction
0	System Control	Controller to Controlled Device
1	System Control Return	Controlled Device to Controller
2	Transport Control	Controller to Controlled Device
4	Preset and Select Control	Controller to Controlled Device
6	Sense Request	Controller to Controlled Device
7	Sense Return	Controlled Device to Controller

The function of the Command2 and data bytes varies with the command. The checksum is the sum of the *numeric value* of the bytes from Command1 through the last data byte before the Checksum.

So to send a command like "Play" the following bytes in hex would be sent:

```
20 01 21
```

In the first byte, 20, the 2 means that the command is a Transport Control message; the 0 means that there are no data bytes. The second byte is the Command2 byte, and is 01 here to indicate a Play command. The 21 byte is the checksum (20+01).

If a controlled device correctly receives and processes a control message with no data, it responds with an Acknowledgment, "Ack," message. If the command message contained data, the receiver responds with a copy of the command and the associated data. If an error occurs, it responds with Negative Acknowledgment ("Nak") and returns associated error data.

Commands

Here are a few of the more commonly used commands.

Stop

```
20  00  20
```

Play

```
20  01  21
```

Eject

```
20  0F  29
```

Fast Forward

```
20  10  30
```

Rewind

```
20  20  40
```

The 2 in the first byte of these commands means "Transport"; the 0 means there are no data bytes in this command. The second byte is the actual command, and the third byte is the checksum.

Cue Up with Data

```
24  31  ff  ss  mm  hh  cc
```

This command cues up a deck to a certain frame number specified in the 4 data bytes. The 24 byte means that this is a transport command, with 4 data bytes. The 31 byte means "Cue Up with Data." The 4 data bytes are coded decimal numbers representing the desired frame, seconds, minutes, and hours, with the most significant nibble of each byte representing the 10s unit, and the least significant nibble representing 1s. The cc above represents the checksum. So, to tell a target device to cue up to 12:23:39:05 (12 hours, 23 minutes, 39 seconds, and 5 frames), we would send a hex message like this:

```
24  31  05  39  23  12  C8
```

where the C8 is the Checksum of all preceding bytes.

Current Time Sense

```
61 0C dd cc
```

It is often desirable to "poll" a target device, asking it to report its current media time. This is the function of the Current Time Sense command. What exactly the target device should return is indicated by the byte shown as dd. The byte shown as dd can have several different values, depending on which bits are turned on in the byte. The function of the bits are:

Bit	Function
0	LTC Time
1	VITC Time
2	Timer 1
3	
4	LTC UB
5	VITC UB
6	
7	

LTC and VITC are different varieties of SMPTE Time Code, which is discussed in detail in Chapter 17, "SMPTE Time Code." UB stands for "User Bits," which can be encoded in the time code. There are many permutations to this table, and each one gets a different response from the target device. Let's look at a common data byte, requesting the time in LTC format. The dd byte would be set to 00h:

```
61 0C 01 DE
```

Because of the 01 data byte, the receiver would respond with an LTC Time Data message.

LTC Time Data

```
74 04 ff ss mm hh cc
```

The target device would then send back up its data in the same format as previously specified.

ODETICS VIDEO DISK RECORDER PROTOCOL

Another de facto video standard is the "Video Disk Recorder Command and Control Specification," by Odetics, a manufacturer of broadcast control equipment. This standard is an extension to the de facto Sony 9-Pin protocol, modifying some commands to address the functionality of a hard-disk-based (instead of tape-based) unit. The data structure, physical interface, connector, and so forth of the Odetics protocol are all the same as the Sony 9-Pin standard.

Instead of adding many new commands, Odetics extended a few existing commands with additional data bytes. They also added the concept of Device ID (needed for advanced applications with multiple units that are possibly on the same link) and IDs, which allow multiple ranges to be recorded and then selected for playback.

Commands

All the commands listed in the Sony 9-Pin section above operate the same way in the Odetics protocol, except the Cue Up with Data command, which Odetics extended and then rendered obsolete, to address characteristics of video disk recording systems. They now recommend the use of the In Preset command instead. Out Preset is also useful for show-control applications.

In Preset

```
4X 14 data cc
```

In Preset operates much like the Cue Up with Data command, presetting the target device to a particular location before playback. The command has a variable number of data bytes, depending on the application. The permutations are:

```
40 14
```

In this usage, with no data bytes, the target device recues itself to 00:00:00:00.

```
44 14
```

In this command, 4 data bytes are added, to allow normal time-code-based addressing on the current "ID."

```
48 14/4C 14
```

With this variation, both the time-code number and an ID number can be specified. The format of the ID data is specified by the manufacturer of the target device.

Out Preset

```
4X 15 data cc
```

Out Preset is similar to In Preset, but instead of presetting the target device to a particular location before playback, it specifies a location at which play should stop. This extension is significant because it adds "play-to-frame" capability. The command has a variable number of data bytes, depending on the application. The permutations are:

```
40 15
```

In this usage, with no data bytes, the target will play until the highest recorded time-code position.

```
44 15
```

In this command, 4 data bytes are added, to allow normal time-code-based addressing on the current "ID."

ES-BUS

ES-Bus was developed by the European Broadcast Union and the SMPTE (hence the name ES) as a master/slave control standard for time-based broadcast video and audio equipment. ES-Bus uses an EIA-422 link and sends its data at a rate of 38.4 kbps; 8064 unique addresses are available. Because of the broadcast nature of the standard, it is not well suited for entertainment control applications, although it may pop up from time to time for broadcast-like applications. MIDI Machine Control is based on ES-Bus.

MIDI MACHINE CONTROL

MIDI Machine Control (MMC), which is covered in detail in Chapter 20, "MIDI Machine Control," is ideal for many performance-video applications. Unfortunately, few video equipment manufacturers seem to have realized its advantages or implemented it.

11

Computer Presentation

Computer presentation applications are sometimes incorporated into live shows, such as corporate meetings and special events.

PRESENTATION SYSTEMS

Presentation software, such as Microsoft PowerPoint® or Macromedia Director® runs on standard computing equipment. Because these programs are generally meant to run in a stand-alone or user-controlled fashion, they typically have minimal external interfacing capabilities. However, as of this writing, one new example of this type of program with external control abilities is Dataton's WATCHOUT™ image presentation software, which was designed specifically for the entertainment and presentations markets.

CONTROL APPROACHES

Some traditional control approaches are supported by presentation programs to a limited extent. Be sure to check carefully about external control capabilities before purchasing or specifying a system.

EIA Serial Standards

Since computer presentation systems use computer platforms, some systems allow access to the machine's serial ports. Using these ports, systems can be used to control a wide variety of equipment.

MIDI

Some computer presentation software packages have the ability to generate or react to MIDI messages from within a show script. Usually the musical MIDI messages, such as note commands and program change messages are incorporated; other, more powerful messages can generally be built up in hex.

SMPTE or MIDI Time Code

Some systems now allow control via external SMPTE or MIDI Time Code (see Chapters 17 and 18). This allows the system to slave off another master time source or, conversely, to generate the master time code.

Keyboard Emulation

Dataton pioneered a unique way of controlling programs that were never really meant to be controlled externally: by emulating the keyboard. By intercepting the keyboard signals on the host computer, virtual keyboard commands can be generated, controlling nearly any aspect of a program.

Commands via TCP/IP

TCP/IP (covered in Chapter 23, "Common Network Protocols"), is a protocol stack used as the core of many networks. It is possible to control some computer presentation systems using commands sent over a network. This type of control is increasingly important, since some new computers have no serial ports.

12

Film Projection

Film projection here includes both static and motion-picture technologies. While video projectors take an electronic video signal and turn it into a projected image, film projectors deal with the projection media—slides or motion-picture film—directly, and are therefore opto-electromechanical systems. As of this writing, film is still going strong in movie theatres and large live shows, but is rapidly being replaced in many new applications by video and computer presentation technologies, which offer easier image manipulation, data transport, and editing. For now, however, film projection is firmly entrenched, so it is included here.

SLIDE EQUIPMENT

"Slides" have been a staple of many types of live performances, from corporate theatre to opera, for many years. Slide media ranges from the relatively small 35mm used in consumer cameras, up to giant, 7-by-7-inch (or larger) large-format slides used for projecting scenic backdrops or transforming a tall building with a projected image.

The basic idea behind a "multi-image" slide presentation is quite simple: At least two projectors are aimed at the same screen, and some sort of control is used to "dissolve" images between the projectors. One projector is dimmed out while the other is faded up, and then the dimmed projector is advanced to the next slide. With control of these two parameters—image brightness and slide selection—remarkably complex presentations have been developed.

Kodak makes the de facto standard 35mm projectors, which use a circular "carousel" to sequence a series of slides, typically 80 or more. Large-format projectors are manufactured by a variety of European companies, each of which has their own media standards. Large-format slides can be static and unchanging throughout a show, with one slide manually inserted into the projector. Alternatively, random-access large-format slide changers can be used, which allow static images to be changed. Another type of large-format image presentation device is the "scroller," which runs one or more scrolls of film media through the projector's gate, allowing the presentation of either a large number of sequential static images, or a continuous, laterally moving image (picture a long train moving by as you observe it through a window). Some scrollers utilize multiple pin-registered or sprocketed scrolls to achieve surprisingly sophisticated effects.

It is easy to vary the brightness of a low-power projector with incandescent projection lamps—the lamp is simply dimmed using a standard dimmer. The electronic device used to control a projector's brightness is called a "dissolver" (or sometimes a "Dove" unit, after a popular dissolver once made by Audio Visual Labs). Brighter light sources, such as arc lamps, however, cannot be dimmed so simply. Instead, they use mechanical "dimming shutters," which use a piece of metal or glass to variably block light output.

KODAK PROJECTOR INTERFACES

The de facto standard for 35mm slide-projector control, pioneered by Kodak, is a crude connector manufactured by EBY; the pin-out is shown in Figure 12.1.

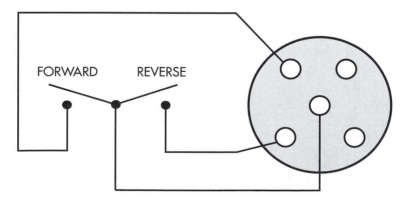

Figure 12.1 Kodak Projector Control Signals (Female Connector Shown)

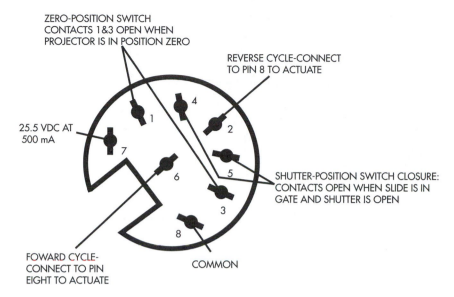

Figure 12.2 Kodak Special Application Receptacle Control Signals (Female Connector Shown)

For more-sophisticated applications, other functions of Kodak projectors can be accessed through the Special Application Receptacle, which is an 8-pin DIN connector. Its control signals are shown in Figure 12.2.

P-COM PROTOCOL

For more demanding applications, Kodak developed a more advanced control method for its Ektapro professional multi-image projectors, which allows direct, random-access serial control of the projector and offers enhanced feedback capabilities. This protocol is known as "P-Com."

Physical Connections/Data Specs

Communications are achieved through the use of the "P-Bus" port, which is a standard 9-Pin EIA-232 interface; see Figure 12.3 for the control signals used. Some projector models have both male and female connectors, which allows easy daisy-chaining of multiple projectors.

Eight-bit words are sent at 9600bps, with 1 start bit, no parity, and 2 stop bits. Projectors are configured as DCE devices; since the control computer is DTE, standard 9-pin serial cables can be used.

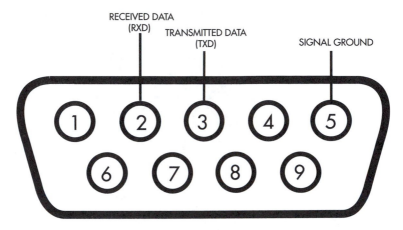

Figure 12.3   Kodak P-Bus Control Signals (Male Connector Shown)

P-Com can communicate to up to 15 projectors directly, or more, through the use of grouping or "all-call" messages. Each projector needs to be set to an address, and most models of projector use a rotary BCD-coded switch, labeled 0-F.

Command Structure

Given the fairly simple functionality offered by P-Com, the command structure used is extremely complex. Three bytes are sent for each command, and the least significant bit is used for "synchronization": the LSB of the first byte is always set to 1, and the LSB of the other 2 bytes is always set to 0. The first byte is always the same format:

```
aaaaamm1
```

Where aaaaa is the address of the target projector, from 0-1Fh. 0-F are normal projector addresses, and 1Fh is a special "global" address, to which all projectors on a link will respond. The next 2 bits denote the "mode" of the command, and there are 4 modes: Parameter Mode, Set/Reset Mode, Direct Mode, and Status Request Mode. The bits for each mode are defined as:

Mode	Bits
Parameter Mode	00
Set/Reset Mode	01
Direct Mode	10
Status Request Mode	11

The remaining 2 bytes, minus the "synchronization" bits, leave 14 bits for commands and data, and the usage of those bits changes depending on the mode.

Parameter Mode Commands

In Parameter Mode, the bytes are in the following format:

```
aaaaa001    ccccppp0    ppppppp0
```

where cccc is the 4-bit Command number, and ppppppp is a 10-bit parameter value. Some common parameter mode commands follow.

Random Access

```
cccc   ppp0 ppppppp0
0000   00n0 nnnnnnn0
```

This command moves a projector to a certain slide-tray position. The tray position, from 0 to 140, is indicated in binary in the n bits.

Set Brightness

```
cccc   ppp0 ppppppp0
0001   nnn0 nnnnnnn0
```

Set Brightness sets a projector's brightness, to a value between 0 and *1000*. The brightness is indicated in the n bits.

Fade Up/Down

```
cccc   ppp0 ppppppp0
0110   00d0 nnnnnnn0
```

Fade Up/Down will fade a projector up or down, depending on the value of the d bit—if this bit is 1, the projector will fade up; if the bit is 0, the projector will fade down. The fade time, from 0 to 12.7 seconds, is set in tenths of a second in the n bits. This command may not be available in older projectors, as it was added in a revision of the protocol.

Set/Request Mode Commands

In Set/Request Mode, the bytes are in the following format:

```
aaaaa011    ccccccs0    ----0
```

where ccccccc is a 7-bit Command number, and s is the "set" bit. The third byte is sent, but the data is not used. The bits indicated by the "-" are ignored, and can be either 0 or 1. A common Set/Request Mode command is the Standby On/Off command.

Standby On/Off

```
ccccccs0
000111s0
```

As you might imagine, this command sets a projector either into or out of standby, as determined by the value of the s bit—if this bit is 1, the projector goes into standby mode, and the lamp and fan will shut off. If the s bit is 0, the projector will come out of standby mode.

Direct Mode Commands

In Direct Mode, the bytes are in the following format:

```
aaaaa101    cccccc-0      ----0
```

where ccccccc is a 7-bit Command number, and s is the "set" bit. The bits in the second and third bytes indicated by the "-" are ignored and can be either 0 or 1. This is one of the more useful command modes, and some common (and self-explanatory) Direct Mode commands follow.

Slide Forward

```
cccccc
000000
```

Slide Backward

```
cccccc
000001
```

Focus Forward

```
cccccc
000010
```

Focus Backward

```
cccccc
000011
```

Focus Stop

```
ccccc
000100
```

Shutter Open

```
ccccc
000111
```

Shutter Close

```
ccccc
001000
```

Status Request Mode Commands

In Status Request Mode, the bytes are in the following format:

```
aaaaa111    cccc--0      ----0
```

where ccc is a 3-bit Command number. The bits in the second and third bytes indicated by the "-" are ignored and can be either 0 or 1. One of the more common status request commands is the Get Tray Position Command.

Get Tray Position

```
cccc
1010
```

The projector, when requested by this command, will send back its tray position and other information. This command may not be available in older projectors, as it was added in a revision of the protocol.

OTHER STANDARDS USED FOR SLIDE CONTROL

There are several other control standards used in the control of slides.

DMX512

DMX is used to control some random-access large-format slide changers, as well as a number of mechanical dimming shutters. In slide-control applications, the range of the DMX signal is often mapped out to specific slides: a specific DMX level equals a specific slide. Using this popular standard, any lighting console can control the slide changers and dimming shutters. While lighting consoles are certainly not the ideal programming device for complex slide shows, they can work adequately for scenic projections and other simple applications.

PROCALL

For many years, the standard for multi-image presentations was Audio Visual Laboratory's (AVL) PROCALL control language. This was a simple control method, where a few shorthand commands could trigger a wide variety of effects. For example, a command of "2D" denoted a 2-second dissolve. With a handful of commands, an operator could program complex shows. After many years of decline, AVL went out of business in 1999, and you are unlikely to encounter PROCALL on anything but the oldest installations.

Audio Track Control

Audio track control, though rarely used today, is a simple, relative control method, where a tone (usually 1 kHz) is recorded on a presentation audio track each time the slides should advance. However, dropout on the tape (or accidental erasure) could cause a tone to be erased and thus cause the controller to get hopelessly out of sync. Since the control method is relative, once an error has occurred, these systems have no hope, short of human intervention, of ever re-syncing themselves. Other, proprietary audio control track approaches overcome some of these problems by recording on tape digital data representing the various projector commands, often using FSK modulation. However, this method, like the analog audio track approach, suffers the same limitations of dropout and other errors inherent in the media.

Show Control

With the development of more sophisticated control protocols such as P-Com, and the de facto standardization of older projectors, projectors in many applications can function directly as target devices for show-controllers. See the show-control section in Part 4 for more information.

MOTION-PICTURE PROJECTION

Slides are slowly being replaced by computer-based displays, and motion-picture projection is being replaced by electronic presentation technologies for many applications. At this point, however, nothing can beat film's high-quality moving images, although some are willing to sacrifice image quality for ease of control and streamlined content creation.

Motion-Picture Projectors

Motion-picture projectors come in a variety of shapes and sizes—ranging from 8mm home projectors to 70mm custom systems such as IMAX® or Showscan®—but motion-picture projectors have not historically been designed for external control. In traditional film applications, the media contains all the information needed for the presentation (image and sound); the projector is started and rolled until the reel is over, at which point the projectionist switches to another reel on another projector.

Modern projection systems in commercial movie theatres generally use "platter" systems in which the entire film is spliced together and laid on its side on a circular platter. The projectionist starts the film by pressing a button on a control panel, checks focus (we hope!), and then goes to start another film in another theatre in the multiplex. Houselights are dimmed automatically based on sensors that read foil-tape tabs on the film, or by other automatic systems.

In film postproduction applications, film has traditionally been synced up to other media using simple, relative sync pulses, pilot tones, or even electromechanical linkages. Film post has traditionally used "dubbers" to record audio onto and play back from sprocketed, mag (magnetic)-coated film; these systems are synced to the film image using tach pulses or pilot tones. As of this writing, however, dubbers are slowly being replaced by multitrack, disk-based recorders using SMPTE Time Code (see Chapter 17) to lock to a video or computer-based copy of the film.

SMPTE-Controlled Film Projection

One approach for entertainment control of film projection was pioneered by the special-effects company Associates and Ferren (A&F)—now part of Disney—in the early 1980s: it manufactured a film projector that could be controlled via SMPTE Time Code. Three components of the projector are automated and therefore available for remote or computer control: the variable-speed motor that drives the film through the projector; the dowser, a heavy piece of metal that acts as a crude dimmer by blocking the light from the lamp; and the changeover shutter (not the regular timing shutter used to block the light during film frame advances). The changeover shutter, a lightweight metal plate, also blocks the projector's light, but it can quickly blackout or open. This shutter cannot be left closed by itself for very long or the light will burn through it. These functions are electrically controlled using a Programmable Logic Controller (PLC); a local control panel connected to the PLC enables manual operation of all the functions, and a remote interface allows interfacing between the PLC and a personal computer, which handles all cuing and time-code functions. Focus, framing, and similar functions are still controlled manually.

In its idle state, the projector has its lamp on, motor off, and dowser and shutter closed. A standard series of cues for the projector is to start the motor and, once the film is up to the proper speed (so that it won't be melted), open the dowser and then the shutter. The reverse sequence is used to shut down the projector at the end of a film segment. Once the system is properly configured with the show's cues, all the operator has to do (barring any problems) is thread the projector at the top of the show, align the film to its starting frame, and monitor the performance. The rest is handled by the computer based on the time code.

Encoding Time Code on Film

In the past, there has been no easy way to encode film media with a time code—attempts to record time code on the film optical sound track were not effective, since the projector might "wow and flutter" significantly. There have been many workarounds, such as counting frames relative to a start point, but with the recent development of optically-encoded digital film sound systems, time code could be recorded as an audio track and simply played back. Additionally, film sound company DTS® has created a processor, which decodes a proprietary DTS time code encoded on the film. Based on this time code, contact closures can be programmed to trigger various effects.

13

Stage Machinery

With the increasing availability of sophisticated, low-cost, computerized controls, stage machinery, mechanized special effects, and "show action equipment" have become increasingly widespread and increasingly automated. Most large productions—whether on Broadway, on the concert trail, or in a theme park—now have some kind of mechanized scenery or stage equipment. Since such systems feature controlled motion, they are often called "motion-control" systems.

Machinery systems generally fall into two types, though the lines between the two can, of course, blur easily. Equipment in the first category, often called "stage equipment," is usually built into a performance space as it is constructed and includes machines such as orchestra lifts, automated rigging systems, turntables, and elevators. The second type is typically installed on a per-show basis, to move scenic pieces across a show deck on a track, "fly" them above the stage, or move them up and down through the stage itself.

Because both types are generally custom-built, and use control approaches that are often proprietary to the manufacturer or shop that built the system, there are few standards in widespread use. But the basics apply to all systems, so an introduction is offered here. Machinery systems generally break down into three basic parts: sensing, control, and drive (see Figure 13.1). Each moving piece in a system is typically known as an "axis" or "effect."

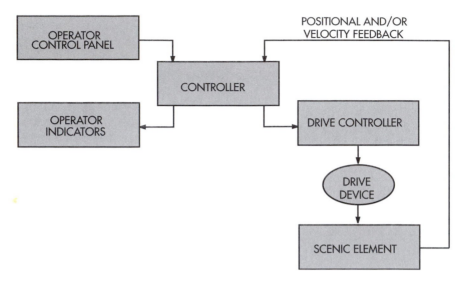

Figure 13.1 Computer-Based Machinery-Control-System Block Diagram

SENSING

In any automated machinery system, one primary aspect determines the system's control design: the type of sensing or "feedback" from the machinery to the control system. Sensing here includes any sort of input to a machinery system.

Operator Controls and Indication

We must, of course, tell a machinery system to do something before it can do it; a wide variety of operator control or "Human-Machine Interfaces" (HMI) are available. Since many of these controls and operator indicators are common to many types of systems, they were detailed in Chapter 2.

Positional Feedback

There are three basic kinds of positional feedback: limit switches, analog encoding, and digital encoding. Each approach indicates to the control system where a machine is in its range of travel; the system can then compare the actual position with a target position indicated by the operator and determine how and in which direction to move the machine.

Limit switches are the crudest, most limited forms of feedback, but they are simple to implement, extremely reliable, and sometimes all that are needed. Limit switches offer absolute positional control and come in a variety of designs, ranging from rotary-cam limit switches to simple mechanical switches mounted on a track or piece of machinery. Both are actuated when the machinery system hits a "limit," or desired target position. Since the limits are indicated by physical switches, the only way to change the target position is to physically move the switch (or the cam or other device actuating the switch). For a simple system, limit switches are adequate; in larger, more sophisticated systems, limit switches are used for backup "end-of-travel" applications.[1]

With analog positional feedback, a proportional analog signal is used to encode the position of the controlled device—a particular signal indicates a specific position. The two primary analog feedback devices are potentiometers and resolvers. Potentiometers ("pots") are simple resistive devices that output an absolute DC voltage proportional to shaft position: 5 volts might mean 15 feet across a stage, 5.9 volts might indicate 18 feet. A resolver is a sort of rotary transformer, with one winding on its shaft and others in the resolver housing. At a certain angular position, a particular AC voltage is induced to the resolver's outputs, and this signal can be decoded into positional information. Both pots and resolvers are absolute devices: a certain position of the device's shaft always equals a certain output, and this is a beneficial aspect for critical systems. This also means that the entire motion of a machinery system must be geared down to one (or a few) revolutions of the resolver or pot. For this reason, and the fact that pots and resolvers are more difficult to accurately interface with digital systems at high resolution, they have fallen out of favor in recent years. Like everything else today, motion control is going digital.

The most common devices for digital positional feedback are rotary shaft encoders or linear encoders. Both encode position, but a linear encoder is laid out in a linear track, while a shaft encoder encloses a rotating disk that interrupts a beam of light to generate electrical pulses. Since much of scenic motion starts with a rotary drive mechanism such as a winch drum, rotary shaft encoders are generally found more frequently in entertainment applications.

Encoders come in two types: absolute or relative. A typical absolute encoder might use eight light beams to send out a discrete digital signal describing where in its rotation the encoder's shaft is—each rotary position of the shaft (to the resolution of the encoder) generates a distinct combination of on and off states (see Figure 13.2). Other systems use a battery-backed relative encoder with integral counters. Even if the power to an absolute encoder is lost, or the system suffers data corruption, the digital value representing the encoder's position is retained by the encoder itself

---

[1]Better to hit a limit switch and stop the system than to hit the physical "end of travel," causing damage!

Figure 13.2 Absolute Encoder Disk (Courtesy Dynamics Research Corp.)

and can be easily reread. Like pots or resolvers, to get a useful signal with no repeated positional data using absolute encoder, you must gear the entire movement of the measured system down to a limited number of revolutions of the encoder.

A relative encoder, on the other hand, simply generates a pulse train when its shaft is rotated (see Figure 13.3). This is also a usable signal for measuring the angular position of the shaft, but only relative to some known starting point. If the encoder's shaft is stationary, we get no signal. If we rotate it 10 degrees clockwise, some number of pulses are generated. So we

Figure 13.3 Relative Encoder Disk (Courtesy Dynamics Research Corp.)

now know that, in relation to the starting position, the shaft (and therefore the system) has moved by that number of pulses, and this data can be translated into a positional value. These types of encoders must be "initialized" to a known start position on power up, and they must use external counters to maintain a positional value. Most relative encoders in use today are quadrature encoders that, when in motion, generate two pulse streams out of phase with each other. By looking at which pulse train makes a low-to-high (or high-to-low) transition first, a controller can determine which direction the encoder is moving.

Velocity Feedback

All the methods we've discussed so far indicate to the control system the *position* of the scenic element; for true motion control, we need to know not only where an object is, but also how fast it is going. In other words, we need velocity feedback. As you might expect, there are both analog and digital methods for generating velocity data.

To generate an analog velocity signal, a generator, or "tachometer," is used. At a particular rotary velocity, a specific voltage is output; the control system can continuously compare this voltage to the target velocity and adjust the system accordingly. Some systems use digital feedback for positional information and (analog) tachometers to close the velocity loop.

In a digital system with enough available computational horsepower, it is now common to derive an object's velocity from the change in the positional information—a virtual tachometer is created.

MOTION PROFILING

Many controllers allow a user (or system) to create a motion "profile," which determines how a motion-control axis will accelerate, what top speed it will reach, and how it will decelerate. This acceleration (change in velocity) is typically either programmed in as a "slope" (slope of the velocity curve if graphed out), or as an acceleration time. "Trapezoidal" profiles have a constant acceleration and deceleration slope; "S-Curve" profiles use more gently changing slopes.

MACHINERY CONTROLLERS

The operator input, positional, and velocity information must all be acted on by some controller, which tells the drive side of the system what to do. Since the factory automation market is so much bigger than the entertainment market, few commercially available systems are able to operate in cue-based modes, but they are useful either for smaller machines, or as a lower-level controller that sits below a master "front end." These fall into two general types: Programmable Logic Controllers (PLCs), or dedicated Motion Controllers.

Programmable Logic Controllers

Simple machinery-control systems today are often built around PLCs: low-cost, heavy-duty industrial computers, with prewired optically isolated inputs and relay, transistor, or solid-state-relay outputs. In a typical application, a PLC's inputs are connected to control or limit switches, and its outputs are connected to motors, indicators, solenoids or solenoid valves, contactors (which can drive heavy loads), or other devices that need to be controlled by the PLC. This internal program is written for each application by the user or system integrator, generally in a language called Ladder Logic, a sort of software-executed relay-logic schematic (graphically, the program looks something like a ladder, hence the name). The PLC is programmed using various types of "elements," which are analogous to relay contacts and coils (from its roots in relay logic). After the PLC reads the input conditions, it evaluates the status of the inputs, processes that data based on the user program, and then executes the states of the output.

Originally designed to substitute for relay-logic control systems, such as those found in controls for elevators and other large machinery, PLCs have recently become remarkably sophisticated, with math, HMI, and sophisticated motion-control capabilities. PLCs are being used increasingly throughout the entertainment industry (see Figure 13.4).

Figure 13.4   Programmable Logic Controller (Courtesy Rockwell Automation)

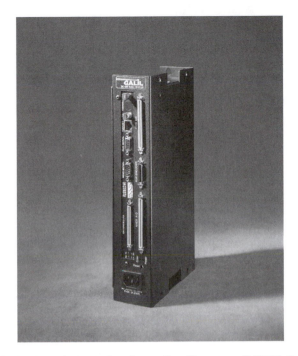

Figure 13.5   Four-Axis Motion Controller (Courtesy Galil Motion Control)

Dedicated Motion Controllers

While PLCs are general controllers, dedicated motion controllers (see Figure 13.5) are intended only for motion-control applications. They connect directly to operator interfaces, encoders, and drive systems, and can either work based on an internal program written by a user, or can respond to external control commands.

These units are often used as the core of entertainment motion-control systems, with a computer used as a "front-end" to handle operator interface, cue editing, data storage, and execution.

Computer-Based Controllers

With the ever-dropping costs of PC hardware, many PLC and Motion Controller systems are being replaced by standard computer hardware running special software. Of course, care must be taken to ensure that operational or safety problems will not be caused by operating system crashes, electrical interference, and other problems common to consumer-oriented PC hardware.

DRIVE DEVICES

We've talked about feedback and controllers, but not yet about the systems that actually do the work—drive devices. Drive here is intentionally vague, as many machinery and motion controllers can control a variety of drive technologies: electric devices, electric motors, and electrically-actuated hydraulic or pneumatic valves.

Relays

While computers and controllers can typically put out small electrical currents for control, we often want to run larger loads. A simple device to do this is a "relay," in which a small current from the controller is used to energize an electromagnet that, in turn, pulls a set of contacts together. These contacts can be designed to handle very large amounts of current, and therefore large devices can be operated from small control signals. Solid State Relays, using transistors, silicon-controlled rectifiers, IGBTs and other devices, are also available. Care must be taken to suppress the inductive spikes caused by the coils in any electromagnetic devices from the control electronics. "Snubbers" are typically used for this purpose.

Solenoids

One of the simplest types of electromechanical drive is the solenoid, which is simply an electromagnet that, when energized, moves a piece of metal. These devices are often used in stage effects for simple, short actuation, and since they are electrical, they are easy to interface with electrical controllers.

Motor Drives and Servo-Amplifiers

Although entire books exist on the subject of electric motors and drives, the entertainment control engineer should understand some of the drives used in entertainment machinery. There are two basic types of motion-control drives: open-loop and closed-loop "servo" systems.

A DC servo "amplifier" is its own closed-loop system. A tachometer coupled to the motor provides velocity feedback to the drive. This information is then used by the drive itself to close the velocity loop—the drive is simply instructed by the controller how fast to go and in which direction. In a DC motor, voltage corresponds to speed, and current determines torque. By varying these two parameters, a DC servo drive can have quite smooth and tight control over a motor's velocity. AC servo drives are also available (as are non-servo DC drives).

With a DC motor, a certain voltage input causes the motor to spin at a certain speed. A "stepper" motor works much differently: the motor has several windings at different angular orientations; applying current to these windings in proper sequence causes the motor to spin. Since sequencing is a task well suited to computers, stepper-motor drives are very easy to interface with digital control systems; a certain number of sequential pulses issued to a motor will equal a certain position. If all is functioning correctly, firing a certain number of sequential pulses should cause a stepper to turn to a certain position; for this reason, stepper motors are generally run in an open loop. Stepper motors are generally available only in small, low-power designs, and are useful for entertainment applications such as props.

AC motors are much cheaper than DC motors, but AC drives are more complex: in an AC motor, frequency determines speed and current corresponds to torque. Three-phase drives are generally run open-loop. Because

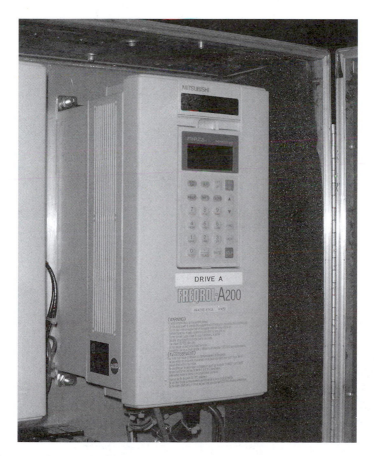

Figure 13.6   Three-Phase AC Motor Drive (Photo by Barbara Wohlsen)

of volume manufacturing, high-power three-phase drives have become available at very low cost (see Figure 13.6).

Fluid Power

Almost all the concepts we've just discussed have hydraulic (oil) or pneumatic (air) equivalents; these systems can be used where tremendous power is necessary but not much space is available (since fluid-power motors are significantly smaller than their electrical equivalents), or where linear motion is desired. Hydraulic and pneumatic systems are, of course, often computer-controlled, and they use many of the same principles detailed above for electrical systems. Feedback can be via electricity or fluid; valves, which can be controlled electrically or mechanically, are used instead of electrical drives and come in both solenoid (on/off only), or proportional (continuously variable) versions. In a solenoid valve, the solenoid is mechanically coupled to the valve actuator, and when energized, the valve either allows or stops fluid flow. Proportional valves are used when variable fluid flow (which usually corresponds to variable speed) is desired. These valves, like electric motor drives, often accept a variable analog or digital continuous control signal (see Figure 13.7).

Figure 13.7 Electrically-Controlled Proportional Hydraulic Valve (Photo by Barbara Wohlsen)

Interfacing with Drive Systems

Today, many drive systems are still run using a simple, but very effective, scheme: +/– 10V DC, with +10 indicating maximum forward velocity, and –10 indicating maximum reverse. No voltage, of course, means no motion. +/– 10V control is very common today for entertainment drive systems, although there are an increasing number of both open and proprietary digital control schemes.

STANDARD INTERCONNECTION METHODS

The process control and factory automation industries dwarf the entertainment technology industry, and so, as in many other areas, we tag along for a ride on their technologies. Factories and refineries need distributed control connection methods for a huge number of sensors, switches, and actuators, and these devices may be distributed throughout a large facility. Many manufacturers have developed networking solutions for these applications, called "field busses."

Today, there are a huge number of competing field-bus approaches, and during the 1990s a major effort took place within the IEC to develop a unified, interoperable standard known as 61158. At a meeting in 1999, competing commercial interests (process control and factory automation are *big* business) derailed the entire project, using procedural manipulations to include eight separate, non-interoperable systems in the now *4000-page* standard. So, there is no standard.

Additionally, no one approach tends to dominate entertainment machinery applications, and you would likely need manufacturer support to implement any of these systems. So only a brief introduction to several commonly-used systems will be offered here.

Allen-Bradley (Rockwell Automation) Data Highway

To connect multiple PLCs, factory automation giant Allen Bradley developed the "Data Highway" system, which is available in three basic versions: Data Highway (DH), Data Highway + (DH+), and Data Highway 485 (DH485). DH is a peer-to-peer LAN for up to 255 nodes running at 57.6 kbps. "Trunk" lines can run up to 10,000 feet, and individual lines can run 100 feet. It uses a modified Token master scheme. Data Highway + is intended for PLC "backbone" communications and runs at 115kbps, serving up to 64 nodes. DH485 is based on EIA-485, runs at 115kbps, and can support 32 nodes.

DeviceNet

The device net system has been standardized by the Open DeviceNet Vendor Association, or ODVA. It is used for field device interconnection, and is an open-network standard based on Bosch's Controller Area Network (CAN), which was originally developed for automotive applications. It runs at data rates of 125kbps for networks up to 500m, 250kbps for up to 250m, and 500kbps for up to 100m, and it uses a linear bus with the power and signal on the same cable to implement both peer-to-peer and multicast operations. It is hot-patchable, opto-isolated, and can accept multiple-power-supplies. Both open and sealed connector types have been standardized.

Ethernet

Ethernet is detailed in Chapter 24 and is being widely used in many different disciplines throughout the entertainment industry. A huge number of remote input/output or "I/O" systems are now available that use Ethernet as a backbone (see Figure 13.8).

LonWorks

LonWorks is a general-purpose control network, and, as such, is described in Chapter 25. It is used for a variety of industrial control applications, and can be distributed over large areas.

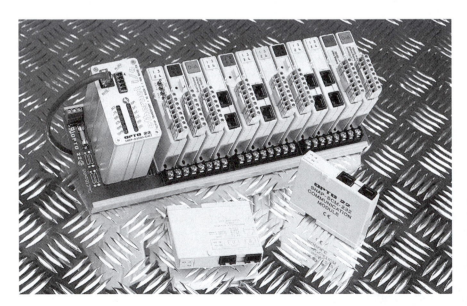

Figure 13.8 Ethernet Distributed I/O System (Courtesy Opto22)

Profibus

Profibus is a German DIN (19245) field-bus standard and is mostly found in Europe. EIA-485 and fiber versions are available and can run at data rates from 26.6-500kbps over distances of 1.2km. The number of nodes that can be linked is 127, but only 32 can be active at any given time.

COMMERCIAL ENTERTAINMENT MACHINERY-CONTROL SYSTEMS

Since few of the components or devices mentioned above are "plug and play," most entertainment machinery systems are designed and installed by a company, which packages standard and custom components into a system suitable for the application.

Controllers for Installed Applications

A number of rigging companies now offer standard controllers for auto-mated control over permanent stage equipment such as turntables, orchestra lifts, and fly systems. They often have PLCs or dedicated motion controllers at their core, and a custom-designed operator interface. Most controllers today have some sort of video user interface, and the requisite emergency stop button (see Figure 13.9).

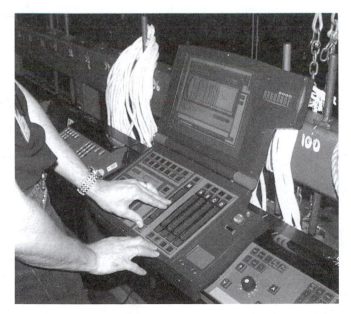

Figure 13.9 Stage Machinery Controller (Courtesy Bytecraft Group)

Figure 13.10 Scenic Motion-Control System and Winch (Courtesy Entolo)

Figure 13.11 Scenic Motion-Control System (Courtesy Hudson Scenic Studio)

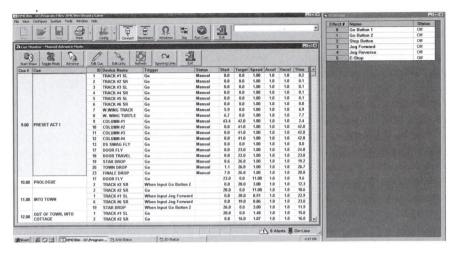

Figure 13.12 Scenic Motion-Control System Screen (Courtesy Hudson Scenic Studio)

Controllers for Production Applications

Many companies now offer machinery-control systems custom-designed for the demands of live production and performance, and these systems are used on Broadway shows, concerts, in theme parks, and other similar venues. Many commercial systems use standard desktop PCs as front ends (see Figure 13.12), with dedicated motion controllers or PLCs located with the drive systems in remote "drive racks." With any machinery-control system, safety is of course of utmost concern; well-designed systems always include extensive emergency stop (or "E-stop") and other safety features (see Figures 13.10 and 13.11).

INTERFACING WITH MACHINERY SYSTEMS

While most machinery systems are triggered manually for safety reasons, some new machinery-control systems can communicate with other devices over a show network using Ethernet, EIA serial standards (discussed in Chapter 6), or MIDI, and some can chase SMPTE Time Code. See Part 4 for more information on MSC, SMPTE, and Ethernet. These external systems should, of course, never compromise system safety.

14

Animatronics

In "animatronics" or "character animation," machines, designed to look like living characters, perform to prerecorded sound tracks.[1] This field incorporates aspects of stage machinery, audio, and computer control systems. Animatronic control systems can generally be broken down into the same general components as stage machinery—sensing, control, and drive—although these technologies are generally used on a smaller scale in animatronics than in stage machinery (see Figure 14.1).

ANIMATRONIC EFFECTS

In an animatronic system, there are two basic types of effects: digital and analog.

Digital

Digital animatronic effects, as you might imagine, can only be turned on or off. They are usually controlled using relatively inexpensive solenoid valves and pneumatic cylinders, or motors that create movement when turned on or off for some period of time. Typical digital functions might be "open/close eyelids," "move arm right," or "move arm left." This approach

---

[1]The term "animatronics" or "audio animatronics" was coined by Disney early in the development of their theme parks.

Figure 14.1   Animatronic Character (with One-Half Skin Removed to Show Mechanism) (Courtesy KX International)

is cost-effective but has limitations: digital effects generally have no speed control, and precisely repeatable positioning is difficult to achieve.

Analog

Analog animatronic effects use some sort of proportional control, and, in higher-end systems, use closed-loop systems with positional, velocity, or advanced feedback systems. Instead of having a digital on/off command such as "move arm right," an analog control would map the range of the arm's motion to a continuous (i.e., 0-10V) scale. In this way, speed, acceleration and deceleration can all be controlled, and the arm can be programmed to start moving slowly, then move quickly, and then move slowly into a precise position.

ANIMATRONIC CONTROL SYSTEMS

Animatronic control systems generally operate in two phases: programming and playback. During the programming period, the character's movements are precisely matched to the audio sound track; during the playback phase, the movements are played back in sync with that sound track. Good programming is key to achieving sophisticated and believable motion in animatronic systems, and most systems use some sort of programming panel (see Figure 14.2) consisting of button panels to turn on and off digital effects, and knobs, sliders, or joysticks to run the analog, proportional effects. High-end systems may even record this performance data from humans with sensors attached to their bodies. As the character's moves are "performed" by a human programmer, the control systems digitally sample and record the performance data.

Generally, each effect (arm, mouth, eyes, etc.) is programmed separately, allowing the programmer to record each "track" just as musicians would perform each part of a song in a recording studio. They might start by programming the mouth, then move on to eyes, head, and so on. If a segment of a track's performance (a few eye blinks) needs to be "punched in" and rerecorded, this can be done in manual or automated ways.

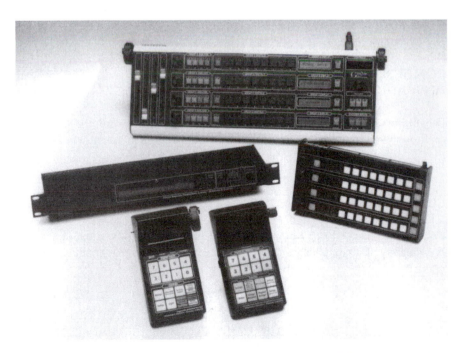

Figure 14.2 Animatronic Programming Panels (Courtesy Gilderfluke & Co.)

The performance can, of course, also be tweaked and polished "off line," and programming systems often feature a number of postproduction-like editing features. For instance, it is difficult for a human performer to exactly anticipate a musical soundtrack, so someone might record a good performance that is slightly late. In some manufacturer's systems, the programmer can simply grab that track and drag it back slightly in time; it will then play back precisely in sync. For things like mouth movement, it is also possible to have the programming system create a movement based on the sound track—whenever the volume on the voice track exceeds a certain threshold, the mouth would move. This track can then be tweaked and cleaned up after processing by the programmer.

During the programming process, most animatronic controllers digitally sample the performance some number of times per second. The higher this "frame" or "update" rate, the more information that needs to be recorded; but higher update rates also typically mean smoother movement, especially with analog effects.

Animatronic control systems are typically either based entirely on a computer with interfacing hardware, which is used both for programming and playback, or they use a computer to create a program that is then "downloaded" into playback hardware. With the latter structure, the expensive PC is only needed for the programming period.

Generally, playback controllers record movements into "shows," which can be triggered on a conditional basis when contact closures, SMPTE frame times, or other signals are received.

CONTROL STANDARDS USED IN ANIMATRONICS

Depending on the effect being controlled, there are a number of control methods used in animatronics either for internal control or interfacing with the outside world.

Contact Closures

Contact Closures (described in detail in Chapter 2) are used extensively in the world of animatronics, both for internal control, and external interfacing.

0-10V DC

For many analog proportional effects, analog control is used, with the effect's range of motion mapped to a 0-to-10VDC scale. For instance, 0 volts might represent a leg fully retracted, while 10 volts might tell the leg to fully extend. Any voltage in between would represent some position between those two extremes.

Since most control systems these days operate digitally even when outputting an analog voltage, a "digital-to-analog converter," or DAC, is typically used. The more bits used for the DAC, the more digital values available, and the more steps from 0 to 10V can be represented. An 8-bit DAC can recreate only 256 steps; a 16-bit DAC has 65,536 possible steps. Typical DACs operate at "precisions" of 8, 12, 16, or even, in some instances, 32 bits. The more bits used, of course, the more data storage required.

DMX512

DMX is well suited to some forms of animatronic control, because it is a simple standard sending continuous information at a fairly high data rate. It also allows an animatronic controller to control lighting equipment, although you would likely want to interface with a larger lighting console for complex shows. Some animatronic manufacturers assign DMX dimmer channels to add error correction to their systems, and this is typically done on a non-standardized, manufacturer-specific basis.

SMPTE Time Code

Many animatronic control systems can "chase" SMPTE Time Code. SMPTE is described in detail later in Chapter 17, "SMPTE Time Code."

MIDI, MIDI Show Control

Some systems, particularly those found in low-cost digital control, use MIDI as a core control signal. They use MIDI notes either to trigger digital on/off or proportional effects (with velocity representing the proportional value). This approach is very cost-effective, and the MIDI messages can easily be recorded into standard musical MIDI sequencers and other devices. If an animatronic system can output MIDI, it should also be able to output MIDI Show Control (see Chapter 19) to control other devices in a show environment.

15

Fog, Smoke, Fire, and Water

This chapter encompasses a grab bag of special-effects systems such as fog, smoke, and flammable gas flame effects, and water (chemical pyrotechnics are covered in Chapter 16, "Pyrotechnics"). These elements are sometimes called "process control," but since that term in industry refers to chemical factories and oil refineries, we'll use "fog, smoke, fire, and water" here.

FOG AND SMOKE EQUIPMENT

The *Introduction to Modern Atmospheric Effects* compiled by the Entertainment Services and Technology Association (ESTA) defines fog as "A mixture of liquid droplets in air that reduces visibility and reflects light," while smoke is "Small, solid particles produced by burning and dispersed in the air. In the context of atmospheric effects, 'Smoke' is used to refer to any aerosol made of solid particles rather than liquid droplets." While smoke effects are occasionally used in performance, fog effects are typically much more easily controlled, and will be the focus here.

A large variety of off-the-shelf fog machines are available that use glycol-based solutions (see Figure 15.1); frozen, liquid, or gaseous carbon dioxide; liquid nitrogen; or other materials. In theatrical-style live shows, fog-generation generally falls under the jurisdiction of the electrics department, and

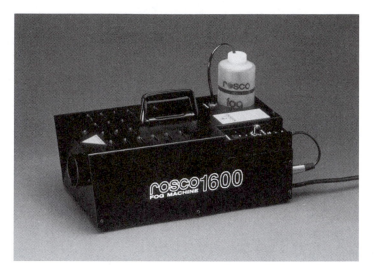

Figure 15.1 Glycol-Based Fog Machine (Courtesy Rosco Laboratories)

in these situations, fog machines are often interfaced to lighting control systems.

FIRE AND WATER

Most fire and water systems are custom-designed and built from the ground up to create spectacular effects for theme park or similar attractions. While many of these are custom, systems are often built using heavy-duty, standardized process, industrial, and machinery-control components such as PLCs (see Chapter 13, "Stage Machinery," for more information). Life-safety concerns, of course, are of utmost importance with any dangerous effect, and common-sense system design is always important. For instance, many flame-effect systems will only release gas if the source of ignition (such as a pilot light) for the gas can be confirmed to be working. Safety standards such as the National Fire Protection Association's "NFPA 160 Standard for Flame Effects Before a Proximate Audience" should always be followed.

CONTROL STANDARDS USED FOR FOG, SMOKE, FIRE, AND WATER

There are no entertainment control standards specifically for control of these elements, but many other systems are used, such as contact closures, DMX512, and field-bus standards.

Figure 15.2 Fog Machine Controller (Courtesy Rosco Laboratories)

Contact Closures

Contact closures, because of their ease of use and reliability, are widely used for simple control applications such as fog. Typical fog systems might include only a machine or two, and because of fog's unpredictable nature, most of these systems are controlled using simple manual controllers (see Figure 15.2) that create contact closures for the machine. Other controllers can also control these machines by interfacing to the remote control port.

4-20mA Current Loop

This is the oldest remote sensing and control approach and is widely used for many applications in industry such as pressure sensing. With this approach, a current loop is established, with a 4mA current flow indicating a setting of 0 percent, and 20mA indicating 100 percent.

Field Buses

The field-bus standards introduced in Chapter 13, "Stage Machinery," are often used in fog, smoke, fire, and water applications, since they offer easy, distributed, remote I/O, and some even have redundant backup loops.

Foundation Field Bus

Because of the quagmire of incompatible field-bus equipment detailed in Chapter 13, "Stage Machinery," the Instrumentation Society of America developed a field-bus standard known as ISA SP50, otherwise known as "Foundation Field Bus." It was designed for real-time field-device interconnection for the process control market and has standard transmission rates at 31.25 kbps, 1.0 Mbps, and 2.5 Mbps. Bus or tree topologies are possible, and data is transmitted using a synchronous current-loop Manchester (biphase) half-duplex modulation scheme.

DMX512

Fog machines from many manufacturers can now accept DMX control, either directly or through the use of an optional interface. Fog on/off, volume, and other parameters can all be assigned to DMX channels. See Chapter 7, "Lighting," for more information on DMX.

16

Pyrotechnics

Pyrotechnics are defined by the National Fire Protection Association as "Controlled exothermic chemical reactions that are timed to create the effects of heat, gas, sound, dispersion of aerosols, emissions of visible electromagnetic radiation . . ."[1] In other words, pyrotechnics create explosive effects for a variety of entertainment productions. Generally, "pyro" refers to smaller, indoor displays for production applications, while "fireworks" are the devices used in large outdoor displays.[2] Safety is of utmost importance in any pyro and fireworks application, and standards such as NFPA's "1126 Standard for the Use of Pyrotechnics before a Proximate Audience" and "1123 Code for Fireworks Display" should always be followed whenever pyro is used.

PYROTECHNIC CONTROL

The fundamental principle of electrical pyrotechnic control is very simple: controlled electrical current heats a small wire, which triggers an explosive reaction of chemicals positioned near the wire. Varying levels of sophistication are used to implement this simple principle, from switch closures to computer-based, time-code controllable triggering systems. Because of safety concerns, and the fact that most shows (except for full-blown fire-

---

[1] *NFPA 1126 Standard for the Use of Pyrotechnics before a Proximate Audience*, 1996 Edition, page 1126-6.

[2] Fireworks are defined in NFPA 1123, "Code for Fireworks Display" as "Any composition or device for the purpose of producing a visible or an audible effect for entertainment purposes by combustion, deflagration, or detonation . . . ."

works displays) generally have only a few effects, pyrotechnics have traditionally been manually controlled. However, computerized systems are becoming increasingly common.

Manual Pyrotechnic Control

A typical manual pyro control system (see Figure 16.1), consists of a controller and a number of effects devices, also known as "mortars," "flashpots," or "holders." The controller has a series of switches, each with "arm" and "test" positions, for the various effect circuits. The mortars hold the "electric match" or "igniter," which is coupled to the controller through a transformer at the pyro device's base. In most temporary pyrotechnic systems, control is distributed using multi-pin XLR cables, each of which can control one or more pyro circuits.

When the switch on the controller is moved to the test position, a very small current (thousandths of an ampere at a low voltage) is applied to the primary of the transformer in the pyro device to measure its impedance. If the electric match is ready and properly installed, continuity will exist on the firing circuit (connected to the transformer's secondary), the transformer will have a low impedance, and the continuity indicator on the controller will light. If the firing circuit is open, the impedance of the primary will be high, and the controller can determine that the circuit is not ready to be fired.

Having the transformer in the circuit has some added safety benefits. Any induced DC voltage on the control distribution wiring will be blocked from the electric match by the transformer, and when the system is idle (no voltage induced through the transformer), the secondary acts to shunt the

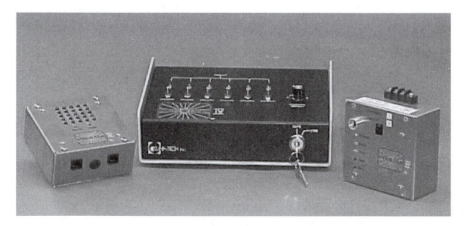

Figure 16.1   Pyrotechnic Controller with Infrared Control Data Distribution (Courtesy Luna Tech)

firing circuit. When shunted, there can be no voltage potential across the electric match; this helps the system resist misfires caused by static electricity or other phenomena.

Once the operator has determined that the circuit is good and the time comes to place the pyro effect into standby, the switch is moved to the arm position. The fire command, for safety reasons, is issued using a key switch; when this switch is turned, voltage is applied to the electric match, causing the effect to fire.

DTMF Systems

In the early 1980s, pyro manufacturer Luna Tech and others implemented a simple but effective pyro-control approach for time-based applications. Luna Tech used dual-tone, multi-frequency (DTMF) signals[3] recorded on a spare track of the show's audio soundtrack; when the proper tones were received by the firing system, the pyro effect was triggered. Safety interlocks were implemented downstream of the firing system.

IR Systems

Recently, manufacturers such as Luna Tech have been creating pyro controllers that use control data distributed by a line-of-sight infrared light link (see Figure 16.1). This approach not only eliminates the need for wiring, but also gets around the international licensing problems associated with radio transmission. Unlike the IR schemes used in audio and video remotes, the PyroPak® protocol is designed specifically for this application, is robust, and uses a 16-bit security code to avoid misfires.

Computerized Systems

In recent years, several manufacturers have developed computerized pyro and fireworks controllers. California-based Pyrodigital Consultants was one of the pioneers in this field, and in the early 1980s they developed a computer-based pyrotechnic control system that breaks pyro control down like a lighting system, with segregated control, digital data distribution, and power devices (see Figure 16.2). The system features either stand-alone or PC-based controllers, which communicate bidirectionally through a proprietary

---

[3]This system is also known as Touch-Tone. A Touch-Tone is actually a pair of dissimilar tones, selected because they are not harmonically related and are very difficult for humans to create. These tones are actually well suited to this task, since it is not likely that they would occur randomly.

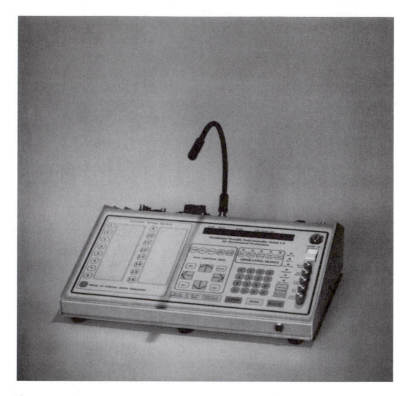

Figure 16.2   Pyrodigital Controller (Courtesy Pyrodigital Consultants)

digital protocol over standard microphone cable to "firing modules." Each firing module is addressable, and handles firing and continuity testing for up to 16 different effects. Continuity checks are done locally on request from the master controller, based on a comparison with the firing instructions; the results are communicated digitally back to the controller. Firing commands are simply digital instructions executed by the firing module; the system is randomly addressable and can fire multiple locations simultaneously.

This approach has a number of advantages for large, complex systems, which for many years have been fired using crude "button boards"[4] connected by multicables (one wire for each effect). With a digital system, the operator can be a safe distance (up to 1000 feet) from the action, with only small control cables leading to the firing site. In addition, since the system is computerized, it is easy to add automated cue control.

Pyrodigital's controllers allow the operator to fire pyrotechnics either manually or based on an internal, user-defined data table, which has a list of

---

[4]Button board may actually indicate a level of sophistication much higher than what often is used: a row of nails shorted with a hot wire.

records similar to cues on a lighting console. The data table contains shell caliber, event trigger time, prefire time,[5] and address. This data table can be generated by "scripting" software, which makes it very easy to create musically (or otherwise) synchronized displays. The console also features extensive group capabilities, which allow simple manual sequential firing, and macros, which allow sequences to be executed with just a few key-presses.

Safety is, of course, of utmost concern in pyrotechnics, and Pyrodigital has taken precautions to ensure that their systems work reliably and safely. Their proprietary control protocol uses extensive error correction, and the system generally defaults to nonoperation in case of a failure (fail-safe). In addition, for technicians' safety, shunting switches are placed on each firing module, which allows the module to be locally disabled; other, larger modules have continuity circuits for perimeter monitoring. In addition, Pyrodigital offers firing modules with independent shunting relays, which can be triggered from a secondary safety system, such as a PLC. This PLC could monitor "in-position" interlock systems, proximity detectors, manual "safe" switches, or any number of other safety interlock devices. Of course, with any pyro system, only qualified and highly skilled personnel should implement it; this is doubly true with automated pyro systems.

CONTROL STANDARDS USED IN PYRO

Because of safety concerns and industry inertia, few pyro systems can be controlled externally, but this has been changing in recent years. Pyrodigital's systems can chase either their own time-code scheme or SMPTE Time Code. MIDI Show Control commands are also supported for event-based control (see Chapter 17, "SMPTE Time Code," and Chapter 19, "MIDI Show Control"). External control allows pyrotechnics to become an integral part of any production. Humans can (and should) always be incorporated in the loop, downstream of the controller, to ensure that the effects are ready to fire safely.

---

[5]Time offset to compensate for the time it takes the shell to travel before exploding.

PART IV

Putting It Together: Standards for Connecting Systems

Most of what we've discussed so far regards only how individual systems communicate internally. Now we can move on to standards and methods of connecting systems together—into show-control systems.

17

SMPTE Time Code

We'll start with one of the oldest and easiest-to-understand show-control standards: Society of Motion Picture and Television Engineers (SMPTE) Time Code (TC). Because it originated in videotape editing, SMPTE Time Code breaks time down into hours, minutes, seconds, and frames; up to 24 hours worth of frames can be encoded. One discrete TC address exists for every frame on an encoded media: a typical address might be 05:20:31:18, or 5 hours, 20 minutes, 31 seconds, and 18 frames. SMPTE Time Code can be recorded on a wide variety of media, and played back for a variety of synchronization applications. It's an absolute standard—from a single SMPTE frame, the entire TC address can be read. If a show starts at 01:00:00:00[1] and a time code of 05:20:31:18 is read, the system can determine that this frame is 4 hours, 20 minutes, 31 seconds, and 18 frames from the beginning of the show.

The development of SMPTE Time Code began in 1967 when, to facilitate electronic videotape editing, the California-based company EECO developed a method of encoding video frames with an absolute time and frame number, based on a method used by NASA to synchronize telemetry tapes from its Apollo missions.[2] The EECO code was successful in the marketplace, and several other manufacturers developed their own proprietary time-coding methods. As in so many other situations already discussed—DMX512, MIDI, and others—this became problematic, as equipment from one manufacturer

---

[1] 01:00:00:00 is a common starting time, because it allows a logical "preroll." If a show were to start at 00:00:00:00, the preroll would have to be in hour 23.

[2] EECO, Inc., *The Time Code Book*, 1983.

would not work with gear from another. In 1969, the SMPTE formed a committee to create a standard time-coding scheme, and the result was eventually adopted by the American National Standards Institute (ANSI) as a national standard. As of this writing, the latest version of this standard is SMPTE 12M-1999, entitled "SMPTE Standard for Television, Audio, and Film—Time and Control Code." This time code, in wide use today, includes binary-coded decimal (BCD) representations of hours, minutes, seconds, and frames, various status flags, and 32 "user bits" that allows any kind of information (such as scene or take number) to be recorded as part of the time code.

AUDIO/VISUAL SYNCHRONIZATION

Because SMPTE has its origins in the film and video world, a brief introduction here to a common film/video time-code application will be helpful, before jumping into time code for live entertainment applications.

Since there are few ways to conveniently record high-quality audio on film (or, in some cases, video), film production traditionally uses a double system: images are recorded on film, and sounds are recorded separately onto an audio recorder. A "slate," on which is written shooting information such as the scene and take, is used to sync the two systems. When shooting, the film camera and audio recorder are both rolled, and once they are both up to "speed," the clapper on the slate is quickly closed to make the familiar "clap" sound. This system provides the editors in postproduction with a visual image of the clapper closing, and the sound of the clapper on the audio recording. They can then manually line up the audio soundtrack with the film to this point, and mechanically link them to run together as needed.

With time code, this process can be greatly simplified. If the camera is capable of generating and recording time code (some even burn it optically on the film outside the image), the TC is sent to the audio recorder and recorded along with the audio. Whenever the camera and the audio deck roll, they both record the exact same time code, frame for frame. The inverse can also be done: the audio deck can generate the TC, which can be sent directly to the camera or to a special "Time Code Slate" with an electronic TC display, which is then filmed for a few seconds each time the camera is rolled. These approaches give the editors encoded time code or a visual image of the time code on film and the time code on the audiotape.

In postproduction, the editors can use the recorded time codes for easy electronic synchronization. For instance, let's say the film from the above example has been dubbed to video, and the editors want to connect video and audio machines together, making them operate as one virtual machine, so that the audio will run in precise synchronization with the image at all times. To do so, a cable is run from one deck to the other carrying the

SMPTE Time Code signal. In this case, a cable is run from the video deck to the audio deck, so that the video deck will "master" the audio deck.

With the machines in the right modes, anytime the video deck is rolled, the audio machine compares the incoming time code from the video player with the time-code position of its own media, and controls and continuously varies its transport speed ("vari-speeds") to lock the two machines precisely together. For example, if "Play" is pressed on the video machine, time code is generated and sent to the audio deck. The audio machine will rapidly start falling behind, will start moving forward quickly to catch up, and then ramp up and down its speed until the two are perfectly synchronized, frame for frame. So, in other words, the audio machine "chases" the video deck, and after a bit of "preroll" time, the audio tracks can be used in perfect sync with the video image.[3]

LIVE ENTERTAINMENT TIME-CODE APPLICATIONS

While the example above comes from the postproduction world, in the live entertainment industry, we oftentimes want to do very similar things. We may want an audio multitrack machine to chase a video presentation, or to have four video decks run separate images to separate screens all in perfect synchronization, along with an audio deck, or to synchronize two audio decks to get more tracks, or to have an animatronic character synchronize exactly to a soundtrack.

We can also use time code to trigger event-based systems. For instance, if we need to synchronize light cues (events) to a sound track, we could record SMPTE along with the audio. Then, whenever the audio deck is rolled, time code would be played back and routed to the lighting console. Many professional lighting consoles today accept time code directly, and each cue can be programmed to trigger at a precise time: cue 18 might be programmed to execute at 07:02:59:23. Whenever the audio track rolls, and the preprogrammed time-code address comes along, the appropriate light cues will trigger. In a similar fashion, many preset-based audio mixers, video routers, pyro systems, playback devices, or other systems can also be triggered. Entire attractions are run from SMPTE Time Code.

TIME-CODE TYPES

Since different media and countries have different framing rates, there are different types of time code. Film is generally shot and projected at 24 frames per second (fps), so there is one type of TC for film—24-frame time code.

---

[3] In the past, a time-code "synchronizer" would have been used to synchronize these two decks; today, this synchronization functionality is simply a feature of the decks.

30-Frame Time Code

Monochrome American video uses the 60-Hz AC line as the basis for its framing rate, and because it is interlaced,[4] the framing rate is exactly 30 fps. This is another type of TC, known as 30-frame time code.

Drop-Frame Time Code

Color video in America was standardized by the National Television Standards Committee (NTSC) and runs at an approximate framing rate of 29.97 fps. If regular 30-fps TC is used to count video frames running at a rate of 29.97 fps, the time-code second will gain 0.03 frames per second in relation to a true second; a cumulative gain of 108 frames, or 3.6 seconds per hour of running time, will result (see Figure 17.1).

This error may be a bit difficult to comprehend, but the key to understanding it is that in a time-code receiver, there is no external clock against which to compare the frame count, because the TC *is* a clock. So, if we're using 30-fps TC to count NTSC 29.97 fps frames, it will take 1.03 actual seconds to reach a count of 30, or 1 time-code second. While an error of +0.03 real seconds per time-code second doesn't seem like much, this accumulates to 3.6 seconds per hour, or 1 minute and 26.4 seconds per day. It would certainly be a problem if a light cue was off by 3.6 seconds at the end of an hour-long presentation.

For this reason, another type of code was developed, known as Drop-Frame-NTSC Time Compensated Time Code (drop-frame TC), and bits in the time code signal are used to indicate when drop-frame compensation is applied, so that receivers can decode the signal properly. Drop-frame TC is so named because the extra 108 frame counts that would accumulate over the course of an hour are omitted. Conceptually, this is similar to a sort of reverse "leap-year," although here we're dropping frames every minute instead of adding a day every four years. Since it is impossible to drop fractional frames, the first two frame numbers of every minute, with the exception of minutes 0, 10, 20, 30, 40, and 50, are dropped:

60 minutes − 6 not dropped = 54 minutes

54 minutes × 2 frames dropped/minute = 108 frames

Even this method still only approximates real time; drop-frame TC still has an error of −3.6 ms every hour.

---

[4] Every other line is scanned first, and then the remaining lines are scanned on alternate "fields." Two fields make up one frame.

COUNTING 30 FRAMES AT 30FPS

COUNTING 30 FRAMES AT 29.97FPS

Figure 17.1   NTSC Framing Rate Error

European Time Code

The video system in Europe is far more logical than the American system: color and monochrome video in Europe both run at exactly 25 fps (1/2 the European 50Hz power line frequency). For this reason, the European Broadcasting Union (EBU) has adopted a time code more or less identical to SMPTE (Europe has no need for a drop-frame version), with a framing rate of 25 fps. Because of the parallel standards, this time code is sometimes referred to as SMPTE/EBU Time Code.

TIME-CODE FORMATS

There are two types of time code—Linear Time Code (LTC) and Vertical Interval Time Code (VITC—pronounced "vitcee").

Linear Time Code

Linear Time Code (which used to be called "longitudinal" time code) is so-named because it was designed to be recorded on an audio track linearly along the edge of a videotape, not helically like the video signal. LTC can be distributed and works like an audio signal. It is encoded using a type of bi-phase modulation, where there is a transition from high to low or low to high at the start (and, because bits are trailed together, at the end) of every bit (see Figure 17.2). A bit with no internal transitions is a zero; a transition within a bit time denotes a one. This bi-phase coding scheme makes the polarity of LTC irrelevant; it also allows the code to be read backwards as well as forwards, and allows LTC to be recorded on a wide variety of audio media.

Each LTC frame is composed of 80 bits, numbered 0-79 (see Figure 17.3); the length of the LTC word is exactly the same as a video frame,

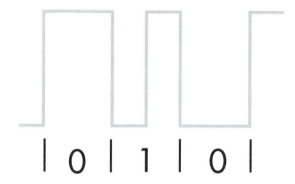

| 0 | 1 | 0 |

Figure 17.2   Bi-Phase Encoding Used in SMPTE Time Code

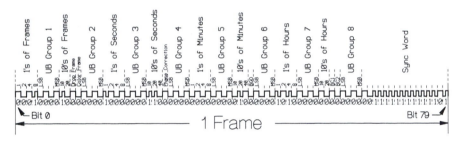

Figure 17.3   Bi-Phase Representation of SMPTE LTC Frame Address
05:20:31:18

and, by specification, the first bit of the time-code word should start on the fifth line of the first field of a video frame, ±1 ½ lines. Because bit timing in the reading of LTC is derived from the actual code read, and not by comparison to an external clock, LTC can be decoded in either direction and at speeds well above (up to 100 times) or below (1/50) its normal speed. At the end of each LTC frame, there is a 16-bit sync word—0011111111111101—which is a series that cannot be repeated anywhere else in the time-code word with any combination of time or user data. When the decoding system encounters this sync word, it knows that this point in the code is the end of one frame and the start of another; the word is also used to derive tape-playback direction.

The standard specifies a "preferred connector" for balanced outputs: a 3-pin XLR. Males are to be used for outputs, females for inputs.[5] The pin-out

---

[5]This may seem backwards if you're not an audio person, but it is the standard sex arrangement for audio connections (because of phantom power emanating from mixers).

follows the AES XLR standard: pin 1 is shield, and pins 2 and 3 are used to carry the differential audio signal (remember, polarity is irrelevant in this bi-phase scheme). The preferred connector specified for single-ended time code transmission is the BNC.

LTC is simple to use and has gained broad acceptance, but it has a number of limitations. If a tape containing LTC is moving extremely slowly or is stopped, the code can be misinterpreted or not read, because the *transitions* in the signal carry the information; with no tape movement, there are no transitions. At high tape-transport rates the frequency[6] of the signal can exceed the frequency response capabilities of standard audio circuitry and become distorted. In addition, LTC generally becomes so distorted and noisy after two generations of recording that it must be "jam-synced," a process in which the TC is read, regenerated, and rerecorded. LTC is generally recorded at a high level in an audio track, and because it is a square wave, crosstalk (interference) with adjacent tracks or even low-level signals in adjacent cables is possible. There are ways to deal with all of these problems (see "Practical SMPTE Time Code" section below), and LTC is used reliably in many audio applications. For video applications, there is another type of time code: Vertical Interval Time Code.

Vertical Interval Time Code

Vertical Interval Time Code was developed in the late 1970s after videotape recorders capable of playing back high-quality still images were developed; as just described, LTC becomes unreadable when the media is not moving. In VITC, time-coding information is inserted as digital data into each frame's "vertical blanking interval," the time during which the electron beam is "blanked" as it "rasters" back to the top of a cathode-ray tube (CRT) after scanning a video field. Because VITC is part of the video signal itself, it can be read and decoded even in extreme-slow-motion or still-frame applications. Additionally, in video-sync applications, VITC does not use up one of the videotape's precious audio tracks.

VITC uses 90 bits to encode the time code instead of LTC's 80; most of these additional bits are used for cyclic redundancy checking (CRC). The VITC code is recorded once for each of a video frame's two fields and can be inserted more frequently. Therefore, at least two copies of the VITC code exist in each frame; this redundancy, in conjunction with the CRC check, means that VITC is much less subject to dropouts and misinterpretation than LTC.

---

[6]At normal speed, the bit rate of 80 bits x 30 frames equals 2400 bps, or a fundamental audio frequency of about 1200 Hz.

Because VITC is encoded within the video signal itself, it can be used only in video applications. VITC must be recorded with the video signal and therefore cannot be changed without rerecording the video. Since video equipment is needed to read VITC, implementations of LTC are generally less expensive for nonvideo applications.

PRACTICAL SMPTE TIME CODE

There are a number of issues to keep in mind when dealing with time code. The recommendations here apply mostly to LTC, which you are more likely to encounter in a live show than VITC.

Hours

Shows that run 24 hours are rare,[7] so it is often more convenient to use the time-code hours for other purposes. For instance, time-code hour might be used for show 1, hour 2 for show 2, and so on.

Regeneration

As mentioned above, LTC degenerates each time it is recorded or rere-corded, especially with analog systems. So it is recommend that *any* time you rerecord LTC you "regenerate" or "jam-sync" it, cleaning up bit transitions through reshaping, and, in some systems, totally recreating the signal to clean up jitter (timing) problems. Some devices incorporate this regeneration as a feature, and stand-alone regeneration units are also available.

Crosstalk

Care must be taken when recording LTC onto analog recorders, because, although the time-code signal uses a specially shaped wave designed to minimize harmonics, crosstalk between adjacent tracks (or wires in an audio snake) could definitely be a problem. For this reason, many users record the LTC signal at a level no higher than –5 VU, –10 VU or lower. As an additional safety measure, it is a good idea to place the time code on a track as far from tracks containing show audio as possible, and you should never record TC with any type of automatic gain control enabled.

---

[7]Although there was at least one in Times Square at the 1999/2000 New Year's celebration. They had to figure out how the machines dealt with rolling over from 23:59:59:29 to 00:00:00:00!

Distribution

To be safe with LTC, you should generally not "two-fer" it; you should instead use some sort of audio distribution amp. This approach solves many potential impedance problems, isolates each output from others on the same link, and ensures that each device receives a clean signal.

Dropouts and Freewheeling

Occasionally, due to tape wear or other problems, time code "dropouts" occur, where the signal momentarily disappears or becomes too corrupted to decode. This is a symptom of a serious problem, but many devices are capable of "freewheeling" through these dropouts, simply rolling on with their own time bases until the code reappears or can be decoded properly again. On any well-designed piece of equipment incorporating this feature, freewheeling should be able to be enabled or disabled, and the number of freewheeling frames should be configurable.

Framing Rate and Drop Frame Mismatches

Framing rate mismatches and drop-frame time-code problems cause more confusion than any other aspect of time code. If you see an error in a system close to the 3.6 seconds per hour described above, then it's likely that either the transmitter is sending drop-frame, and the receiver is not properly configured for it, or vice versa. Many entertainment control applications—even those incorporating video—simply use 30-frame time code, even if it runs at the 29.97 rate, to avoid problems. After some period of time, the time-code *number* and the *actual* time will drift apart slightly. But if we're simply triggering light cues, it really is fine if light cue 18's time-code address doesn't exactly match the actual show time, as long as the cue is executed properly.

The most important thing in any time-code application is to be sure that the framing rate is chosen and agreed upon well in advance, everything is double-checked, and time is left for testing. Time-code test equipment (see "Distripalyzer" section later in this chapter) is invaluable for solving these problems.

Offset

It is often desirable to be able to "offset" time code, adding or subtracting time to it. This might be useful when you want to transfer one show to another, or when you have latency problems somewhere in a system.

Chasing

Another feature of well-designed equipment that handles SMPTE time code is the ability to somehow *disable,* or not listen to, the incoming time-code stream. This is extremely useful when you are trying to work on a system and someone else is doing something that causes the time code to roll. There is nothing more annoying than being deep into programming a cue and having the console start executing other cues based on incoming TC!

SMPTE TIME-CODE HARDWARE

Because of the large broadcast equipment market, and the wide acceptance of the SMPTE Time-Code standard, there is a large variety of specialized time-code generation, processing, distribution, and interfacing hardware.

Time-Code Generator

A time-code generator (see Figure 17.4) is used in many applications to create a master time-code source. Some generators can even synchronize themselves to the Global Positioning System (GPS), which has very accurate time services. Many live shows do not need a generator in performance, but they might use one in the studio to create the code recorded on the audio or video media. Other shows use an externally controllable generator as a master, with all other devices as slaves to it.

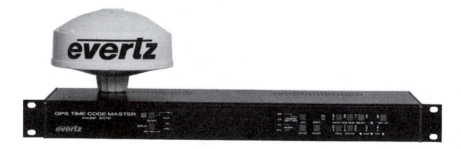

Figure 17.4 Time-Code Generator with GPS-Sync Capability (Courtesy Evertz Microsystems)

Figure 17.5 Time-Code Regenerator/Analyzer/Distributor (Courtesy Brainstorm Electronics)

Distripalyzer

One unique and invaluable device for any time-code application is the Distripalyzer (see Figure 17.5), made by Brainstorm Electronics. In addition to performing standard functions like jam-syncing and time-code distribution, this unit features some built-in test equipment (which is also available separately). The Distripalyzer can analyze an incoming time-code stream, and measure and display the frame rate, the time-code format, the drop-frame status, and a number of other parameters. The device can even display user bits (if encoded in accordance with a SMPTE-recommended practice). The unit is not cheap, but it could save you hours of troubleshooting on a job site if you encounter a problem.

SMPTE to MIDI SPP

While rarely used today in show applications, devices are available that allow MIDI's Song Position Pointer (SPP) system to be locked to SMPTE Time Code. These devices convert the incoming TC into MIDI Timing Clock and Song Position Pointer messages, based on a tempo map that is programmed into the converter by the user. The SPP approach is of little use for entertainment control applications, because when even simple real-time (not tempo-based) changes are made, an entire tempo map must be reprogrammed.

SMPTE to DCC/GPI

There are a variety of SMPTE interfacing devices with programmable "hit lists," which allow contact closure or other events to be programmed and triggered at specific times. Some of the MIDI SPP devices have this functionality as well.

SMPTE Display Units

One invaluable device is a SMPTE display, which simply shows the current time-code addresses as they roll by. This is a very useful device for troubleshooting and for system monitoring.

SMPTE to MTC

Many devices only take MIDI Time Code (described in Chapter 18). There are a variety of converters that will generate MTC messages from an incoming SMPTE stream.

OTHER TIME CODES

In addition to the widely-used SMPTE Time Code, there are a number of other "time codes." For instance, many computers now incorporate some sort of internal time code for CD-ROM, DVD, and DVD-ROM. However, these are mostly used inside a computer, between the drive and the application software.

Sync or Tach Pulses/Pilot Tones

For simple, relative synchronization, a "sync" or "tach" pulse is sometimes used. For example, a camera might send out a square wave pulse when it exposes each frame. Or, a motorized system might send out a pulse train that varies in frequency as it runs. With either of these systems, the sync pulse can be received by another device, which can synchronize to the pulses. Another analog approach, found in older film production equipment, is the "pilot tone." With such a system, a tone is recorded on a media's track. As the device moves slowly, a low-frequency tone will be generated; as the device speeds up, the frequency will increase. Alternatively, a device could look at something like a SMPTE stream, and synchronize itself to the SMPTE address data without synchronizing to the addresses themselves. Sync-pulse synchronization schemes are highly unstandardized.

18

MIDI Time Code

Since SMPTE TC is an analog audio signal, machines that only have digital inputs (computers) must sample and convert the analog signal somehow in order to extract the time-code data. To encode the time-code data instead as digital MIDI messages, MIDI Time Code (MTC) was developed in 1986 by Evan Brooks and Chris Meyer, of the audio/synthesizer companies Digidesign and Sequential Circuits, respectively. MTC breaks the analog SMPTE TC frames into MIDI messages and digitally transmits them directly down a MIDI line.

MTC MESSAGES

MIDI Time Code is transmitted in two formats: full messages and quarter-frame messages. Full messages contain a complete time-code address and are sent whenever a system starts or stops. Quarter-frame messages transmit pieces or "nibbles" of the current TC address, and as the name implies, they are sent out at the rate of four per TC frame. Eight quarter-frame messages are used to communicate one full TC address, so the time-code count can be fully updated only every other frame. However, a receiving system can still *sync* four times per TC frame, by examining the timing of the quarter-frame messages.

The 11110001 (F1h) status byte is used as the MTC quarter-frame system-common byte. After this MTC status byte is sent, a data byte is sent, which can contain a nibble for the message number, a nibble representing one of the TC digits, or a nibble containing other data. See Table 18.1 for complete details.

Table 18.1 MIDI Time Code Messages

Function	Status Byte Binary	Status Byte Hex	Data Byte(s) Binary	Data Byte(s) Hex	Where
Full Frame Message	11110000	F0	01111111	7F	System Exclusive
			00000001	01	Real Time System Exclusive
			00000001	01	MIDI Time Code Sub ID#1
			0tthhhhh		Full Frame Sub ID#2
					tt = TC Type (00=24, 01=25, 10=30 DF, 11=30 Nondrop)
					hhhhh = Hours, 0-23
			00mmmmmm		mmmmmm = Minutes, 0-59
			00ssssss		ssssss = Seconds, 0-59
			000fffff		fffff = Frames, 0-29
			11110111	F7	End of System Exclusive
Quarter-Frame Frame Count LS Nibble	11110001	F1	0000dddd	0d	dddd = Frames LS Nibble
Quarter-Frame Frame Count MS Nibble	11110001	F1	0001uuud	1d	uuu = Undefined; set to 0 d = Frames MS nibble
Quarter-Frame Seconds LS Nibble	11110001	F1	0010dddd	2d	dddd = Seconds LS nibble
Quarter-Frame Seconds MS Nibble	11110001	F1	0011uudd	3d	dd = Seconds MS nibble
Quarter-Frame Minutes LS Nibble	11110001	F1	0100dddd	4d	dddd = Minutes LS nibble
Quarter-Frame Minutes MS Nibble	11110001	F1	0101uudd	5d	dd = Minutes MS nibble
Quarter-Frame Hours LS Nibble	11110001	F1	0110dddd	6d	dddd = Hours LS nibble
QuarterFrame Hours MS Nibble/TC Type	11110001	F1	0111ttdd	7d	tt = TC type (same as above) dd = Hours MS nibble

Table 18.2 MIDI Time Code User Bits Message

Function	Status Byte		Data Byte(s)		Where
	Binary	Hex	Binary	Hex	
User Bits Message	11110000	F0	01111111	7F	System Exclusive
			00000001	01	Real-Time System Exclusive
			00000012	02	MIDI Time-Code Sub ID#1
			0000aaaa		User Bits Sub ID#2
			0000bbbb		aaaa = First User Bit Group
			0000cccc		bbbb = Second User Bit Group
			0000dddd		cccc = Third User Bit Group
			0000eeee		dddd = Fourth User Bit Group
			0000ffff		eeee = Fifth User Bit Group
			0000gggg		ffff = Sixth User Bit Group
			0000hhhh		gggg = Seventh User Bit Group
			000000ii		hhhh = Eight User Bit Group
			11110111	F7	ii = Group Flag Bits
					End of System Exclusive

So, a full-frame MTC message containing the time-code address 05:20:31:18 (sent in 30 nondrop) would break down in hex as follows:

```
F0  7F  01  01  65  14  1F  12  F7
```

SMPTE USER BITS IN MIDI TIME CODE

The MTC standard provides a method for encoding SMPTE TC user bits in MTC, as shown in Table 18.2.

PRACTICAL MIDI TIME CODE

MIDI Time Code is actually capable of *higher* resolution than SMPTE, because it uses four quarter-frame messages per single SMPTE frame. At a normal framing rate of 30 fps, 120 MTC messages would be sent out each second. However, since MIDI is a simple point-to-point interface, there is no mechanism built-in to ensure that these messages arrive at the receiver in a predictable amount of time, especially if MIDI processing equipment is used in line.

While it is possible that some MTC messages could be delayed in a MIDI merger or other device due to heavy traffic, this might only result in a particular MTC message or two coming in a few milliseconds late, (except in extreme cases). Correspondingly, a light cue might end up being a few milliseconds late, and for many entertainment applications this would not be a problem worth dealing with, and some receiving devices can even free-wheel over such a timing error. However, if timing is critical in a particular application, a dedicated MIDI link should be run directly from the generating device to the receiver, with no other MIDI traffic allowed on that segment. If the MIDI link is simply a piece of cable with no other traffic, it will have a predictable latency.

MTC messages are simply standard MIDI messages, and the distribution topologies and other recommendations found in Chapter 9 apply.

19

MIDI Show Control

MIDI was embraced by the professional sound industry soon after its introduction in 1983, since the sound and music businesses have always been intertwined. Many musical MIDI messages are well suited to sound control—a program change command applies as well to an audio processor as it does to a musical synthesizer.

The entertainment lighting industry jumped on the MIDI bandwagon in the late 1980s, with musical-equipment manufacturers such as Sunn, which made club and small touring lighting systems, leading the way. Other companies such as Electronic Theatre Controls and Strand, and moving light companies such as Vari*Lite, soon caught on. However, standard MIDI messages don't translate well to disciplines like lighting control: what message do you use to initiate a cue? How do you control a submaster? How do you fire a macro? How do you set a grand master level?

Some lighting companies used implementations where program-change messages triggered cues; moving light-oriented companies often based their implementation on note commands, where arbitrary notes were assigned to various buttons on the console. These note messages could be recorded into some sort of sequencer and played back later to initiate complex cue-based operations. These varying implementations led to a situation very similar to the state of the music industry in the days before MIDI, or the lighting industry before DMX—similar devices had similar control capabilities but spoke different languages. In this case, it was more like different dialects, because, though all the controllers spoke MIDI, few could be interconnected in a logical way.

Talk of creating a standard MIDI implementation for show applications came to a head at the "MIDI Mania" panel discussion at the Lighting Dimensions International trade show in Nashville in 1989. Andy Meldrum, a programmer for Vari*Lite, put forth a proposal for an open, standard implementation of System Exclusive messages that would allow controllers from any manufacturer to be connected and controlled. Participants were excited about the possibilities of a standard protocol, and in December 1989, Charlie Richmond, of Canada's Richmond Sound Design, organized a "Theatre Messages" working group within the MIDI Manufacturer's Association (MMA) and got a forum set up on the USITT's Callboard electronic bulletin-board system for development.

Through contributions on Callboard and a great deal of footwork on Richmond's part, a formal standard known as "MIDI Show Control," or MSC, was developed and sent to the MIDI Manufacturer's Association for voting in 1991. The standard was approved by the MMA and sent on to the Japanese MIDI Association for final, international approval; MIDI Show Control Version 1.0 became a standard in the summer of 1991. The current release is 1.1.

MIDI Show Control is the only open, standardized protocol for peer-to-peer show-control applications. As such, MSC does not replace any controller-to-device standard, such as DMX512, or even musical MIDI messages; in fact, it works well in conjunction with most other standards and protocols. MSC has been kept as open as possible—the bare necessities have been rigidly defined, and there is ample room for expansion.

MSC COMMAND STRUCTURE

MIDI Show Control contains show commands such as "Light Cue 34 go" and "Sound Resume," and the messages are standard MIDI SysEx, using the Universal Real-Time System Exclusive ID, with a reserved Sub-ID of 02h assigned by the MMA. Commands can vary in length, up to a maximum of 128 bytes.

MSC Message Format

The general MSC command format (in hex) is:

```
F0 7F [Device ID] 02 [Command Format] [Command] [Data] F7
```

MIDI Show Control messages all start with an F0 byte to indicate that the message is Universal System Exclusive. The next byte is a 7F, which denotes Real Time (all MSC messages are real time); then a Device ID is sent. This Device ID determines to what address a message is intended, but since MIDI is a broadcast standard, all messages go to all devices on a link. The MSC Sub-ID, 02h, is sent next. This second Sub-ID byte may seem to really belong immediately after the 7F byte, but it is placed here so that the messages conform with the Universal System Exclusive standard. After the Sub-ID, the Command Format is sent; this tells the receiver what type of message to expect—whether lighting, sound, machinery, or a myriad of other types. Next the actual command is sent; these commands include simple messages such as "Go" and "Stop" as well as more esoteric commands. Finally, any associated data, such as the cue number, is sent. The message is closed out with an F7 End of SysEx byte.

Device ID

The Device ID, as just detailed, is used to indicate the intended receiver of a particular message. In equipment of any reasonable design, the Device ID will be user-configurable, although this flexibility is not specifically called for in the standard. Every device must respond to at least one of the 112 individual device IDs (00-6Fh), or the 7Fh All Call number, which is used to transmit global messages to all receivers in the system. Additionally, a receiver can respond to commands issued to one of 15 groups (70-7Eh), which allow groups of devices to be addressed simultaneously. This feature is not required by the standard. A group of Device IDs exists for each Command Format.

Command Format

In one sense, the Command Format byte indicates which type of equipment is to be addressed by a particular message; however, what is really being indicated is what set of commands are being used. Basic commands such as Go and Stop have been globally defined (more on that below), and the existence of the Command Format allows commands that are specific to a particular type of control to be implemented. A large variety of Command Formats have been defined in the standard, and room has been reserved for expansion (see Table 19.1).[1] Each command format type has a "General Category" number and subsections. A conventional lighting control console, for example, would use commands of format 01h; a moving-light controller, or even a moving light itself, might use format 02h (although, in fact, most use 01h). Looking at the category list, you might notice what appear

---

[1] Ironically, no "Show Control" command format was designated. This may finally be addressed in MSC Version 1.2.

Table 19.1 MIDI Show Control Command Formats

Hex	Command	Hex	Command
00	Reserved for extensions	30	Video—General
		31	Videotape Machines
01	Lighting—General	32	Videocassette Machines
02	Moving Lights	33	Videodisc Players
03	Color Changers	34	Video Switchers
04	Strobes	35	Video Effects
05	Lasers	36	Video Character Generators
06	Chasers	37	Video Still Stores
		38	Video Monitors
10	Sound—General		
11	Music	40	Projection—General
12	CD Players	41	Film Projectors
13	EPROM Playback	42	Slide Projectors
14	Audio Tape Machines	43	Video Projectors
15	Intercoms	44	Dissolvers
16	Amplifiers	45	Shutter Controls
17	Audio Effects Devices		
18	Equalizers	50	Process Control—General
		51	Hydraulic Oil
20	Machinery—General	52	H_2O
21	Rigging	53	CO_2
22	Flies	54	Compressed Air
23	Lifts	55	Natural Gas
24	Turntables	56	Fog
25	Trusses	57	Smoke
26	Robots	58	Cracked Haze
27	Animation		
28	Floats	60	Pyro—General
29	Breakaways	61	Fireworks
2A	Barges	62	Explosions
		63	Flame
		64	Smokepots
		7F	All-Types

to be holes in the types of equipment you could want to use; for example, in the sound category, you might think that samplers had been omitted. However, these devices already have a standard command set: MIDI. The existence of a Command Format here, of course, does not mean that equipment exists now (or ever will); it simply means that the designers of the specification left room for that type of equipment.

Commands

The heart of a MIDI Show Control message is the single-byte command that follows the Command Format byte. There are 127 possible commands for each Command Format; see the detailed descriptions that follow for more information. Each command can contain up to 128 bytes, which allows for a wide variety of data to be transmitted. Two types of data are globally defined in the standard: cue numbers and time numbers.

Cue Numbers

The cue number is a vital part of MIDI Show Control. Cues are addressed via a Cue Number and an optional Cue List and Cue Path. Cue Path indicates from which of the available media the Cue List should be pulled; Cue List indicates to the receiver in which of the currently "open" Cue Lists the Cue Number resides. Optionally, lighting equipment may use the Cue List number to indicate which submaster or playback control is being used to execute a particular cue. For instance, if a lighting console had two crossfaders, one labeled A-B and the other labeled C-D, a Cue List value of one could be used to tell the console to execute the cue on fader A-B; Cue List two could denote the C-D faders.

The actual numeric cue data is encoded using ASCII, with the 2Eh ASCII decimal-point character used for its intended purpose. The Cue Number/List/Path data is sent sequentially with 00h delimiters. If the Cue Path or List is not needed, it is simply omitted; however, a Cue Path cannot be sent without a Cue List. If a receiving device is not able to deal with Cue Paths or Lists, it simply discards that data.

To indicate that a particular device should select Cue 47.3 on Cue List 2 from Cue Path 37, the following hex bytes would be sent:

```
34  37  2E  33  00  32  00  33  37
```

More than one decimal point may be used: numbers like 67.3.4 are valid. If a particular piece of equipment cannot support the multiple decimal points, subsequent sub-cue numbering is discarded.

Time-Code Numbers

Time is also globally defined in the MSC spec. The coding method is the same as that used in the MIDI Time Code and Machine Control specs, with the same units of hours, minutes, seconds, frames, fractional frames: hr mn sc fr ff. There are actually two implementations of the subframe data in the spec. The first is as listed above, the second uses the fractional frame byte for "status" data. This second type is rarely used.

RECOMMENDED MINIMUM SETS

While manufacturers may decide which of the commands defined in the spec to implement, there are logical groupings that help indicate to an end-user how deeply a manufacturer has implemented MSC. The commands are grouped into three recommended minimum sets, designed to help equipment of various sophistication be compatible. Recommended minimum set one contains only three commands: Go, Stop, and Resume; set two has "full data capability" but does not contain any time-code commands; set three contains all the commands defined in the specification.

MSC COMMANDS

Since MIDI Show Control is such an important standard for entertainment control, all the commands defined in the standard are detailed here. Data in <angle brackets> is optional.

As shown above, the general MSC command structure (in hex) is:

```
F0  7F  [Device ID]  02  [Command Format]  [Command]  [Data]  F7
```

Only the command and data bytes are detailed below. To make a complete message, you would have to know the target Device ID, Command Format, Command, and related data (cue number, etc.).

Messages for All Types of Equipment

The first group of MIDI Show Control commands is common to nearly any cue-based system—lighting controllers, slide controllers, or anything else controlled using cues.

Go

```
01 <Q_number> <00> <Q_list> <00> <Q_path>
```

This command's function is fairly self-explanatory: it starts a transition to a preset cue state. If a cue number is not specified, the controlled device simply executes the next cue in its Cue List. The transition time is stored in the controlled device; if you want to send transition time as well, you should use the Timed Go command below.

Stop

```
02 <Q_number> <00> <Q_list> <00> <Q_path>
```

This command is also fairly self-explanatory: it simply stops the specified transition. If no cue is specified, it stops all cues currently in progress.

Resume

```
03 <Q_number> <00> <Q_list> <00> <Q_path>
```

Resumes the specified cue, or resumes all stopped transitions if no c number is specified.

Timed_Go

```
04 hr mn sc fr ff <Q_number> <00> <Q_list> <00>
   <Q_path>
```

The time communicated in this Go message is generally either the cue transition time or the time at which the cue should be executed, depending on the implementation. If a receiving device cannot deal with a Timed Go command, it should simply execute the cue (Go) with its prerecorded time. Here, hr mn sc fr ff is the time, down to fractional frames.

Load

```
05 <Q_number> <00> <Q_list> <00> <Q_path>
```

This command might also be known as Stand By. The cue specified in the message is loaded and placed in a ready mode for execution. This might be necessary for a sound system, for example, where a sound might have to be cued before the cue can be executed.

Set

```
cc cc vv vv <hr mn Sc fr ff>
```

This command "defines the value of a generic control," which is intentionally vague because of the command's potentially broad application. In the above composition, "cc" denotes a 2-byte Generic Control Number, which might be thought of as a sort of sub-Device ID, sent least-significant byte first. Here, "vv" denotes a Generic Control Value. This is one of those commands that is important but hard to define without a specific manufacturer's implementation, so you should consult your manufacturer's manual for more information.

Fire

```
07 mm
```

This command is primarily designed to fire console-based macros, as might be found on a lighting controller. Here "mm" denotes a 7-bit (128 values) Macro Number.

All Off

```
08
```

Restore

```
09
```

Reset

```
0A
```

All Off kills all outputs but leaves the controllers in a restorable condition. This command might be useful when a stage manager or director is yelling "Hold please!" or in emergency situations. The 09 Restore command restores the controlled devices to the conditions existing before an All_Off command was issued; Reset terminates all running cues and resets addressed controlled devices to a starting condition. Controlled devices are reset to a "top-of-show" condition.

Go_Off

```
0B <Q_number> <00> <Q_list> <00> <Q_path>
```

This command sends a selected cue to an off condition. If no cue is specified, all currently running cues are terminated. Go_Off would be useful in a situation where a cue contains a loop that runs until a certain event takes place; once that event takes place, you want to shut the cue down (fade-out the sound, dim the lights, and so on) in a controlled fashion.

Sound Commands

A second set of commands, known as "sound" commands, is defined in the spec. While these commands are rooted in the sound realm, many are quite useful for other applications. At the time of the standard's creation, Charles Richmond, chief architect of MIDI Show Control, was one of the only manufacturers involved with the standard who was making open show-oriented controllers that functioned in a cue-based mode. For this reason, many of these commands are derived from the operation of his systems, which have an internal clock running from the moment the software is invoked, or when set or reset by a command. This clock can run on its own, be synced to external sources such as MIDI Time Code, be reset for each cue, or be ignored altogether.

Go/Jam Clock

```
10 <Q_number> <00> <Q_list> <00> <Q_path>
```

This command executes a cue and syncs, or "jams," a controlled device's internal clock to the cue's time number, which is stored in the controlled device.

Standby +

```
11 <Q_List>
```

Standby –

```
12 <Q_List>
```

Standby_+ is similar to the Load command detailed above, but it sets the next cue in a Cue List into a ready mode, awaiting execution. Standby_– works the same way as Standby_+, except that it loads the previous cue in the list.

Sequence_+

```
13  <Q_List>
```

Sequence_–

```
14  <Q_List>
```

If you have multiple cues with the same base number, such as 1, 1.25, and 1.3, the 1 component of these cues is called the "parent" cue. Sequence_+ loads the next parent cue to standby operation. Let's say you have a cue series of 2.0, 2.5, 2.6, 3.0, and 3.8. You're in scene 2 (cue 2.5), an actor forgets his blocking, and you need to jump on to scene 3 (cue 3.0) without speeding through the cue actions in cue 2.6. Sending a Sequence_+ command will send the system to cue 3.0. The Q_List selection optionally selects which Cue List you want to act upon. Sequence_– functions the same as Sequence_+, except that it places into a standby mode the parent cue previous to the current cue. If you have cues 2.3, 2.5, 3.0, 3.1, and 4.8 and are currently executing cue 3.1, executing Sequence_– would call up cue 2.3.

Start_Clock

```
15  <Q_List>
```

Stop_Clock

```
16  <Q_List>
```

Zero_Clock

```
17  <Q_List>
```

Set_Clock

```
18  hr mn sc fr ff  <Q_List>
```

Start_Clock starts a controlled device's internal clock. If the clock is already running, this command is ignored. In some controlled devices, multiple Cue Lists can each have their own independent clock; the optional Cue List parameter of this command selects which Cue List to act upon. Stop_Clock stops a controlled device's internal clock, holding the current time value. Zero_Clock resets a Cue List's clock to a value of 00:00:00:00.00 (the last set of 0s denotes fractional frames). If the clock was running when it received the command, it will continue running from the 0 value; if it was stopped, it will remain stopped but be reset. Set_Clock sets a controlled device's internal clock to a particular value. Optionally, this action takes place only on a specific Cue List's clock. Like the Zero_Clock command, Set_Clock does not care whether the clock is running or stopped.

MTC_Chase_On

19 <Q_List>

MTC_Chase_Off

1A <Q_List>

MTC_Chase_On instructs a controlled device's internal clock to follow an incoming MIDI Time-Code data stream. By specifying an optional Cue List, this command affects only a specific Cue List's clock. If no MTC is present in the MIDI stream when the command is received, the internal clock is unaffected; however, once MTC appears, the internal clock must follow the time code. MTC_Chase_Off stops chasing incoming time code, then returns the clock to its previous mode with the last MTC value received.

Open_Cue_List

1B Q_List

Close_Cue_List

1C Q_List

These commands "open" or "close" a Cue List, making it available for operation.

Open_Cue_Path

1D Q_Path

Close_Cue_Path

1E Q_Path

These commands "open" or "close" a cue path for use by the system.

Sample Messages

To show you how all this goes together, let's put together some sample messages. Remember, the general MSC command format (in hex) is:

```
F0 7F [Device ID] 02 [Command Format] [Command] [Data] F7
```

First, let's look at a message that would tell a lighting console, configured to respond to messages on Device ID #1, to execute cue 18.6 on fader 2 (many light boards use the Cue List bytes to indicate fader numbers). The Device ID is simply 01h. The Command Format would also be 01, which means Lighting. The command for Go is simply 01. Cue 18.6 in ASCII would be 31 38 2E 36 (2E is the ASCII decimal point character), and the Cue List would be 02. A 00 delimeter would be placed between the Cue Number and Cue List. Adding the "overhead" bytes F0, 7F, 02 and F7 we get:

F0	7F	DeviceID	02	Command Format	Command	Data	F7
F0	7F	01	02	01	01	31 38 2E 36 00 02	F7

To tell the same lighting console to run cue 25 on the fader 1, we'd only have to change the cue and Cue List bytes:

F0	7F	DeviceID	02	Command Format	Command	Data	F7
F0	7F	01	02	01	01	32 35 00 01	F7

To tell the same lighting console to stop cue 25 on fader 1, we would only have to change the Command byte:

F0	7F	DeviceID	02	Command Format	Command	Data	F7
F0	7F	01	02	01	02	32 35 00 01	F7

This is easy, right? Once you get the basic structure in and working (it's always worth testing your syntax before going further), it's easy to make minor changes.

Let's look at one more. Let's tell a Sound Controller on Device ID 6 to execute a Go on cue 11, Cue List 30, and cue path 63.

F0	7F	DeviceID	02	Command Format	Command	Data	F7
F0	7F	06	02	10	01	31 31 00 33 30 00 36 33	F7

LIMITATIONS OF MIDI SHOW CONTROL

The MIDI Show Control standard can certainly not be all things to all people; it is however, a tremendously versatile and powerful protocol. As of this writing, it is the only standard designed specifically for show-control applications. Some have criticized it for being based on the MIDI platform; they are concerned that the response time of MIDI may not be adequate.

Command Response Time

This argument has some merit: while all MSC commands are designated "real time," there is no reason that some data-hogging device on a MIDI Link couldn't bog down the system enough to cause important messages to be delayed. However, this is a problem easily avoided by not putting too many devices on a single MIDI link. Also the MSC messages, even with the tremendous overhead, are pretty fast. If a "light cue 362 go" command is given to Device 1, the following bytes (in hex) would be sent:

```
F0 7F 01 02 01 01 33 36 32 F7
```

This is 10 bytes, each 8 bits with start and stop bits, for a total of 100 bits. At 31,250 bps, this message would occupy the network for 100/31,250 seconds, or just over 3 ms. This means that 100 such messages could be sent in 300 ms, which is probably about how long it takes the average board operator to press a Go button after hearing a human stage manager's "Go" command. In any case, if your application is more time-critical than a few milliseconds, you should probably be using another standard.

Open-loop

Standard MIDI Show Control commands are completely open-loop: no feedback or confirmation of any kind is required for the completion of any action. When a controller sends a message out, it has no idea if the target device even *exists* (although in most shows someone should eventually notice such a problem).[2]

This open-loop approach was chosen for a number of reasons, first and foremost of which was to keep the standard simple to use, easy to implement, and fast—an open-loop approach keeps traffic on a MIDI link to a minimum. In addition, with an open-loop system the failure of any one

---

[2] And, of course, confirmation systems can be easily designed for critical purposes or for start of day checkups.

device in a show network should not affect any other system on the network; there is no reason that a properly functioning sound computer should not be allowed to execute its cue on time because the system is waiting for a response from a broken lighting controller. As for MSC applications that could be potentially life-threatening, the philosophy of the standard is clearly spelled out (in all capital letters) in the specification itself:

> IN NO WAY IS THIS SPECIFICATION INTENDED TO REPLACE ANY ASPECT OF NORMAL PERFORMANCE SAFETY WHICH IS EITHER REQUIRED OR MAKES GOOD SENSE WHEN DANGEROUS EQUIP-MENT IS IN USE. . . . MIDI SHOW CONTROL IS NOT INTENDED TO TELL DANGEROUS EQUIPMENT WHEN IT IS SAFE TO GO: IT IS ONLY INTENDED TO SIGNAL WHAT IS DESIRED IF ALL CONDI-TIONS ARE ACCEPTABLE AND IDEAL FOR SAFE PERFORMANCE. ONLY PROPERLY DESIGNED SAFETY SYSTEMS AND TRAINED SAFETY PERSONNEL CAN ESTABLISH IF CONDITIONS ARE ACCEPTABLE AND IDEAL AT ANY TIME.[3]

TWO-PHASE COMMIT

To address safety and other issues, MIDI Show Control version 1.1 was developed, which added some additional commands to allow a new type of operation: Two-Phase Commit (2PC). This 2PC approach was primarily developed by Ralph Weber, then of Digital Equipment Corporation, with assistance from Charlie Richmond. 2PC is a communications approach that allows systems to proceed with absolute certainty; in 2PC, all actions are acknowledged before execution and after completion. The two phases are Standing By, when devices are readied for action, and Go, when the actions are executed. These are the same two phases used in communications between stage managers and system operators in the theatrical world. While the general concept of 2PC operation is very simple, implementation of 2PC systems could fill an entire book.

The standard, released in 1995, has, as far as I know, never been implemented in any system or product. Theme park system designers consider it simultaneously too complex and not sophisticated enough, and theme parks were the key market for this standard. So, while the 2PC commands are basically dead on arrival, a brief introduction is included here since it is part of the standard, and the control concepts are interesting. Full details, of course, are available in the full MIDI spec from the MMA—a document well worth owning (see the contact information in Appendix C).

---

[3] MIDI Show Control 1.1 Standard, page 8.

Basic Structure

Two-phase commit operation assumes that a master/slave device relationship exists between the master controller and individual controlled devices, and that a detailed script has been created and is resident in both master and slaves. Both the controller and the controlled devices must have significant native intelligence to monitor operations and communications.

2PC Commands for Normal Operation

Four messages are used for normal 2PC operation: Standby, Standing_By, Go_2PC, and Complete.

Standby

```
20 Checksum Seq_Num Data Q_Number <00> <Q_List> <00>
   <Q_Path>
```

The Standby message is the first message sent by the master to a slave to initiate a cue. The receiving slave device must respond with either a Standing_By or an Abort message: Standing_By indicating that the device is now ready to execute the cue; Abort meaning that either the data packet is corrupt or the controlled device is not ready for the cue for some reason. The controlled device has two seconds to respond to the Standby message; if two seconds elapse and the controller has not received a message back from the controlled device, it proceeds as if an Abort message were received.

Standing_By

```
21 Checksum Seq_Num Cue_Time <Q_Num> <00> <Q_List>
   <00> <Q_Path>
```

Standing_By is sent from the controlled device back to the controller to acknowledge that it is ready to execute the cue specified in a previous Standby command. If the controller is not ready, it sends an Abort command. The cue number does not need to be returned to the controller, since the returned sequence number must match that in the Standby message. Cue_Time here communicates to the master controller the maximum amount of time the slave could take to execute the specified cue; this is used by the controller to determine a timeout for the controlled device for this specific cue. This time can be longer than the actual time required, but it obviously cannot be any shorter. The time is sent in 5 bytes: hours, minutes, seconds, frames, and fractional frames.

Go_2PC

```
22 Checksum Seq_Num Data Q_Number <00> <Q_List> <00>
   <Q_Path>
```

This is the core command of 2PC control—the Go command. This command, sent by the master, must be preceded by a Standby command. The controller must also have received a Standing_By message with the same sequence and cue numbers before issuing the Go_2PC message. As this command is issued, a clock is started in the master controller, which times how long it takes until the Complete command is received from the slave. If the timer exceeds the amount of time specified in Cue_Time in the Standing_By command, the transaction is cancelled and the master sends a Cancel message.

Complete

```
23 Checksum Seq_Num <Q_number> <00> <Q_List> <00>
   <Q_Path>
```

This message is sent by the controlled device to the master controller to confirm that a cue transaction has been successfully completed. If the cue and sequence contained in the Complete message do not agree with that in a pending Go_2PC message in the controller, the Complete message is treated as an Abort.

2PC Commands for When Things Go Wrong

Three commands are included in 2PC for when things go wrong: Cancel, Cancelled, and Abort.

Cancel

```
24 Checksum Seq_Number Q_number <00> <Q_List> <00>
   <Q_Path>
```

Cancel is sent by the master controller if, for some reason, execution of a cue must be terminated; it is acknowledged by the controlled device with a Cancelled message. Cancel must follow either a Standby or Go_2PC message (there must be some action to cancel); if the controlled device was in standby on receipt of the message, the transaction is simply stopped. If the cue transition was in progress, there are several courses of action for the controlled device, which are determined by the device's manufacturer: the cue can run to completion and stop; the cue can "pause" awaiting further execution; the cue can terminate immediately; or the controlled device can reverse operation. In any case, the controlled device should send a Cancelled message, containing an appropriate status code for the type of cancellation.

Cancelled

```
25 Checksum Status_Code Seq_Number
```

This message acknowledges that a cue transaction has been cancelled; it is sent in reply to a Cancel message. The message's Status_Code specifies several different types of cancellation; the sequence number must be that of the Cancel message.

Abort

```
26 Checksum Status_Code Seq_Number
```

This message, normally sent by a controlled device, indicates that the slave has failed to execute a Standby, Go_2PC, or Cancel command, or that a checksum error has occurred. The type of abort operation is indicated using the status code. Sequence number is used to indicate which sequence has caused the abort condition.

MIDI SHOW CONTROL 1.2?

As of this writing, work is underway on MSC Version 1.2. Topics being discussed for inclusion include the long-needed addition of a show control command format, and several message types for certain types of communication. If all goes well, this version should be voted on in 2001; contact the MMA for more information.

20

MIDI Machine Control

Developed in the late 1980s, MIDI Machine Control (MMC) was adopted by the MMA in 1992. MIDI Machine Control is a standard way of controlling transport-oriented equipment, such as audio or video machines. MMC is based on the broadcast control standard ES-Bus and was primarily created to give music sequencers control of SMPTE-based tape machines. However, MMC is useful for interfacing with a variety of audio and video devices for show-control applications. Because MMC is very complex, it cannot be covered fully here—the standard is over 100 pages long. If you're interested in more details, please get the full spec from the MMA.

MMC SYSTEMS

Systems built using MIDI Machine Control can take many forms. The basic structure, however, is fairly simple: A master control computer running sequencer software (or entertainment control software in entertainment control applications) sends MMC commands to a tape deck, which contains a SMPTE Time-Code track (see Figure 20.1). The SMPTE TC is converted to MIDI Time Code and sent back from the tape deck to the control computer, over an optional closed-loop MIDI line. In this way, the master controller can determine the time-code location of the tape and make decisions based on that and other information. MMC can operate in either open- or closed-loop modes; because MIDI is unidirectional, a return MIDI line must be included in any system where closed-loop operation is desired.

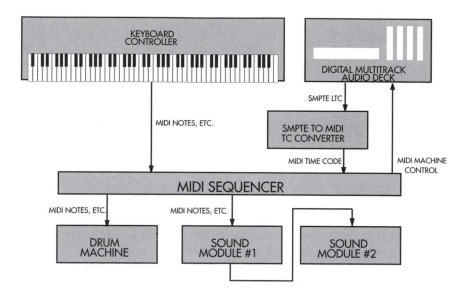

Figure 20.1   Typical MIDI Machine-Control System

COMMAND/RESPONSE STRUCTURE OF MMC

MIDI Machine Control messages fall into three categories: commands, responses, and information fields. Master controllers send commands; slave devices respond with responses. Information fields are sort of a hybrid; they are registers, maintained by controlled devices, that can report their contents when polled by the master. Some of these registers are read-only and send their data back to the master on request; others can be written by the master. Data contained in the registers include the current time-code address of the controlled media, execution status of recently received commands, and so on.

MMC MOTION CONTROL

MIDI Machine Control commands fall into several groupings. Two of the more interesting groups for show-control applications are Motion Control States and Motion Control Processes.

Motion Control States

An audio or video machine can do only one type of thing exclusively at one time—it can't fast-forward while in rewind mode. For this reason, some

MMC commands are gathered into a mutually exclusive group; these commands are known as the Motion Control State (MCS) commands. Executing an MCS command cancels any other currently running motion-control mode and starts the newly desired action as soon as possible. In this way, the master controller doesn't have to care what state the controlled device is currently in; it simply commands it to the newly desired state. However, if the master wants to know the current state of the machine, it can find out by querying the Motion Control Tally information field. The basic MCS commands are Stop, Pause, Play, Fast Forward, Rewind, Search, and Eject.

Motion Control Processes

Two other mutually exclusive commands are the Motion Control Processes (MCP)—Locate and Chase—that cause the controlled device to go into a special mode, capable of issuing its own Motion Control State commands. Locate causes the deck to move to a specific time-code frame on the media; Chase causes the machine to lock itself to a time-code source. When in either of these modes, the controlled device may issue any number of Motion Control State commands internally to position the media.

MMC MESSAGE STRUCTURE

Like MIDI Show Control, MMC is made up of Universal Real-Time System Exclusive MIDI messages, and two Sub-IDs have been designated for MMC: 06h and 07h. Messages with an 06h ID are commands sent from a controller to a controlled device; the 07h ID denotes responses sent from slave devices back to the master.

MMC messages use the real-time command structure:

Commands: `F0 7F [Destination ID] 06 [Command String] F7`

Responses: `F0 7F [Source ID] 07 [Response String] F7`

Note that the ID's meaning is dependent on its context. The ID refers to the address of the target-controlled device if sent in a command by a master controller; in a response from a controlled device, the Device ID is the address of the sender—the target is assumed to be the master controller.

Command/Response Lengths

The number of data bytes in an MMC message is variable and is either implied by the command number, or designated within the message itself through the use of a "count" byte. Count is simply a count of the subsequent data bytes (in hex), not including the count byte itself or the F7 end of a system exclusive message. For instance, a Return to Zero command to an audio or video machine would include a count byte:

```
F0 7F 01 06 [Locate] [Count = 06] [Target] 60 00 00 00
   00 F7
```

MMC also allows more than one command or response to be sent within a single 48-byte SysEx MIDI message or, conversely, long single messages to be sent across multiple SysEx messages. This is known as "segmentation," and two special messages (Command Segment and Response Segment) are included for this purpose.

Guideline Minimum Sets

As in MIDI Show Control, no commands are mandatory for inclusion in an MMC-capable device; however, MMC has four Guideline Minimum Sets. Implementing a particular set's commands implies that a device is generally capable of a certain level of operation. The Guideline Minimum Sets are as follows:

1. Simple Transport; open loop, no TC reader.
2. Basic Transport; closed loop possible, no TC reader.
3. Advanced Transport; closed loop possible, TC reader, event-triggering control, track-by-track record control.
4. Basic Synchronizer; closed loop possible.

COMMON MMC COMMANDS

In this section, we'll go through some MMC commands and responses most useful for live entertainment applications. The overhead (F0 7F, etc.) bytes are not included. (See MMC Message Structure above.)

Stop

01

Play

```
02
```

Fast Forward

```
04
```

Rewind

```
05
```

Eject

```
0A
```

These Motion Control State commands are self-explanatory.

Chase

```
0B
```

This Motion Control Process causes the selected device to chase an incoming time-code stream. Chase mode is cancelled by the receipt of an MCS or MCP command.

Pause

```
09
```

The command places the controlled deck in pause mode, where the device stops as soon as possible and can restart as fast as possible. On video decks, this command causes the device to stop "with picture."

Locate

```
44 [Count] [Sub-Command] [Information Field/Target
   Time Code]
```

When the subcommand byte is 00h, Locate causes the deck to move the media to the time-code position indicated in the specified information field. If a subcommand of 01h is sent, the target time-code address is specified within the Locate command.

21

SDX

The SDX protocol was designed for continuous control of large or potentially dangerous entertainment devices such as fountains or stage machinery by Richard Gray, then of R.A. Gray, Inc., and Robert Harvey, of The White Rabbit Company. While privately developed, the standard was released in 1992 for use by anyone willing to license it. The Communications Company, which bought R.A. Gray, now handles licensing.

WHY SDX?

DMX512 has no error correction, which is fine since it is intended for controlling lighting dimming systems. If bad data causes a dimmer to momentarily "burp," who cares? It's not likely that any equipment would be damaged, and few would notice the transient change in lighting levels anyway. However, some dimmer-like devices could react catastrophically to corrupt control data: if a valve controlling a high-pressure fountain system received a control glitch, the plumbing could be damaged or destroyed, and, in the worst case, people could be injured. SDX was invented to handle these critical low-level applications.

DATA SPECS

SDX is a synchronous protocol: each system component's time-base frequency matches the master controller's. The system uses Manchester-like bi-phase encoding, and the code is symmetrical, and therefore has little or

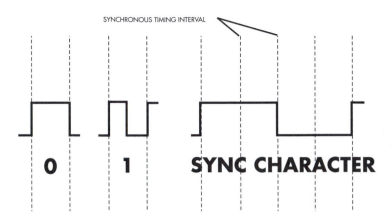

Figure 21.1 SDX Data Encoding

no DC component (see Figure 21.1). This simplifies isolation and distribution schemes since no active repeaters are necessary—simple transformers can be used instead.

SDX runs at a basic data rate of 192,000 bps; like DMX, SDX continually updates transmitted data. Unlike DMX, and due to SDX's synchronous nature, the carrier is transmitted at all times—there are no variable-length break signals as in DMX. A carrier frequency of 192 kHz was chosen because it is frequency-related to other standards like DMX, SMPTE Time Code, and video signals; this allows for easy conversion between the various standards.

SDX uses "sync characters" to indicate the beginning and end-of-data blocks. A sync character is simply a signal sent at half the carrier frequency. SDX packets contain bits for odd-parity error correction, which is adequate for detecting most errors; data "blocks" themselves can also have error correction for further reliability. Receivers pass data to the rest of the control circuitry only when a data block is complete and checked; since all receivers are synchronous, the entire system should act on the transmitted data at once.

SDX transmits data in 64-, 128-, 256-, 512-, or 1024-byte-frame "blocks"; 512-byte blocks are the preferred size. Eight-bit data bytes are sent least significant bit first, followed by the odd-parity bit, and sync characters are sent when there is no data to send. The framing rate can vary from 20 frames per second up to 331 fps. Blocks of 512 and 1024 bytes can have optional system bytes, containing time code or other information.

Physical Connections

SDX uses 3-pin XLR-type connectors in conformance with the AES audio XLR standard: pin 2 is SDX+, pin 3 is SDX−, and pin 1 is shield. SDX's peak-to-peak voltage can be anything between 5 and 10V; output impedance of a transmitter is less than 20Ω. Receivers are transformer-coupled and have a resistive load of about 2000Ω; shield is tied at the transmitter end only. R.A. Gray now manufacturers SDX regenerators, distribution amplifiers, and fiber-optic interface transceivers; a single-chip SDX encoder is also in the works.

SDX DATA BLOCK TYPES

SDX defines a number of data types that will cover most applications: bit device, interlocked switch, lighting, level, image projector, general device, position device (such as a moving light), and ASCII device. Information in a data block is sent with the first user data byte first; system bytes close out the block.

The simplest data block is the "bit-device" block, designed to control devices that take on one of two states—relays, valves, and so forth. Bit devices are controlled using a simple 8-bit byte structure; since 512-byte blocks are standard, there are 4096 bit "addresses" that can be set in a given system. The interlocked switch block is meant for control of devices that have mutually exclusive control modes, such as audio or video decks. Interlocked-switch data types can be either 1 or 2 bytes and can exist in several formats: 1 of 2, 1 of 4, 1 of 8, or 1 of 16. Unused bits should always be set to 0. Like DMX, the lighting device block type uses an 8-bit word to indicate dimmer level. The 255 possible levels are matched to a 0 to 100 percentage scale using the level-translate table in the USITT "ASCII Text Representation for Lighting Console Data" specification. A level device block is similar to lighting device blocks, but only 6 or 7 bits are used, giving 64 or 128 possible levels, depending on what is required. The unused high bits can be used as a bit device. One byte of the 2-byte "image projector" device data block type is used to control lamp intensity; the other represents "image position." Image position could be the number of a slide in a tray or the position of a scroll of images or color. The general device block, as you might guess, is a 1- or 2-byte device intended for a variety of generic applications. One byte can be used to present 256 values, as either 0 to 255 or –127 to +127 (–128 is not used). Two bytes can represent 0 to 65,535, or –32,767 to +32,767, with –32,768 unused. The positioning servo device block is a 2- or 4-byte type used to transmit an unsigned value from 0 to 65,535, scaled to the range of a motion-controlled device. The user must define the "home" position of the device, as well as the count range. Finally, the ASCII device block is used to transmit 7-bit ASCII characters over an SDX link.

CURRENT USES OF SDX

As of this writing, SDX has been implemented in large R.A. Gray fountain and other control systems. Because of its robust nature, it is well suited for some low-level entertainment control applications.

PART V

Networks Used for Entertainment Applications

So far, we've discussed point-to-point entertainment system applications. The chapters in Part 5 cover general-purpose *networks* and their applications for entertainment control systems.

22

General Network Concepts

Networks are designed to connect a number of devices, or "nodes," together, allowing them all to communicate with each other. Networks can be highly efficient, allowing a large number of devices to be connected with a small amount of cable. Figure 22.1 shows how many connections would have to be made and managed to connect a group of devices together in a point-to-point fashion. In a network, many of these connections can be made virtually rather than physically.

In the entertainment industry, we are generally interested in building small, secure networks[1] that are "deterministic," or able to deliver data in a predictable amount of time. However, most of the rest of the world is interested in building huge, open networks capable of moving non-time-critical data around the world. In recent years, the proliferation of office-networking technologies has dominated the world of datacom and networking. In datacom equipment designed for a typical office environment, cost considerations come before almost everything else, and office network equipment is designed to be cheap, but not necessarily robust. Additionally, latency is typically not a concern in an office situation: if a spreadsheet takes a second or two to load up, or longer when the office is busy, that's not a big deal.

---

[1]It could be embarrassing or dangerous if someone outside a show got control over show systems!

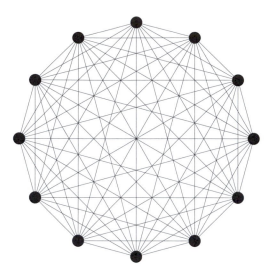

Figure 22.1 Connections Without a Network

In addition, equipment gets abused backstage on shows in ways worse than might be found in many factory or military environments, and yet, the audience expects the systems to continue working no matter what, and producers want everything to be as cheap as possible. Equipment designed to survive such a rough environment is expensive, and so, because of cost concerns, the entertainment industry is increasingly using office networking equipment in applications and environments for which it was never intended, pushing it in ways never imagined by its designers. We are not alone in adapting these office networking techniques—the huge factory automation and process control markets, which previously used only specialized industrially-robust systems, are doing the same thing. Keep all this in mind when reading these next sections, because we are now in this industry doing many things that we would not do if given a cost-effective alternative. The phrase you hear many times today is, "It's so cheap, just be sure to keep lots of spares on hand."

OPEN SYSTEMS INTERCONNECT (OSI) MODEL

As datacom and network systems grow increasingly complex, it becomes useful to break systems down into functional "layers," each of which only has to be able to communicate with adjacent layers above and below. The most commonly used layering model is the Open Systems Interconnect (OSI) model.

Work on OSI started in 1977 in the International Standards Organization, (ISO), as a model way to connect networks together. The ISO 7498 standard, finalized in 1984, consists of seven discrete layers, each performing one part of the communications and networking task, building on the services offered by the next lowest layer. The OSI layer approach is complex and represents an idealized model; many network systems today (such as TCP/IP in Chapter 23) combine or leave out layers altogether, and do not strictly follow the model. However, OSI is helpful for understanding the functions of networks, and you may hear its terminology used, so a section is included here.

Through OSI, a layer in one device can communicate with its counterpart layer in another device, even though the only actual connection between the two devices is through the physical layer. The OSI layers, from lowest to highest, are physical, data link, network, transport, session, presentation, and application.

1—Physical   The Physical layer defines the nuts and bolts (or bits and volts) of the network, including bit timing, data rate, interface voltage, mark and space values, connectors, and so on. The physical layer has no intelligence about what kind of data is being sent; data is simply treated as raw bits.

2—Data Link   Data Link is the layer that packages raw data for transport; it is responsible for synchronization, error detection, byte framing, start and stop bits, and so on.

3—Network   The Network layer is the traffic control center for the network; it might determine how a particular message can be routed and where it will be sent.

4—Transport   The Transport layer is responsible for ensuring reliable end-to-end transfer of data; multiplexing is one of the transport layer's responsibilities.

5—Session   The Session layer is responsible for managing and synchronizing the overall network "conversation" and concerns things such as the communications format (full duplex, half-duplex, etc.).

6—Presentation   The Presentation layer is responsible for presenting the raw data to the application layer; file and data transformation and translation are the responsibility of this layer, allowing different applications to access the same network.

7—Application   The Application layer presents resources for applications programs run by users. Application is the top layer in OSI and includes resources for things like transferring files, messages, or electronic mail.

OSI is powerful but also confusing—it is often difficult to discern separate functions for some of the layers, especially the ones near the middle. Fortunately, we leave this task to the networking experts; you will likely never have to divide layering tasks, but it is important to understand the general concept.

NETWORK TYPES

There are several general types of networks, each covering a specific application. As in so many other areas, the lines between the network types gets blurry, but we can generally break networks down into three types: Local Area Network (LAN), Metropolitan Area Network (MAN), or Wide Area Network (WAN). Some of these also cross over into the "Internet" or "Intranet" category.

Local Area Network

A Local Area Network, or LAN, covers a "small area," like a single building, or a small group of buildings, and is typically owned and maintained by one organization. Typically, LANs use broadcast technology, where all nodes receive all transmissions, and each node deals only with messages correlating to its address. Typically, in entertainment applications, LANs are used.

Metropolitan Area Network

A Metropolitan Area Network, or MAN, is similar to a LAN, but covers a larger geographic area such as a campus of buildings. MANs, like LANs, also generally use broadcast technology and are similar enough for our purposes here that only LANs will be referenced in this book.

Wide Area Network

A Wide Area Network, or WAN, covers long distances or a "wide area." They typically use a "common carrier" like a phone company for at least some of their connections, and therefore rarely are totally owned and operated by a single organization. WANs are a separate area of specialty, mostly outside of the scope of this book.

Internet

The "Internet" is basically a network of networks. To the user, the Internet appears to be one giant network, but, in fact, the user's network, created by their Internet Service Provider (ISP), is connected to many other networks, and this is how communications are achieved.

Intranet

Many large corporate WANs or MANs are referred to as internal private "Intranets" to differentiate them from the public Internet.

LAN TOPOLOGIES

The way in which a network is physically connected, or laid out, is the network's "topology." While many modern network control protocols are topology-independent, the concept is still important to understand. The three predominant network topologies are the star, the bus, and the ring, each named for its schematic appearance.

Star Topology

Each node in a star topology network (see Figure 22.2) is "home run" to a central device, which either resends each incoming message to all connected nodes, or somehow routes particular messages to particular nodes.

A phone exchange is a prime example of this topology: cable is run from each customer's home (node) to the central office, which handles all the switching and routing for the entire network. Star topology networks are ideal for any application in which simultaneous multiple pathways between various nodes are desired. If a single node in a star topology network fails, other

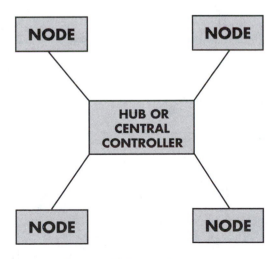

Figure 22.2 Star Topology

nodes will typically not be affected. On the other hand, if the central "star" device fails, communications to all the nodes connected to that device will fail.

Bus Topology

The bus topology is a simple scheme in which all nodes are connected to a single network cable "bus" (see Figure 22.3).

For electrical reasons, this is the topology used in most unidirectional control standards—a "daisy chain" is created through all the nodes, with the final node terminating the line. A variation of the bus topology is the tree, where several independent buses are connected together via a "backbone," schematically giving the topology a tree appearance. Bus topology can also be found inside personal computers, connecting internal expansion and peripheral devices.

Bus topology networks are easy to wire, but suffer some distance limitations if the signal is not amplified or repeated at any point. Buses also have the disadvantage that a problem on any one node can take down the entire network.

Ring Topology

In the ring topology, all nodes are connected with a loop of network cable; network data is passed from one node to another around the ring sequentially (see Figure 22.4).

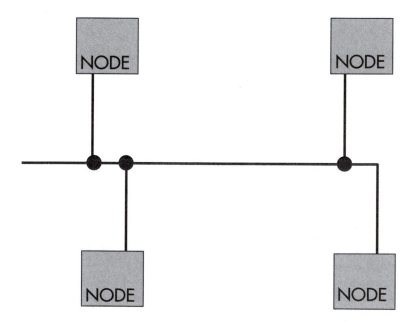

Figure 22.3   Bus Topology

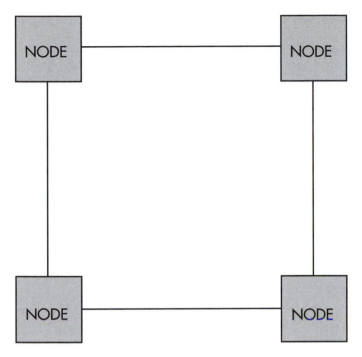

Figure 22.4 Ring Topology

Ring topologies can cover greater distances than some other topologies, since data is repeated and amplified as it is passed around the ring. Like other topologies, however, the ring also has the disadvantage that the failure of a single node, or a failure between nodes, can bring down the entire network. For this reason, critical ring networks often employ complete backup rings, active at all times. Another disadvantage: the ring structure makes it difficult to add stations to the network after initial installation, since the entire network must be shut down to do so.

Combinations

Of course, it is also possible to combine various topologies—you could have a ring of stars, a bus of rings, and so on. A network where any topology is allowed is often referred to as a "free" topology system.

LAN HARDWARE

There are a few types of LAN hardware common to many systems, and we'll go through a brief introduction here.

Network Interface Card

The Network Interface Card, or NIC, is the actual interface between a computer and a network. The NIC, in many ways, is actually the node, although, functionally, the whole device that encompasses the NIC can also be thought of as the node.

Repeating Hubs

A hub is the central connection point for a "hub and spoke" (star) topology. The repeating hub has a number of "ports." It takes networking messages from any port, connects the transmit-and-receive lines correctly, and copies and repeats those messages to all the other ports on that hub. One port on the hub can be run some distance to another hub, allowing networks to be expanded considerably. Although, in general, repeating hubs do not contain any routing intelligence, some are capable of detecting collisions and generating a special collision presence signal.

Switches

"Switches" or "switching hubs" are sophisticated versions of multiport hubs, having enough resident intelligence to know the "address" of each connected device. With that knowledge (either configured or found automatically), the switch will route to a node only the messages intended for that particular node, creating a virtual "private channel." This approach can dramatically improve performance of a network, particularly those that use CSMA/CD protocols (discussed later in this chapter), since the switch can reduce or eliminate collisions on a segment. As of this writing, switches are dropping in price dramatically, and for many applications, the performance benefits are worth the small increase in price (see Figure 22.5).

Direct Connection Cables/Passive Hubs

For a network of only two nodes, it is possible to connect the two devices simply by switching the transmit and receive lines (as done in Null Modems for the EIA serial standards) in a network cable, or inside a "passive hub." Today, however, repeating and switching hubs are so powerful and inexpensive that they are often worth the comparatively minor extra expense. In addition, the use of hubs means that all cables will be exactly the same and interchangeable, and you won't run into problems with special "turned around" cables.

Figure 22.5 Switching Hub and Cat 5/RJ-45 Cables (Photo by Charles Scott)

Bridge

A bridge is used to connect together multiple network segments. A properly configured bridge can understand whether a particular network message belongs on this segment of the network, or on the segment on the other side of the bridge. Bridges allow networks to be "partitioned" for enhanced performance and reliability.

Router

Routers are used to connect LANs together, typically into WANs. Routers have processing capabilities sufficient to route messages from one LAN or segment to another.

Media Converter

A media converter typically is a two-port device, with one type of media on one port, and another type on the other. For instance, a media converter might convert cable on one port to fiber on the other.

BASIC NETWORK CONTROL SCHEMES

We've discussed the physical layout of a network, but you can't simply plug devices together and have them work; we need some sort of "protocol" to manage how the nodes communicate with each other. While some network topologies lend themselves to particular protocols, modern protocols are typically independent of topology.

Command/Response

In a "command/response" protocol, communications take place between a master device and a number of slave devices, which speak only when spoken to. To ensure that data is gathered from slave nodes, the master is often configured to request data from the slaves at a regular interval; this process is known as "polling." Command/response networks only allow slaves to report their data directly to the master; if a slave needs to communicate with another slave node, it must send its data to the master, which then passes it on to the target node.

Command/response protocols are easy to implement and are generally reliable, but are not particularly efficient or responsive, since data can be received from a slave only once per polling interval. Slow, however, is a relative concept: a few milliseconds might not matter for a cue-status update, but the same few milliseconds would be critical in a mechanical servo-control application.

Interrupt Driven

"Interrupt-driven" protocols are refinements of the command/response protocol. In these systems, whenever slaves need to send data, they send an "interrupt" signal to the master, using either a dedicated hardware line or a software control code. Upon receiving an interrupt, the master can poll the node needing attention. This approach makes interrupt protocols faster than straight polling protocols, since the master needs to initiate a poll only when necessary, and polling can stop when data is found.

Token Passing

Network control in a "token-passing" protocol is implemented using a sequentially circulating "token," which acts as a sort of mail carrier, moving from node to node, with one of its bits identifying whether or not it is available to carry data. If a node needs to send data, it waits until it receives the token in an "available" state, and then inserts its data into the token frame. The token is passed from node to node around the network until the destination is reached. Data is then moved out of the frame, and the token is sent back to the sender, which then passes the token onto the next node in line. If the next node needs to send data, it puts its data in the token and passes it on; otherwise, the token is passed on to the next node. In this manner, each node has equal access to the network, since the available token moves sequentially from node to node around the network. Token-Passing protocols are often used with "ring" topologies; you often hear of "token-ring" networks. Token-passing networks are reasonably efficient, but not quite as efficient as CSMA/CD protocols.

Carrier Sense Multiple Access/Collision Detection (CSMA/CD)

Carrier Sense Multiple Access/Collision Detection (CSMA/CD) protocols allow any node to take control of the network and transmit its data frame to any other node, as long as it checks first to see if the network is busy. If the network is found to be busy, the node will wait until the link clears and then transmit its data.

It takes time for a data signal to propagate through a cable, and this speed is measured in "propagation velocity"—a percentage of the speed of light. A cable might have a propagation velocity of 66 percent, and this means the signal moves about a foot in 1.5 nanoseconds.[2] That is extremely fast, but computer processors work faster, and so it is possible that nodes sharing the same "domain" can have "data collisions." For example, look at Figure 22.6. In "Time 1," Node 1 has some data to send. It checks to see if the network is busy, and, finding no other traffic, it begins sending its data.[3] At "Time 2," Node 4 also has some data to send, and it checks the network. Since the message from Node 1 has not yet arrived, it determines that the network is free and it begins sending its data. At "Time 3," a data collision occurs, corrupting the data.

All the nodes are watching the network and will eventually see the collision. Afterwards, if each node with data to transmit simply waited for all transmissions to stop, and then started transmitting after a preset period of time, data collisions could again occur. Instead, in CSMA/CD, each node with data to transmit waits or "backs off" a random amount of time before starting to transmit again. The random element ensures that each network node will maintain equal access to the network—if fixed back-off times were assigned to each node, nodes with shorter times could dominate the network. To speed this whole process up, CSMA/CD network nodes, upon collision detection, can transmit a "jamming" signal to ensure that no other node starts transmission until the problem has been cleared up.

CSMA/CD protocols can be highly efficient, since the network is occupied only when data needs to be sent, and there is no overhead involved in

---

[2]A nanosecond is .000000001 seconds. The velocity figure is from Stephen Lampen's *Wire, Cable, and Fiber Optics for Video and Audio Engineers*, page 38 (see Bibliography for more information).

[3]Note that, for clarity, this diagram shows a bus topology, but many CSMA/CD networks can use a variety of topologies.

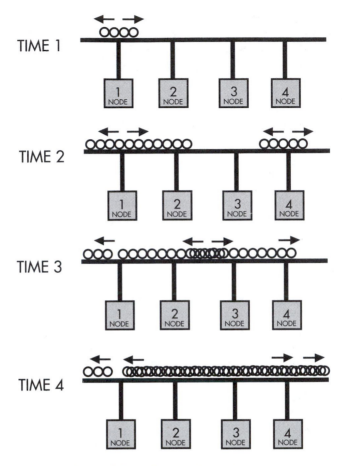

Figure 22.6 Data Collision Sequence

circulating tokens or in polling slave devices. However, access and response times are not predictable or "deterministic," since both parameters are tied to possible data collisions, and therefore the random time element. Additionally, with heavy network utilization, the number of collisions may increase, and network performance will then decrease. So CSMA/CD networks are generally said to be "nondeterministic," although there are ways in network infrastructure to get around this problem. Ethernet, described in detail in Chapter 24, "IEEE 802.3—'Ethernet,'" is based on CSMA/CD.

23

Common Network Protocols

Modern network protocols have given rise to the Internet, which can transport a message from one system to another, traveling across a variety of networks, platforms, routers, and so on, all transparently to the user. Many of these protocols handle complex routing details beyond the scope of this book, but some of these internetworking protocols are used in control system applications, so their general principles are included here.

TCP/IP, UDP/IP

Some of the most common protocols in use for control system networks are the Transport Control Protocol (TCP), User Datagram Protocol (UDP), and the Internet Protocol (IP). TCP, UDP, and IP are all separate protocols, but are often used together in a protocol "suite." This suite existed before OSI and is in enormously widespread use today.[1] The suite does not strictly comply with OSI, since not all layers are necessary or mandated in any application; for

---

[1] According to networking guru William Stallings in *Data and Computer Communications, Fifth Edition* (page 520; see Bibliography for more information), when OSI was being developed, manufacturers had to either wait for OSI, or use the existing TCP/IP stack. Many chose TCP/IP, and it soon became the dominant protocol model in the world, party because the U.S. Department of Defense mandated the use of TCP/IP in all its systems in the 1980s and 90s. And, of course, the DOD based the Internet on TCP/IP. So the TCP/IP model is actually in wider use today than any OSI-based system.

instance, an application might deal with IP directly, bypassing the other layers. However, TCP and UDP can be thought of as occupying OSI Layer 4—Transport, with IP on OSI Layer 3—Network. The TCP/IP or UDP/IP stack sits below user applications (Layers 5–7), such as web browsers, e-mail programs, or lighting or show control software, and above networks (Layers 1–2), such as Ethernet (see Chapter 24). User programs might use protocols, such as Hyper Text Transport Protocol (HTTP), File Transfer Protocol (FTP), or the e-mail transfer system Simple Mail Transport Protocol (SMTP).

Message Handling

Let's look at a simplified version of a TCP/IP message exchange. For TCP and IP to successfully handle a message transmission, the unique "address" of the destination must be known. TCP sits above IP, so it needs to know both the "IP address" of the destination machine, and the "port" number, which can be a software process residing on that destination machine. TCP takes data from the user or originating system, adds some header information including the destination port address, and passes it to the IP layer along with the IP address. IP adds a header containing the IP address, and sends the message along to the network, which adds header information of its own. The network carries the data to the destination machine, strips the network header information off, and hands it up to the destination machine's IP service. The IP protocol in the target machine then strips off the IP header, and hands the message up to the TCP protocol. TCP then strips its header off and hands the information off to the user service in the target machine. That sounds like a lot of work and overhead, but remember that systems are extremely fast today, and so are networks. The message process described above happens millions of times every second on the Internet.

Reliable vs. Unreliable

IP is an "unreliable" protocol that is connectionless—no continuous stream of information is established between sender and receiver; each "packet" of data travels on its own. IP makes no guarantee to services above it that a packet will get to a particular destination; it simply makes its "best effort," while higher layer protocols such as TCP can provide a "reliable" end-to-end service. TCP establishes a "connection" to the target device and guarantees to the layers above it that a message sent will make it to its destination somehow, or else it will notify the upper layers that the transmission failed. However, TCP adds some complexity to a communications transaction, and some applications don't need those reliable services. For "unreliable," "connectionless" service, the much simpler UDP was developed.

IP Addressing

While most entertainment control technicians are unlikely to have to deal with the inner workings of TCP/IP or UDP/IP, they may have to deal with IP addressing. So an introduction is warranted here.

The IP address is simply a unique 32-bit number assigned to a particular system. The IP address is broken down into two parts: a network identifier, and a "host" or local address for a particular device (server, workstation, etc.) on that network. The routers that deal with network traffic only look at the network ID; the receiver in the local network deals with the rest of the information.

There are five classes of IP address, and the first few bits indicate the class of service:

Class A, for large networks with many devices:

0	7-Bit Network ID	24-Bit Host (Local Address)

Class B, for medium sized networks:

10	14-Bit Network ID	16-Bit Host

Class C, for small networks:

110	21-Bit Network ID	8-Bit Host

Class D, for multicast applications:

1110	Multicast Address (28 Bits)

Class E, for future use:

1111	Reserved for Future Use (28 Bits)

IP addresses are usually expressed as "dotted decimal" numbers, with each decimal number representing 8 bits of the address.[2] Viewed in dotted decimal format, the Classes lay out as follows:

Class	Range
A	0.0.0.0 to 127.255.255.255
B	128.0.0.0 to 191.255.255.255
C	192.0.0.0 to 223.255.255.255
D	224.0.0.0 to 239.255.255.255
E	240.0.0.0 to 255.255.255.255

---

[2] If you've used the Internet, you've used IP addresses. However, a "Domain Name System" maps easier to remember text addresses like www.zircondesigns.com to specific numeric IP addresses.

With the explosive growth of the Internet, all the original network IDs in the classes (especially Class B) have been getting used up. So "Classless Inter-Domain Routing" (CIDR) was created, which allows larger network IDs to be used. In CIDR, additional information is added to the IP address, indicating how many of the bits in the IP address indicate the network address. Because of the leading bits that indicate the IP address class, this approach doesn't interfere with the other classes.

While CIDR allows more network addresses, many networks need even more local addresses. For example, Class B allocates many of the bits available to the local "host" address, and many networks are constructed using "subnets," with many hosts on each subnet. So subnet "addressing" or "masking" is often implemented. For example, in a Class B address, the first 8 bits of the host ID might be used to indicate a particular subnet instead of a host number, with the last 8 bits only indicating the host number.

IP addresses are typically either configured by the user and are "static," or are assigned dynamically by networking systems. Dynamic addressing allows large Internet users such as Internet Service Providers to assign a particular user whatever IP address they have available at a particular time. So each time you log on, you might get a different IP address.

Keep in mind that these IP addresses are for Internetworking purposes, and machines or NICs may have their own physical address (such as the "MAC address" in Ethernet; see Chapter 24). So the TCP/IP suite includes the Address Resolution Protocol (ARP), which allows a network administrator to create a table that maps IP addresses to physical machine addresses.

As of this writing, IP version 6 has been released, which extends the address to 128 bits. This should resolve many of the addressing limitations and workarounds discussed here.

SIMPLE NETWORK MANAGEMENT PROTOCOL

The Simple Network Management Protocol (SNMP) was developed in the early 1990s for, not surprisingly, network management. SNMP communications take place between a "Network Management Station" and a "Network Element, " which would traditionally be a router, hub, network printer, and so forth. The software running on the network management station is known as the "agent." Since so much of modern entertainment control systems are being built on standard networks, SNMP has applications for our market.

SNMP runs over UDP, and most of the communications involve the setting or polling of simple variables as defined by the manufacturer of a Network Element in a "Management Information Base" (MIB). SNMPv1, which, as of this writing, is most commonly used, is very simple: it is made up of only five messages.

SNMP Messages from Manager to Element

A single network manager might control many Network elements. The three commands sent by the manager are:

get-request

Fetches the value of a variable in the target Network Element.

get-next-request

Fetches the value of the next variable in a series in the target device.

set-request

Sets the value of a variable in a Network Element.

SNMP Messages from Element to Manager

Network Elements can either respond to a "get-request" command, or send up data for certain situations.

get-response

Returns the value of a variable polled by get-request.

trap

Notifies the manager that something happened at the agent. Trap commands can be sent even when data is not requested.

Entertainment Applications of SNMP

While SNMP may not be complex enough to handle live, real-time control of entertainment systems, it is more than adequate for non-time-critical system configurations and network management. Peak Audio, designer of Ethernet-based CobraNet (see Chapter 24) uses SNMP for remote management of their systems, and they have defined and published an MIB, including variables such as Current Level, Source, Destination, and so forth.

TELNET

Telnet is a way to establish virtual client-server "terminal" sessions over a network, allowing a user to type and receive characters just as if he or she were sitting at a remote computer. In the "old days" this is the way we connected to mainframe computers, but back then it was over dedicated modem lines. Now, of course, this can be accomplished over a TCP network. Telnet is used in some entertainment control applications to connect with devices such as "port servers," which can hang a large number of EIA serial ports onto a single Ethernet connection.

24

IEEE 802.3—
"Ethernet"

Ethernet has taken over the computing world and is now starting to conquer the entertainment industry as well.[1] Today, you will find Ethernet carrying lighting control information even in small performance venues; transporting multichannel digital audio and control data throughout entertainment facilities; and connecting together components in scenic motion-control systems.

Ethernet was developed in the 1970s by Xerox, to allow users at their "workstations," then a radical concept, to transfer files using a network. In 1983, Ethernet was first standardized by the Institute of Electrical and Electronic Engineers (IEEE), and the 802.3 Ethernet working group is still very actively developing extensions and new systems today. Since "IEEE 802.3" is such an unwieldy mouthful, the network will be referred to in this book simply as Ethernet.

Ethernet breaks down into three general layers: Logical Link Control (LLC), Media Access Control (MAC), and Physical Layer (PHY). LLC and MAC can be thought of as occupying OSI Layer 2—DataLink, while the Ethernet PHY layer of course fits into OSI Layer 1—Physical.

---

[1] It's not that we wanted it in the entertainment world. Ethernet wasn't designed to be deterministic; it generally uses plastic connectors that don't survive well in the harsh backstage environment; and it was pushed forth by consumer computer giants rather than industrial control firms. However, because Ethernet has such a huge momentum in the rest of the world, it's here to stay, and we've figured out how to overcome many of its limitations for entertainment applications.

LOGICAL LINK CONTROL (LLC)

In Ethernet, Logical Link Control takes data from a user application or upper-level protocol such as IP and passes it on to the Media Access Control layer for physical transmission on the network (of course, data also flows in the other direction). LLC is part of the IEEE 802 group of standards, and can run in several different modes. LLC shares functionality with HDLC and other data link control standards beyond the scope of this book.[2]

MEDIA ACCESS CONTROL (MAC)

The Media Access Control layer connects between the LLC layer (and, therefore, everything above it) and the shared Ethernet media. CSMA/CD is part of the MAC layer.

CSMA/CD

CSMA/CD (described in detail in Chapter 22) is what actually controls access to the network and was developed in conjunction with Ethernet.

MAC Frame

The MAC Frame is the actual package of data sent over the Ethernet network. The MAC frame includes addressing information, the data from the LLC layer, and error correction. The MAC frame consists of a Preamble, Start Frame Delimiter, Destination Address, Source Address, LLC Data Length, LLC data, Pad, and Frame Check Sequence.

Preamble	Start Frame Delimiter	Destination Address	Source Address	LLC Data Length	LLC Data	Pad	Frame Check Sequence

Preamble

The preamble consists of 7 octets, in an alternating 1/0 pattern. These bytes are used by the receiver for synchronization purposes.

---

[2] See William Stalling's excellent *Data and Computer Communications* in the Bibliography for more information.

Start Frame Delimiter

After the Preamble, a special Start Frame Delimiter octet of 10101011 is sent. This byte indicates the start of the frame to the receiver.

Destination/Source Address

Next in the MAC frame are two groups of either 2 or 6 bytes, which indicate the address of the destination and sending nodes. Depending on the implementation, the address might be a physical "MAC address," permanently burned into an Ethernet NIC at the factory, or it could be a group or global address.

Length

Two octets are sent next indicating the length of the variable-length LLC data to follow, or the packet type.

LLC Data

This section of the MAC frame contains the data packaged by the LLC layer above.

Pad

The Pad is used with some LLC data to ensure that the frame is long enough for collision detection to work properly.

Frame Check Sequence

The Frame Check Sequence occupies the final 4 octets of the MAC frame and is a CRC check of all the octets in the frame except the preamble, the start frame delimiter, and the FCS itself.

SEGMENTS/COLLISION DOMAIN/NETWORK DIAMETER

Before we get into the details of various types of Ethernet, we should define a few terms related to physical network topologies. A connection between a node and a hub, or two nodes, is called a network "segment." Since Ethernet uses a broadcast approach, any group of nodes capable of simultaneously receiving a frame forms a "collision domain," since any two (or more) of the connected nodes could cause a collision affecting all the nodes in that domain. The "network diameter" is the physical distance in meters from the two most distant nodes in a single collision domain. More nodes in a collision domain means more potential collisions, and a physically larger collision domain means longer transport times for messages, which means a longer time window for potential collisions. So the size of the collision domain and network diameter are closely related to the performance of the network.

PHYSICAL DETAILS

There are a wide variety of Ethernet types, each notated by:

```
[Data rate in Mbps][Signaling method][Maximum segment
    length in 100's of meters/physical media type]
```

For example, "10Base5" means 10megabits per second data transmission rate, baseband transmission, and 500-meter segment length.

10BASE5 — "ThickNet"

10BASE5 or "ThickNet" was the original Ethernet, and was often called "Frozen Yellow Garden Hose" because the 13mm-diameter, 50 Ω coaxial cable was huge, hard to work with, and yellow. 10BASE5 uses baseband Manchester signaling at 10Mbps, and has a maximum segment length of 500 meters. Each node had to physically tap into the coax cable. You might find this type of Ethernet in older office buildings, but you are highly unlikely to encounter it in a modern entertainment application.

10BASE2 — "ThinNet"

10BASE2, or "ThinNet," was the second-generation Ethernet. It uses 5mm diameter 50 Ω coax and BNC connectors in a bus topology to send 10Mbps Manchester-coded data over network distances of 200 meters. Each node is connected using a "T" BNC connector, and the ends of a line must be electrically terminated. The smaller, more flexible 5mm coax is much easier to work than the older 13mm variety, and with fairly robust BNC connectors, 10BASE2 was adopted by many entertainment manufacturers early on. However, as 10BASET (see the following) became more popular, it became harder to find 10BASE2 distribution components, and so most modern entertainment networks use 10BASET.

10BASE-T

10BASE-T is one of the most widely used networks in the world today. It sends Manchester-coded data at 10Mbps over two pairs of "UTP," or unshielded, twisted pair cable (T in the description stands for twisted pair). These days, 10BASE-T is typically implemented on inexpensive and high-performance Category 5 cable and RJ-45 connectors in a star topology, with repeating or switched hubs connecting everything together.

10BASE-FL

10BASE-FL allows 10Mbps data to be sent over multimode fiber in a point-to-point fashion up to 2000 meters. Two pieces of fiber-optic cable are used in each link, one for data in each direction. 10BASE-F is generally used in entertainment for special applications, such as long-haul links, or where extreme electrical noise immunity or lightning protection is needed. Manchester coding is employed, with a "high" state indicated by light on, and a "low" indicated by light off. There are other variations on 10BASE-F, but, as of this writing, you are not likely to see them in typical entertainment applications.

100BASE-T — "Fast Ethernet"

100BASET is the general class name for "Fast Ethernet," which is a star-topology system running at a data rate of 100Mbps. There are several variations of 100BASE-T; the most common for entertainment applications are 100BASE-TX and 100BASE-FX.

100BASE-TX

100BASE-TX uses two twisted pairs in a cable, one pair for transmission, and one for reception, over Category 5 UTP or STP.

100BASE-FX

With 100BASE-FX, two multimode optical fibers are used, one for transmission and one for reception, with maximum segment lengths of 2000m.

1000BASE-T/1000BASE-SX — "Gigabit Ethernet"

As of this writing, a new version of Ethernet is coming on the market in commercial devices—1000BASE-T, or Gigabit Ethernet. This implementation, designed primarily for extremely high-bandwidth "backbone" applications, can send data at a blinding 1000Mbps over fiber, or amazingly, over all four pairs of Category 5 copper cable.

SWITCHED ETHERNET

A traditional 10 or 100Base-T network using standard repeating hubs is called "Shared" Ethernet, since every frame appears at every node, no matter where that frame is addressed. "Switched" Ethernet is a topology using only switching hubs, which memorize the address of each device connected to each port, and route only messages destined for a node to that node (see Figure 24.1).

Switched Ethernet is important for entertainment applications, because it can overcome some of the random latency problems inherent to Ethernet, and deliver messages in the "real time" fashion so critical for our applications. Because of the predictable latency, and the availability of industrialized switches, switched Ethernet is also becoming popular in industrial applications, process control, and factory automation.

In a network with all switched hubs (no "repeater" hubs), nearly point-to-point communications can be achieved, since each node only sees traffic destined for it, and many virtual communications channels can be active simultaneously. Full-duplex switched networks take the switching concept one step further, disabling collision detection and avoidance mechanisms, and allowing each node to transmit and receive simultaneously.

Switched networks can also be made more robust than typical shared networks using "spanning tree" or "trunking" methods. In the spanning-tree approach, network controllers can be aware of their topology, and duplicate links can be enabled or shut down when needed or not needed. Ring topologies are possible in spanning tree topologies, and if one segment of the ring fails,

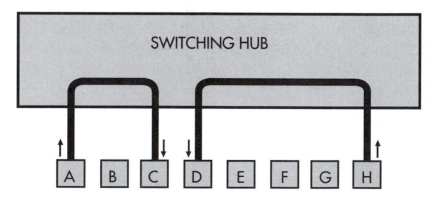

Figure 24.1 Switching Hub Operation—Multiple "Conversations" Happening Simultaneously

messages can be routed over the other ring segments. Trunking approaches allow multiple links between switches, with the load shared between the two. If one link fails or is cut, the switch can load traffic onto the other link.

ETHERNET NETWORKS FOR ENTERTAINMENT

As with any other data communications technology, the entertainment industry is distilling down what will work for our applications from the larger computer industry. There are many ways to implement the common networking standards. It is totally possible that a network component fully compliant with industry standards will not work at all with a piece of entertainment hardware, especially since so many entertainment manufacturers are only in their first- or second-generation of Ethernet products. Ethernet, like many digital systems, typically either works perfectly or not at all, and the "not at all part" can arise unexpectedly. So it is more important than ever to follow manufacturer's instructions carefully, as well as the guidelines for implementing their systems. Fortunately, in this age of Web access, a lot of specific information regarding manufacturer's products is available online.

Before planning any entertainment Ethernet installation, you should purchase the ESTA *Recommended Practice for Ethernet Cabling Systems in Entertainment Lighting Applications*, and the *Supplement to the Recommended Practice for Ethernet Cabling Systems in Entertainment Lighting Applications* (see the contact information in Appendix C for more information). These documents go into specific detail of recommended topologies appropriate for a variety of applications in entertainment.

As of this writing, the most common Ethernet implementations found in the entertainment industry are 10BASE-T, 10BASE-FL, 100BASE-TX, and 100BASE-FX.[3] Typically, for entertainment applications, the fiber implementations of 10BASE-FL and 100BASE-FX are used only for vertical "backbones" in large systems, or for applications where extremely long cable runs are needed.

ENTERTAINMENT LIGHTING ETHERNET IMPLEMENTATIONS

A typical production "tech table" might have several monitors for the lighting designer, and a remote console entry unit. Backstage, we might want a few DMX outputs on one side of the stage for some dimmer racks, a few more DMX outputs over the stage for some moving lights, and a remote monitor for the stage manager. In the catwalks, we might want a few DMX outputs, and a connection for a remote focus unit. Each of these devices

---

[3]The most recent ESTA networking Recommended Practice as of this writing specifically recommends against 10BASE-2 and 10BASE-5 ("ThickNet" and "ThinNet").

would typically need a different type of cable run separately to or from the main lighting controller, and some sort of patching and distribution in the control room. With an Ethernet-based system, a single Ethernet network can be run throughout the performance facility, and the appropriate lighting "node" is simply connected wherever you need data, a monitor, or a remote entry or focus station. Even though shared Ethernet cannot guarantee timely arrival of real-time data due to its CSMA/CD nature, the Ethernet bandwidth is so great for this relatively simple application (10Mbps is 40 times faster than DMX) that it is more than adequate.[4]

Many lighting manufacturers now make systems for exactly these purposes, but, as of this writing, none of the implementations are compatible with any other (sound like a familiar situation?). Work is underway in ESTA to solve this situation with ACN (see Chapter 25). In the meantime, here is some information on a few commercially available systems (in alphabetical order).

Electronics Diversified Integrated Control Environment

Electronics Diversified partnered with Amazing Controls to create its I.C.E. Ethernet implementation. Using a variety of Ethernet types and topologies, the system can simultaneously carry 10,240 channels of DMX, and each "node" can transmit or receive 1536 channels. A variety of devices can be connected to the network, including control consoles, dimmer racks, remote video monitors, architectural controls, and ports for SMPTE, MIDI, and analog I/O. A Macintosh-based system is used to manage and configure the net.

ETC ETCNet2

ETCNet2 is based on TCP/IP running over 10BASE-T and can carry up to 64 universes of DMX, or 32,768 DMX channels. It can also carry ETCLink talkback data for dimmer status, remote video, remote focus control, and other signals (see Figure 24.2).

Strand ShowNet™

Strand's "ShowNet" system works on 10BASE-2, 10BASE-T, or 100BASE-TX, using compressed, broadcast data over UDP. The network can connect directly to consoles or a variety of "SN" series nodes (see Figure 24.3),

---

[4]This is a general comparison—it would be hard to get a typical (especially nonswitched) network to send data at 10Mbps at full duty cycle.

Figure 24.2   ETCNet2 DMX Node (Courtesy Electronic Theatre Controls)

Figure 24.3   ShowNet Networker Node (Courtesy Strand Lighting)

which can provide remote video, remote fader input, remote handheld device connection, MIDI ports, and, of course, DMX In/Out. The system can carry 36 universes of DMX (18,482 channels), and only changing level information is transmitted to save bandwidth.

ENTERTAINMENT AUDIO ETHERNET IMPLEMENTATIONS

Ethernet has tremendous potential in the audio world as well, either carrying audio data and control messages, or carrying proprietary control information to and from a remote mixing desk.

Peak Audio CobraNet™

Peak Audio developed CobraNet to carry a large number of high-quality audio channels over Ethernet. The system has been licensed by QSC for their Rave™ system, and by Peavey for connection with the MediaMatrix system (and therefore, also by Crest which is now owned by Peavey). Other licensees include Crown (Harman), Eastern Acoustic Works, Level Control Systems, Rane, and Whirlwind. CobraNet has many applications, although at this point the system has found a home mostly in larger facilities and applications, where the cost and complexity of an Ethernet cabling infrastructure is lower than a similar system implemented with traditional audio wiring. Each CobraNet device can transmit and receive 32 channels of audio at sample rates ranging up to 48kHz, with word lengths from 16 to 24 bits.

To solve the problem of the nondeterminism of CSMA/CD, CobraNet inserts a layer above the MAC layer and uses a special message structure. CobraNet was originally developed in the days before switched networks were inexpensive and commonplace, and first-generation CobraNet systems needed dedicated 100BASE-TX networks with no other potentially conflicting traffic. With the availability of cost-effective switched networks, new versions of CobraNet can now be run on switched networks along with other traffic, and the number of channels is only limited by the network infrastructure. Audio network management in CobraNet is accomplished through SNMP.

OTHER ENTERTAINMENT ETHERNET IMPLEMENTATIONS

There are a virtually unlimited number of possible uses for Ethernet in the show environment.

E-Show™

With E-Show, Richmond Sound Design has extended their ShowMan™ show-control software to connect and control a wide variety of devices over Ethernet, or any network that can transport TCP or UDP/IP (this means connection to the Internet is possible, but not advised by the company). E-Show is based on MIDI messages, and, as of this writing, supports a variety of Ethernet-based distributed I/O systems and PLCs (see Chapter 13, "Stage Machinery"), serial port servers (see the following), and, of course, any device that can accept MIDI. The system has a highly extensible architecture, and new devices can be added and supported easily.

Figure 24.4 Serial Port Server (Courtesy Comtrol Corporation)

Serial Port Servers

"Serial Port Servers" or "Serial Hubs" allow a large number of serial ports to be connected to any Ethernet network (see Figure 24.4). Each of the multiple ports can send or receive data over EIA standard interfaces, and a single Ethernet could support a huge number of virtual serial port channels.

Machinery Systems

As Ethernet gains broader acceptance in the industrial control market, many types of devices are becoming available that can be hung on an Ethernet. Dedicated motion controllers, motor drives, I/O devices, and rigging controllers are all now available with Ethernet ports.

25

Other LANs

As of this writing, Ethernet is finding the most widespread use of any network in the entertainment industry. Since so much of entertainment control is increasingly computer-based, there are other networks and interconnect methods you might encounter, and these are introduced in this chapter.

ECHELON® LONWORKS®

LonWorks is a networking system designed by Echelon for distributed-control system applications, such as embedded control, building management systems, transportation, consumer/home controls, and utility automation. It can be transmitted over a wide variety of media, including IP-based networks, and hardware and networking management software solutions are available from Echelon and a variety of OEMs. In recent years, the system has been gaining acceptance in some sectors of the entertainment industry.

The heart of a typical LonWorks device is the Neuron® networking chip. Embedded in this chip is processing capacity for customer applications, and also the LonTalk® protocol stack (standardized as ANSI/EIA 701.1), which contains all the control intelligence needed for distributed-control applications. Echelon offers several different development tools as well as a client/server network management architecture called LNS™. With just a few lines of code, an engineer can configure the network for a wide variety of applications.

Up to 32,385 nodes can be addressed in a single LonWorks "domain," and each Neuron chip can reside in two domains. Transceivers are available for communicating over a variety of media, including twisted pair, power line, IR, RF, and fiber optics, and routers are available for switching between different media types. Echelon recently released the iLON™ 1000 Internet Server, a combination router and Web server that operates on any IP-based data network, including 10BASE-T Ethernet.

Entertainment Applications

LonWorks is generally embedded in products and devices by OEMs, or created into special systems by authorized systems integrators. A trade association—LonMark®—has been created to handle common application development for any interested industry. Entertainment lighting manufacturer ETC has adopted LonWorks for dimmer monitoring and configuration and as part of their architectural control system. Apogee, Bose, Meyer Sound Labs, Renkus-Heinz, and TOA have all licensed the system for monitoring and control for their products (for more information, see Chapter 9, "Sound"). However, none of these systems are interoperable.

UNIVERSAL SERIAL BUS — USB

USB was standardized in 1995 by a consortium of computing manufacturers as a "plug-and-play" and "hot-patchable" standard, designed primarily for connection between a computer and a few desktop peripherals such as keyboards, speakers, video capture boards, and even Ethernet adaptors or standard EIA ports. It was not designed to network computers, and is not well suited for many entertainment control applications, but you may encounter it on computer peripherals in the show environment.

USB supplies 5-volt power on its four-wire USB bus (the other two wires carry the data) to power peripherals. You can connect up to 127 individual USB peripherals onto a single USB bus, but you may be limited to less because some devices reserve USB bandwidth. USB can provide both "isochronous" (bandwidth-guaranteed) or asynchronous (non-bandwidth guaranteed) service. USB can operate at two speeds: "full" speed USB devices run at 12Mbps, and "low" speed devices use a 1.5Mbps subchannel. USB uses two types of nonlocking plastic connectors, types "A" and "B." Type A connectors are typically found on computers, hubs, or other devices that supply power. Type "B" connectors are usually found on peripheral devices that consume power. Standard cables connect type A to type B, and cable length at full speed is limited to 5 meters; low-speed devices can run only 3 meters. To connect more than one device to a single USB connection, a hub is used. Hubs can be incorporated into monitors or be stand-alone devices. It is possible to connect two computers together using a special USB "bridge," which acts as a sort of null modem and adds some power isolation. The USB link has a built-in CRC check.

Entertainment Applications

As of this writing, USB is not finding applications directly for entertainment control, but many computer peripherals and hardware keys are now available in USB versions.

IEEE 1394–"FIREWIRE™"

IEEE 1394 was originally developed in the mid-1980s by Apple Computer as "FireWire" (an Apple trademark), a high-performance, real-time, isochronous transport system for connecting devices,or peripherals to computers. FireWire became an IEEE standard—1394—in 1995. The standard is gaining acceptance as a high-speed digital interconnect and can carry a huge number of high-quality digital audio and video channels simultaneously. With this kind of bandwidth, transporting control data in a timely fashion is a trivial task, and there are currently 1394 protocols to transport serial data and MIDI.

1394 works at blistering speeds of 100, 200 and 400 Mbps, and the recently developed 1394B offers data rates up to 3.2Gbps. That's fast! Up to 63 nodes can be connected to up to 1024 buses, giving a total of about 64,000 possible nodes. 1394 can address up to 16 *petabytes* (1 quadrillion bytes) of memory space, is hot-pluggable, and is plug and play. Cables and connectors can have either 4 or 6 conductors; the 4-pin connector doesn't carry any power, but the 6-conductor version does. Data is transmitted on two shielded twisted pairs, with one pair for data and the other for synchronization. Six-conductor cables have an additional pair for power and ground. Unfortunately for entertainment applications, cables are limited to 4.5 meters; however, fiber-based solutions to this limitation exist.

1394 offers both guaranteed-bandwidth "isochronous" and asynchronous transfer services. This isochronous delivery is critical for the successful transport of digital audio or video, and once bandwidth is guaranteed, it remains available until no longer needed. Nodes connect in a peer-to-peer, equal-access hierarchy, and CRC error correction is implemented on data transmission.

Entertainment Applications

1394, as of this writing, has not yet found wide use in entertainment control systems. However, Seattle-based Digital Harmony Technologies is a major supplier and proponent of 1394 technologies for multimedia transport for consumer and professional applications. Fortunately for us, Digital Harmony's founders come from the professional entertainment industry. So our needs will certainly be considered in any of their projects.

ESTA ADVANCED CONTROL NETWORK (ACN)?

As of this writing, the Entertainment Services and Technology Association is hard at work on a network with the working title of "Advanced Control Network" or (ACN). If ACN succeeds, it could completely change the way devices are controlled on both large and small shows, and allow for new and highly sophisticated control not seen before in our industry.

ACN is being designed to be completely "plug and play," allowing a network of devices to be plugged together with no configuration by the user. A controller could then "discover" the devices on the network, with each device appearing on the screen, waiting to be addressed and programmed for the needs of the show. The actual protocols are being designed to be platform-and network-independent, but Ethernet will certainly be one of the first and primary networks used for the standard, since it is so ubiquitous today and has such a large installed base.

The task group developing ACN is primarily made up of representatives from lighting manufacturers, but the group is keeping in mind other applications, and liaisons have been made with the Audio Engineering Society to consider the standard for the transport of audio control messages. First applications are likely to be transport of dimmer-control data, reporting of dimmer-status data, and moving-light control.

Let's wish success to the ESTA Control Protocol Working Group's ACN task group. ACN would be hugely beneficial to our industry, and it would clean up the current mess of incompatible, proprietary Ethernet implementations.

HIGH-PERFORMANCE NETWORKS

We've covered a lot of networking information, but there are still dozens of other networks that are not included here. Since many of these technologies are only used in Wide Area Networks or seriously high-performance applications, you are not likely to encounter them in any but the most serious, high-end entertainment applications where you would be likely to hire a specialist for implementation. But they're worth a mention here so you understand the buzzwords.

Asynchronous Transfer Mode (ATM)

Asynchronous Transfer Mode (ATM) (also known as cell relay) is primarily used as a "backbone" between slower networks like Ethernet, or to carry multiple virtual Ethernets. ATM runs at 155.520 or 622.080 Mbps (and a 10Gbps ATM version is in the works). That's serious—existing ATM networks could carry (hypothetically, of course) between 100 and 600 10BASE-T Ethernet networks! ATM supports multiple, guaranteed classes of service, virtual channels, and offers isochronous operation. As such, ATM could offer guaranteed channels for real-time video, and still transfer files in the background.

Fiber Distributed Data Interface (FDDI)

Fiber Distributed Data Interface, or FDDI, is a token-ring-based network, typically distributed on fiber (but other modes are possible). It runs at data rates of up to 100 Mbps, and it is typically used as a backbone for LANs, or for connection of high-performance workstations. It can run over distances of *200 km*. FDDI uses a token-ring protocol and can connect thousands of nodes.

Fibre Channel

Fibre Channel was designed to combine direct connections and networks. It uses two fibers for full-duplex operation and can run at speeds up to 1Gbps over distances of 10km. Fibre Channel is ideal for connecting systems to shared storage devices such as "RAID" arrays, and it is viewed by some as a successor to SCSI.

Frame Relay

Frame Relay was originally designed for use with ISDN (Integrated Services Digital Network) and is used in both public and private WANs. It can run at data rates of up to 2Mbps over T-1 lines or other media.

T-Carriers

Although "T-Carriers" are not actually networks, they are often encountered in many telephony/internet applications, and were introduced by the Bell System in the 1960s. The T-Carrier system uses time-division multiplexing to carry multiple channels of voice or data simultaneously. "T-1" lines run at 1.544Mbps and use dedicated circuits to offer 24 channels, each with 64kbps bandwidth. "Fractional" T1 allows you to buy only some number of the 24 channels. A "T-3" line operates at 44.736Mbps. T-Carriers can run over two pairs of wire (for full duplex operation, one send and one receive), coax, or fiber.

PART VI

Systems

We've covered basic concepts, datacom, production element control, and networking. Now we'll move on to how all those elements can be combined—we're going to cover system design.

26

System Design Concepts

We've been focusing throughout this book on hardware and implementation considerations. Now, let's step back a bit and look at *design* issues for systems. These topics are mostly related to entertainment control system design, but they also apply to many kinds of systems.

JOHN'S DESIGN PRINCIPLES

The process of design is one of going from the general to the specific. Here are my general design principles when designing any kind of system (from the most important to the least important):

1. Ensure safety.
2. The show must go on.
3. Simpler is always better.
4. Strive for elegance.
5. Complexity is inevitable; convolution is not.
6. Leave room for unanticipated changes.

Some may disagree with this list, but hey, it's my book! Of course, these are highly generalized principles, and, as we know, there are always exceptions to any rule (except rule number 1—Ensure Safety).

Ensure Safety

"Safety is no accident" is the cliché. But like many clichés, this one is true—safety can only exist if considered for every situation, every action, from the top of a system, process, or design to the bottom. Safety should always override any other consideration: If you can't afford the resources (time, money, etc.) to do it safely, you can't afford to do it.

The Show Must Go On

This is second nature to those of us in the entertainment industry, and while the rest of the world is getting more like our industry all the time, many designers still fail to take this principle into account. Entertainment systems must be designed to be flexible, easily understood, diagnosed, repaired, and even bypassed or run manually if necessary. Murphy usually strikes about 3 minutes before show time.

Simpler Is Always Better

I have rarely seen a situation where a more complicated solution is better when a simpler system can achieve the same result. Simpler systems are easier to design, easier to install, easier to program, and easier to troubleshoot (and all that generally adds up to less expensive). No one will be ever impressed by a complex system that no one can troubleshoot, no matter how many blinking lights it has.

Strive for Elegance

An elegant solution is one that uses minimal resources to accomplish a task in the best possible way.

Complexity Is Inevitable, Convolution Is Not

Big systems are inevitably complicated. But there is *never* a reason to have a convoluted system; convoluted systems are generally the result of poor design, planning, implementation, and documentation, all of which lead to an unsightly mess that no one can ever figure out—except, of course, for the creator. But everyone I've ever known who has created convoluted systems as a means of "job security" has been fired eventually when they were not able to fix the system—eventually even they couldn't decipher their own convolution.

Leave Room for Unanticipated Changes

The cost of a piece of cable is extremely low relative to the costs of engineering that cable, the labor involved in putting a conduit in place to contain the cable, and the labor involved in pulling and terminating the cable. Always run spare cables, order extra terminals, and buy spare parts. Do this even if you cannot imagine any possible way the system could need expansion—someone will soon figure that out for you. I've never heard anyone complain that spares were in place, but I have heard plenty of complaints about not having expansion capacity. While it's often difficult to convince the bean-counters, it's much cheaper to put in room for expansion now than it will be later.

CONTROL SYSTEM SAFETY AND RELIABILITY

On the advice of their massive legal departments, few of the big entertainment producing and presenting organizations will discuss safety. This is unfortunate, since they really are the safety experts, and run thousands of shows and performances a year, exposing actors and audience to potential risks. Yet the percentage of accidents is very low, and this is because they have very well engineered safety systems and procedures.

There are a few general safety principles that I apply in my designs. Use these if you agree, but of course, I make no representation that following these principles will make anything safe! Safety is, of course, up to you—the system designer.

Single-Failure-Proof Safety Design

Whenever possible, systems should be designed so that the failure of one single component will not cause the system to fail in a dangerous way. This is called "Single Failure Proof Design," or "Fail-Safe Design."[1] This approach can be used for both mechanical and control systems.

Emergency Stop Systems

Emergency Stop or "E-Stop" systems are critical for any dangerous effect, and generally work by disconnecting power to or from drives, at very low levels in a system. E-Stop systems should generally be very simple, and

---

[1] Consultant Olaf Sööt is responsible for giving this term widespread use in our industry.

should be external to any computerized control system, but should report their status to such a system for monitoring. When something is moving, E-Stops should only be used in true emergencies, because large, dangerous effects oftentimes will not stop smoothly, and catastrophic damage to a system (possibly causing further unsafe conditions) can occur due to large inertial loads or other factors. Many systems have a controlled stop mode for less serious cases, and the E-Stop for true emergencies.

Humans in The Loop

In my opinion, humans should *always* be in the control loop of any entertainment effect or system that could hurt someone. In factory automation and robotics, they simply build big fences around dangerous robots, and add interlocks so that if someone opens the fence gate, the machine stops. This approach is useful in some entertainment applications (for example under a stage or behind a glass window), but there are many effects, particularly on a stage, that we can't fence in. While a control system could be used to deal with effect timing and cueing issues, a dangerous effect should never be allowed to operate without some positive action from some human somewhere, on or offstage. "Enabling" systems are often used to incorporate this human feedback into control systems.

Effect-Enabling Concepts

A concept developed for theme park control is the "enabling" system, which allows humans to authorize or "enable" dangerous effects. For example, a control system could continuously monitor a number of safety sensors, and if all the sensed conditions are safe at the appropriate time in a show, the system can open a "window" for the operation of a dangerous effect. When this window opens, the effect is then enabled (usually a button lights up), and the operator can then fire the effect at the right moment only if he or she confirms that conditions are safe. Alternatively, the operator could press a button on a console enabling the computer system to fire the effect at a preprogrammed time. Or, the computer could open a window, an operator could enable the effect, and the *performer* could actually fire it, by stepping on a switch or some other means. Through the use of enabling systems (and appropriate system design, of course), a single operator or "technical director" often controls entire theme park attractions full of potentially dangerous equipment.

Operator Issues

In theme parks, where shows may run many times a day, system designers also have to take operator boredom or complacency into consideration. Well-designed enabling systems typically look for some sort of transition (button pressed, button released, or button pressed and released) from the operator's control, not just a steady state. If the transition is not seen by the system, the effect will fail into a safe condition, or go into some sort of "graceful abort" mode. This keeps operators or performers from doing things like putting rocks on a safety switch to hold it down. Another technique to counteract operator fatigue is to place part of the operator's control system inside or near the dangerous effect. For instance, to be sure an operator looks at the right part of an attraction when they are supposed to, the "enabled" warning light might be built into the set, or placed adjacent to the dangerous effect.

27

Typical Commercial Show-Controllers

This chapter offers a brief introduction to some commercial control systems. This discussion is by no means meant to be comprehensive; rather, I've chosen a few systems that represent some widely varied approaches to entertainment show control. This is not a buyer's guide! The companies are listed in alphabetical order; be sure to check http://www.zircondesigns.com for the latest company contact information.

SHOW-CONTROLLERS

These companies make control systems specifically designed for entertainment applications.

Alcorn-McBride

Alcorn-McBride, based in Orlando, has made show control equipment since 1986. Their control systems grew out of the market for control of laserdiscs, and today, in addition to the popular V series of controllers (see Figure 27.1), the company makes a variety of digital audio and video playback equipment. Their show-controllers are programmed offline on a Windows-based programming system, and the compiled program is transferred to the

Figure 27.1 V16 Show-Control System (Courtesy Alcorn McBride)

show-controller over a serial link. The system features as standard a number of serial MIDI and I/O ports, and can support other protocols such as DMX or Ethernet through the use of optional hardware.

Anitech Systems

Anitech show-control systems are found mainly in theme parks and similar applications; many of their systems are based on large, modular, centralized controllers (see Figure 27.2). A wide variety of plug-in devices are available, including protocol and PLC interfacing cards, lighting controllers and sound playback devices. Programming is accomplished offline, and is downloaded to the control units. Anitech also makes character-animation programming panels and software; the company is based in California.

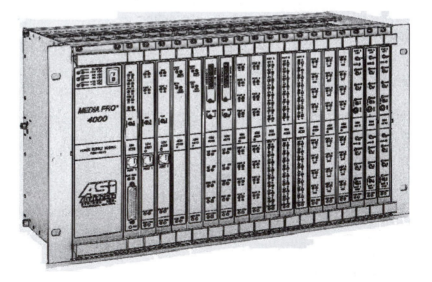

Figure 27.2 Media Pro Show-Control System (Courtesy Anitech Systems)

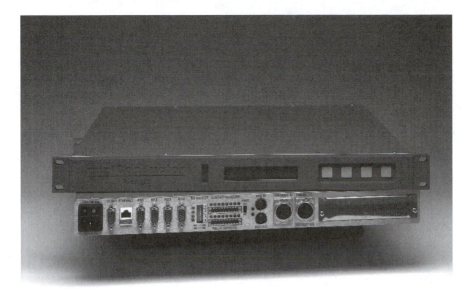

Figure 27.3   miniConductor Show-Control System (Courtesy Avenger Systems)

Avenger Systems

Avenger Systems, based in Belgium, makes the Conductor and miniConductor show-control systems (see Figure 27.3). The highly versatile Conductor is a large-scale, modular system that can house a number of interface cards to support a wide variety of protocols. The miniConductor has a range of fixed I/O and one expansion slot for standard Conductor cards. Programming is accomplished offline on a PC in a powerful Windows-based environment, and the compiled program is downloaded into the unit either over a serial or Ethernet connection. Extensive system monitoring, virtual control-panels, and multiple units can all be networked via Ethernet. Through the use of "instruments," a variety of devices can be easily controlled.

Richard Bleasdale

Richard Bleasdale is the creator of the "SAMSC" Macintosh-based show-control software (see Figure 27.4). The system communicates via serial, MIDI, and other protocols, through standard Mac-interfacing ports, and has been used primarily on Broadway, West End, and other shows. The software integrates Quicktime functionality, and allows easy control of many lighting consoles, the internal CD-ROM drive, or any MIDI Show Control device. Extra hardware allows interfacing to DMX, relays, and other signals. Richard Bleasdale is based in London.

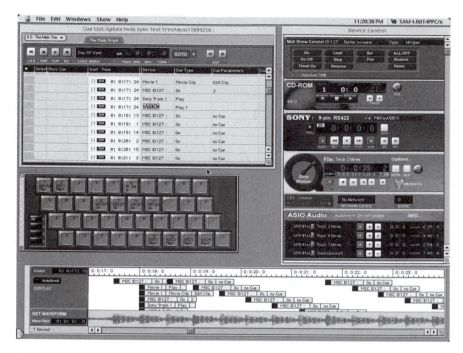

Figure 27.4 SAMSC Show-Control System Screen (Courtesy Richard Bleasedale)

Dataton

Dataton has deep roots in the multi-image market, and their Macintosh-based TRAX® control software communicates with "SMARTPAX QC" control units (see Figure 27.5). Each SmartPax unit has four ports, which can connect to and control a huge variety of devices through various interfaces available from Dataton. The system "tracks" the current status of all connected devices, and this structure makes it ideal for media presentations, since the whole system can be easily and quickly reset to any point in the show. Dataton, based in Sweden, also makes a variety of touch-screen, push-button, and other controllers, and recently introduced WATCHOUT™, a new kind of presentation and control software.

Gilderfluke & Co.

The roots of Gilderfluke & Co. are in animatronic and audio playback systems. Gilderfluke shows can be programmed using Windows-based software (see Figure 27.6), and can be either run from a PC, or downloaded as

Figure 27.5 SMARTPAX QC and TRAX Show Control Software (Courtesy Dataton)

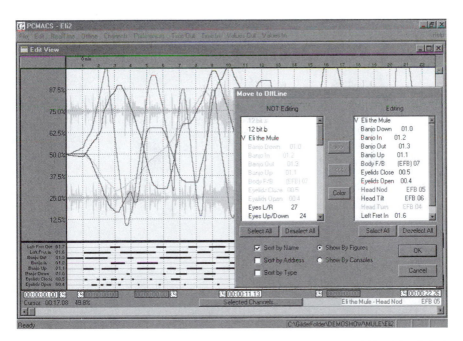

Figure 27.6 PC*MACs Show Control System Screen (Courtesy Gilderfluke & Co.)

shows into stand-alone "Bricks" to be triggered by a variety of protocols and standards, from contact closures to SMPTE. The California-based company also makes a variety of animatronic programming panels for input to their animation software.

Laservision Macro-Media

Australia-based Laservision is an attractions and presentation company that developed the Sinodial-series control system. Once recorded, shows are played back from a hard-disk-based "Digital Data Pump" (see Figure 27.7), which synchronizes and controls a wide variety of equipment including laser systems.

Figure 27.7 Sinodial Show-Control System (Courtesy Laservision)

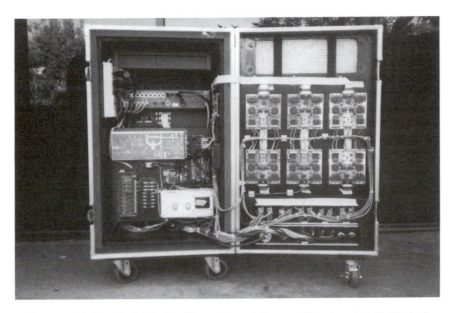

Figure 27.8 MediaMation Show Control System (Courtesy MediaMation)

MediaMation

California-based MediaMation makes a variety of control equipment (see Figure 27.8), ranging from cost-effective MIDI-based control systems up through programmable, interactive PC-based controllers capable of running entire attractions. MediaMation systems can be programmed or operated from MIDI sequencers or directly from any computer with an Ethernet connection. The company also makes animatronic programming and control systems.

Richmond Sound Design

Richmond Sound Design (RSD) makes multipurpose, computer-based, live show-control systems and has existed since 1972; its products run attractions and shows around the world in theme parks and theatres alike. RSD systems were originally based on the multitasking Amiga, but recent products such as ShowMan™ (see Figure 27.9) run under Windows NT or 2000. ShowMan can communicate with any MIDI-controllable device, or nearly any other type of device through the Ethernet-based E-Show™ networking system. Through E-Show, any device that can speak TCP/IP or UDP/IP can be controlled, and through serial port servers or standard, off-the-shelf industrial Ethernet I/O devices, a wide variety of devices can be controlled. The company's AudioBox™ product can also act as a show-controller.

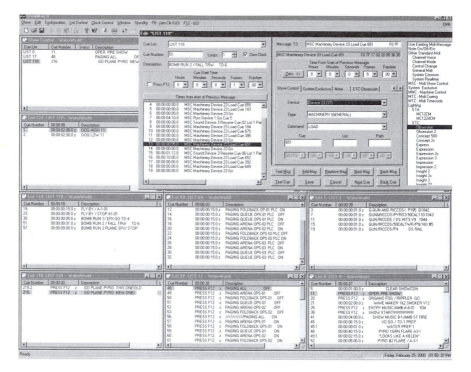

Figure 27.9 ShowMan Show-Control System Screen (Courtesy Richmond Sound Design)

Stage Research

Stage Research's Windows-based SFX software (see Figure 27.10) was primarily designed for theatrical sound effects playback, but, in recent years, the system has expanded to include show-control functions. SFX can output any MIDI or serial message, and, through standard ports, can connect with and control a wide variety of equipment. Stage Research is based in Ohio.

Triad Productions

Iowa-based Triad has been making software and hardware show-control systems for theme parks and other similar applications since 1980. The Triad system is programmed using standard PCs, and shows can be downloaded into a variety of stand-alone controllers for animation, lighting, multi-image, and other applications. Triad also makes animatronic panels, programming software, and controllers (see Figure 27.11). Triad is, as of this writing, developing a Linux-based system.

Figure 27.10 SFX Show-Control System Screen (Courtesy Stage Research)

Figure 27.11 Triad Show-Control System Hardware (Courtesy Triad Productions)

RELATED CONTROLLERS

While the systems in this section were not designed specifically for show control, they are used in many entertainment applications, especially as a "front end" for users or operators.

AMX by Panja

AMX control systems from Panja Corporation are multipurpose systems designed primarily for installation and board-room applications, although the systems do have limited live-control capabilities. The systems are increasingly Internet-connected, and AMX systems are based around either a central rack-mounted controller or a multipurpose card frame into which a variety of interface and control devices are plugged. AMX control surfaces include custom-configured touch-screen displays (see Figure 27.12) and a variety of button and slider panels. Panja is based in Dallas.

Figure 27.12 Touch-Screen Controller (Courtesy Panja)

Crestron

New Jersey-based Crestron makes multipurpose control systems for a wide variety of control applications, primarily for boardroom and home-theatre remote-control applications. Recent products feature sophisticated Internet connectivity. Crestron makes a number of wired and wireless touch-screen and other controllers for their systems (see Figure 27.13).

Figure 27.13 Touch-Screen Controller (Courtesy Crestron)

PART VII

Show Control System Examples

The control methods and protocols discussed so far are best understood within the context of realistic applications, so to bring what we've covered into focus, Part 7 examines a few practical entertainment control problems and solutions. Each of the systems and approaches covered here was selected to illustrate specific points, and please only take these systems as *possible* solutions to the problems presented. One of the most fascinating (and simultaneously daunting) aspects of entertainment control is that there are a hundred different ways to achieve any particular goal.

Although the names have been changed to protect the innocent (and the guilty),[1] the components, devices, and systems in these hypothetical systems are generally based on real products and applications. Wherever possible, I've leaned here towards off-the-shelf rather than custom solutions.

GENERAL SYSTEM DESIGN CONSIDERATIONS

When designing an entertainment control or show control system, the designer should evaluate each possible approach in light of the given application. Here are few general considerations we will use in these examples:

1. What is the master control information source?

2. Should the system be event-based, time-based, or a hybrid?

3. Does the show include life-threatening elements?

Think about questions as you read through the problem descriptions.

---

[1] And to protect me from litigation. No resemblance to any real person, corporation, product, or venue is intended!

28

A Theatrical Thunderstorm

A huge flash of lightning illuminates the stage and, seconds later, "Kaboom!" and the audience's seats shake as a huge thunderclap rolls through the theatre. Ephraim Cubit, his three sons, and the girl next door are all huddled under the kitchen table as the storm continues. From the ever-shortening time between the lightning flashes and thunderclaps, we can tell that the storm is fast approaching. "I sure wish I had cut down that big, dead oak tree next to the house!" shouts Ephraim. As the word "house" leaves his lips, there is a blinding flash and simultaneous thunderclap. Seconds later, an oak branch smashes through the window upstage. As the sound of the giant thunderclap decays, Ephraim suffers one final indignity: his lights go out, leaving the stage in blackness.

THE MISSION

This musical version of *Desire Under the Oaks* is being produced at a major regional theatre. The director will "spare no expense" to ensure that this sequence comes off perfectly night after night, although she has also insisted that the sequence not be "canned." We must keep in mind that "sparing no expense" in the regional theatre world is equivalent to sparing every expense at a theme park; controls will be selected with an eye on keeping the cost as low as possible while still achieving the director's goal.

The show will run for 4 weeks, and there are lighting, sound, and props run crews already on contract to the theatre. Any entertainment control system will be used only to ensure accurate timing for this critical sequence; the rest of the show will be run manually by the operators on cues from the stage manager.

General Considerations

Now, let's look at our system design considerations:

1. What is the master control information source?

   The stage manager is in charge of the run of the show; he will call all cues, including those in the thunderstorm sequence.

2. Should the system be event-based, time-based, or a hybrid?

   Given the fact that the director doesn't want anything "canned" and that there are live actors involved, the system should be event-based. However, the delays between lightning flashes and thunderclaps add a time-based element.

3. Does the show include life-threatening elements?

   The large, scenic tree branch effect could be potentially life-threatening, and care should be taken to ensure that the effect cannot be triggered accidentally.

THE EQUIPMENT

Given these considerations, let's look at the various systems and equipment on hand for the show.

Lighting

For the production, the master electrician has rented a DMX512-controllable lightning-effects generator. The theatre already has a lighting console that outputs DMX512; the ancient dimmers, however, have analog-control electronics and are interfaced to the console using a DMX512-to-analog converter. The lightning generator is connected to the console's DMX512 output through an opto-isolator/splitter rented for the production. The master electrician requested the opto-splitter so that any failure in the high-power lightning effect will not be transmitted back up the DMX line and take out the console (see Figure 28.1).

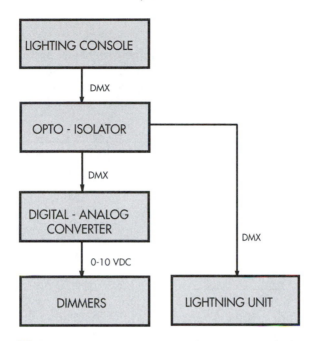

Figure 28.1 *Desire Under the Oaks:* Lighting System Block Diagram

The console, which is backstage, is capable of triggering cues based on MIDI Show Control commands and has been configured to receive those commands as MSC device #1. The console, in addition to receiving MSC commands, also generates MIDI messages as its front-panel buttons are pressed. This could be useful for our thunderstorm, since MIDI Note On/Off messages are generated when the submaster bump buttons are pressed and released. The following cues have been programmed into the board:

Cue	Effect	MIDI Command
218	Lightning Strike 1	MSC Cue 218 Go
219	Lightning Strike 2	MSC Cue 219 Go
220	Lightning Strike 3	MSC Cue 220 Go
220.5	Big Lightning Strike	MSC Cue 220.5 Go
221	All Lights Out	MSC Cue 221 Go

The lightning strike "looks" from cues 218 to 220.5 have also been loaded into submasters 1-4; when the submaster bump buttons are pressed on this console, the appropriate lightning effect is triggered and a corresponding MIDI Note is sent out the MIDI port. The lightning flashes last as long as the operator holds down the bump button.

Sound

In addition to a traditional musical-reinforcement sound system, the theatre has purchased a MIDI-controllable sampler, which it will use for this production and then add to its stock of equipment. The sound designer has recorded and loaded into the sampler a number of sounds, each mapped to a different MIDI note.[2]

Sound	Keyboard Note	MIDI Note Number
Thunderclap 1	C2	18h
Thunderclap 2	D2	1Ah
Thunderclap 3	E2	1Ch
Big Thunderclap	F2	1Dh
Tree Falling	G2	1Fh
Glass Breaking	A2	21h

The sound designer has programmed the sampler so that each sound has infinite sustain; in other words, once a Note On message is received, the sound will play through to completion. The sampler has been set to receive MIDI on channel 1, and its audio outputs are connected to inputs on the mixer, so the operator must remember to bring up those faders to the prescribed levels for the cue sequence. Since this is a live show, the sound-mix position is in the back of the orchestra seats.

Props

The theatre's technical director has devised a simple but effective way of electrically releasing the tree branch. The base of the branch is mounted on a pivot and weighted so that, without restraint, it will fall through the window. A simple electrical solenoid is mounted so that, without power, the branch is held in the "out" position; when power is applied to the solenoid, the branch falls. (This is a fail-safe design—a power failure will not cause the tree to fall.) Through experimentation, the Technical Director (TD) has determined that the solenoid must be energized for at least 1 second to give the branch time to fall past the solenoid's shaft. For safety, a manual release pin has been installed next to the solenoid, so that unless the pin is released,

---

[2]Notes on keyboards and other MIDI devices are often referred to using their musical note name and a number. In this case, C2 does not denote the hex value of the number but rather the second C note from the left on a keyboard. This is not standardized, however: every keyboard manufacturer implements it differently (except those that conform to the General MIDI spec).

the tree cannot fall. Once the actors are safely onstage and under the table, the pin is manually released by the prop crew, "arming" the effect.

The solenoid is controlled by the light-board operator, using a pushbutton station positioned next to the light board. The master electrician had considered firing the effect using a dimmer controlled by the console, but all the dimmers in the theatre were already in use for the show lighting.

As the branch effect falls, it doesn't make realistic tree-crashing sounds, so its fall must be augmented with a sound effect. For safety reasons, stage glass is used in the window through which the branch crashes, and since this fake glass doesn't make much sound when it breaks, a glass sound effect is also necessary.

SHOW-CONTROL SCRIPT

To clear up any confusion, the stage manager precisely scripts out the whole sequence. Working closely with the lighting and sound designers, he prepares the script shown in Table 28.1.

APPROACH 1

The design team decides to test the entire sequence using the equipment already on hand. The light board will be used as a master MIDI source, triggering the sampler; the tree will be triggered manually using a pushbutton

Table 28.1 Desire Under the Oaks Control Script

Actions	Trigger	Control Messages
First Lightning Strike	Stage Manager	Light Cue 218
First Thunderclap	2-Second Delay	Sampler Note C2
Verify Safety Off Tree	Stage Manager	Verbal Headset Confirmation
Second Lighting Strike	Stage Manager	Light Cue 219
Second Thunderclap	1-Second Delay	Sampler Note D2
Third Lightning Strike	Stage Manager	Light Cue 220
Third Thunderclap	$1/2$-Second Delay	Sampler Note E2
Big Thunderclap	End of "House" Line	Lights 220.5/Note F2
Tree Falling/Sound FX	Stage Manager	Solenoid/Sampler Note G2
Glass Breaking	Tree Through Window	Sampler Note A2
Lights Out	Stage Manager	Lights 221

controller operated by the electrician, on command from the stage manager. All system interconnection is done via MIDI, and since the light and sound boards are more than 50 feet apart, an inexpensive pair of MIDI "line drivers" is purchased, allowing the MIDI data to be sent safely from backstage to the mix position in the house (see Figure 28.2).

For the test, the four lightning/thunderclap effects are triggered by the electrician using the console's submaster buttons, on cues from the stage manager. The MIDI output from the console is routed through the line drivers to the input of the sampler, so that pressing a submaster button triggers both the lightning effect and the appropriate sound. In order that the delay between lightning flash and thunderclap will be consistent night after night, the sound designer records silence at the beginning of each sound effect, to delay each thunderclap. Once the stage manager confirms that the tree effect has been armed, he calls the cue for the falling branch over the headset to the electrician; the sound operator is cued by a cue light for the falling-branch sound. The breaking-glass sound is executed as a visual cue by the sound operator as he sees the tree poke through the window.

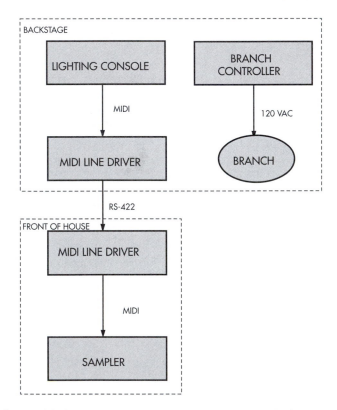

Figure 28.2 *Desire Under the Oaks:* Approach 1 Block Diagram

The Results

The director and design team are delighted with the results of the test, but there are a few problems. Because of lag time in the lighting console's submasters, the electrician is not able to consistently control the duration of the lightning flashes, and the director now feels that the timing between the first three thunderclaps should be exactly the same every night, regardless of what the actors are doing (in other words, she wants to "can" the effect). During the test, the big thunderclap was so loud that the electrician never heard the "Tree Release Go" command and missed the cue. Finally, the director thought that the lightning for the big blast was not bright enough, so an additional lightning machine is rented.

APPROACH 2

The sound designer figures out a way to solve many of the first approach's problems. She brings in a sequencer from her home studio and programs in MIDI note commands for the sampler and MIDI Show Control messages (as hex strings) for the light board. She is now able to remove the dead time from the start of each thunderclap sample and adjust the delay between the lightning flashes and the thunderclaps using the sequencer. Using the MIDI line drivers already in place, she sends data from the sequencer at the sound position to the lighting console backstage and connects the sequencer to the sampler with a short MIDI cable (see Figure 28.3).

To fire the tree effect reliably, the electrician buys an inexpensive MIDI-to-dry-contact-closure (DCC) interface, which can fire the solenoid using a MIDI Show-Control Set command on MSC device 2. The line-voltage solenoid is wired to a relay, which is controlled by the output of the DCC interface. Since MIDI is already run from the sequencer to the light board backstage, the DCC interface is simply placed next to the console and given a MIDI input from the MIDI Thru jack on the light board (since this project is still in the testing phase, they don't get a splitter for the MIDI).

The sound designer programs into the sequencer two sequences that the sound operator will execute with single button presses. For the sampler, she programs both Note On and Note Off commands, to ensure that there are no "stuck" notes.

Sequence 1 contains the messages for the first three lightning strikes, each followed by the appropriate note commands for the sampler (see Table 28.2).

Sequence 2 consists of the simultaneous lightning effect and the huge thunderclap, followed by the release command for the tree and the falling-tree sound effect (see Table 28.3).

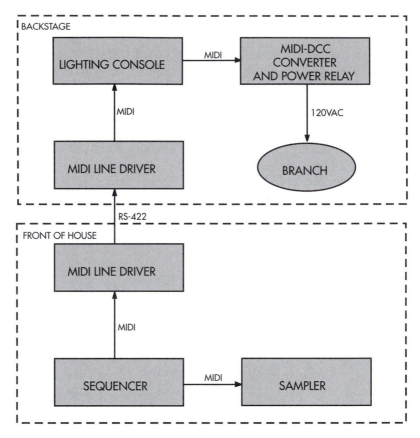

Figure 28.3 *Desire Under the Oaks:* Approach 2 Block Diagram

These two sequences allow the entire thunderstorm to be run with two simple Go commands. Since the rate at which the tree branch falls is not predictable, the breaking-glass sound cue is still taken visually by the sound operator and triggered using buttons on the front of the sampler. The final "lights out" that ends the act is called by the stage manager and taken manually by the light-board operator.

The Results

This new approach works well, but the additional lightning machines generate a huge static blast through the sound system, and the sound operator was so busy pulling down radio mic channels to kill the static that he was late in executing the second tree-falling sequence. Flustered, he missed the breaking-glass sound altogether.

Table 28.2   *Desire Under the Oaks* Lightning Strikes Sequence 1

Effect	Action	MIDI Message (in hex)
Lightning Strike #1	Lights 218 Go	F0 7F 01 02 01 32 31 38 F7
2- Second Delay		
Thunderclap #1	Note C2 On	91 24 3F
	Note C2 Off	81 24 3F
15- Second Delay		
Lightning Strike #2	Lights 219 Go	F0 7F 01 01 01 32 31 39 F7
1- second delay		
Thunderclap #2	Note D2 On	91 25 3F
	Note D2 Off	81 25 3F
10- Second Delay		
Lightning Strike #3	Lights 220 Go	F0 7F 01 01 01 32 32 30 F7
$^1/_2$- Second Delay		
Thunderclap #3	Note E2 On	91 26 3F
Note E2 Off		81 26 3F

Table 28.3   Desire Under the Oaks Lighnting Strikes Sequence 2

Effect	Action	MIDI Message (in hex)
Big Lightning Strike	Lights 220.1 Go	F0 7F 01 02 01 32 32 30 3E 31 F7
Big Thunderclap	Note F2 On	91 27 3F
	Note F2 Off	81 27 3F
Tree Release	Set 01 On	F0 7F 02 02 20 01 00 00 01 F7
1- Second Delay		
Tree Release Reset	Set 01 Off	F0 7F 02 02 20 01 00 00 00 F7
Tree Falling Sound	Note G2 On	91 28 3F
	Note G2 Off	81 28 3F

APPROACH 3

To overcome all these problems, the team decides to rent a show-controller to run the entire sequence. The light-board operator will run the controller, to which the sound designer will transfer her MIDI sequences. The MIDI line drivers are used to run data from the show-controller backstage, which has multiple, isolated outputs, to the sampler at the mix position; local cables are used to run MIDI from the controller to the light board and to the

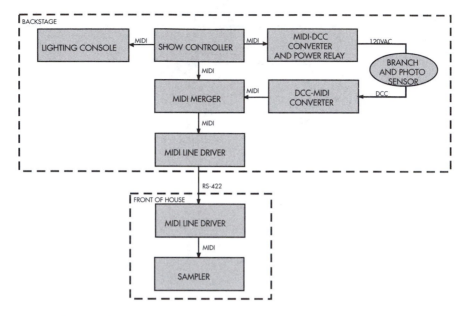

Figure 28.4 *Desire Under the Oaks:* Approach 3 Block Diagram

DCC interface (see Figure 28.4). This same approach could have been implemented using the sound designer's sequencer, but the user interface on the show-controller is better suited to the task than the sequencer, which was designed for music production.

This leaves only the problem of triggering the breaking-glass sound effect. Since the sound operator is no longer running the rest of the sequence, he is free to run the cue manually, but he could be tied up at any point with unanticipated problems. So the sound designer decides to trigger the sound automatically. The tree does not fall at a predictable rate, so she installs a photoelectric sensor across the window; when the falling tree breaks the beam of light, the photo sensor generates a contact closure. A DCC-MIDI interface is used to generate a MIDI Note On when the sensor beam is interrupted and a MIDI Note Off when the beam is cleared. The sampler now needs to receive MIDI control messages from both the show controller (running the thunderclaps) and the DCC interface (triggering the glass break), so a MIDI merger is added to merge the two signals.

The Results

This approach works beautifully. To execute the entire sequence, the light-board operator simply hits a button on the show-controller when commanded by the stage manager; the rest of the sequence runs automatically.

29

Put on a Happy Face

"Put on a happy face," booms the voice from the screen. "Xylenol is the one for you!" Xylenol's trademark yellow smiley face appears on the screen, and suddenly two spotlights follow a loud swoosh sound, sweeping from behind the audience to the screen. The spots highlight the main screen, which is rotating to reveal a pile of old car batteries. The houselights come up, and the room full of doctors, some humming the catchy Xylenol theme music, line up for free Xylenol merchandise handed out by scantily clad models.

This is how Michael, marketing VP for the pharmaceutical giant Klaxo, wants to end the pitch for Xylenol, the antidepressant drug manufactured from used car batteries. Klaxo's chief stockholder, Mr. Schumaker, is flying in from Germany to approve this presentation, which will be used to pitch the drug to doctors at an upcoming trade show. Michael, understandably, is very anxious for the show to come off perfectly.

THE MISSION

Michael wants this show to be different from others on the trade show floor—he wants it to have a more "theatrical" feel, although to keep costs down, the presentation will have to be fully automated. Ralf, presentation manager for Klaxo, has been assigned the task of making Michael's dreams a reality. Ralf is well versed in many computer programs and boardroom control systems, but controlling equipment beyond the realm of the computer screen is a bit of a mystery to him, so he has hired a show-control consultant.

General Considerations

Let's look at our general design considerations:

1. What is the master control information source?

   The show will be "canned," but there will probably need to be some sort of manual start button to start the show.

2. Should the system be event-based, time-based, or a hybrid?

   Since the whole presentation has to chase a video presentation that never varies, it will be completely time-based (once started).

3. Does the show include life-threatening elements?

   The turntable is potentially dangerous.

THE EQUIPMENT

Klaxo has contracted with an exhibit firm to make the booth for the show, but it is producing the show in-house and will rent any necessary control, video, or audio gear from a staging company.

Scenery

The exhibit firm is building the booth that houses the show and is handling the projection screens. The turntable is being manufactured by a theatrical scene shop and will be integrated into the booth by the exhibit firm at their headquarters. The motion-control systems will be handled by the scene shop.

Video

Video is a key element of the show. Klaxo's corporate communications department has contracted a video producer to produce the video elements, which will play on three screens across the front of the theatre. The producer wanted to use videotape, but on the show-control consultant's recommendation, they go with three video "servers" for playback instead. The video servers can take Sony 9-Pin control commands, cue and recue very quickly, and store video and two tracks of audio on a hard disk.

Lighting

Klaxo has rented four moving lights: two for the "swoosh" effect and two others for house and ambient lighting. The fixtures can be controlled using DMX 512. Although the show-control consultant recommends renting a moving-light console, Ralf decides that there is not enough money in the budget to do so, that the lights will be run directly from the show-controller, and that he will program the lighting cues himself. The show-control consultant gladly takes him up on this, and together they decide on the channel assignments shown in Table 29.1.

Audio

The video servers will act as the primary audio source for the show—each of the three servers can output two-channel stereo sound. The video stu-

Table 29.1 Lighting Channel Assignment

DMX Channel	Unit	Function
1	1	Dimmer
2	1	Pan
3	1	Tilt
4	1	Color
5	1	Gobo
6	2	Dimmer
7	2	Pan
8	2	Tilt
9	2	Color
10	2	Gobo
11	3	Dimmer
12	3	Pan
13	3	Tilt
14	3	Color
15	3	Gobo
16	4	Dimmer
17	4	Pan
18	4	Tilt
19	4	Color
20	4	Gobo

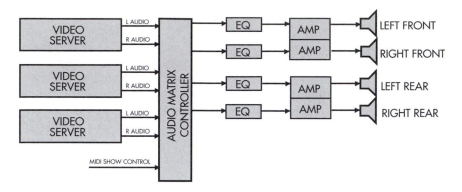

Figure 29.1 Put on a Happy Face: Sound Control Block Diagram

dio's sound designer is in charge of the audio for the booth, and he routes the stereo tracks from the main server to a pair of self-powered speakers located left and right of the main screen, where they are used for stereo sound effects and music. For the swirling swoosh sound effect that moves behind and around the audience to the front speakers, the show-control consultant and the sound designer decide to rent a computer-controlled audio matrix system that can move the sound wherever desired and be triggered by MIDI Show Control commands (see Figure 29.1).

Machinery

The scene shop that built the turntable has supplied a system that can accept two simple ASCII serial commands: "C1" and "C2." When "C1" and a carriage return are received by the unit, the turntable rotates to the post-show "battery" position; C2 resets the turntable to the preshow screen position. The 10-foot-diameter turntable rotates 180 degrees in about 5 seconds. A manual control console is also provided.

On the show-control consultant's advice, Ralf has the turntable control system built with a simple manual "enable" control, which will be operated by the attendant responsible for loading the doctors into the room. The attendant must be holding down the button for the turntable to operate; if any drunken doctors get up and try to ride or grab the turntable while it's in motion, the attendant will simply release the button and the turntable will stop. For safety reasons, the turntable is manually reset at the end of the show.

To ensure that the attendant knows her cue, an indicator lights just before the effect needs to be armed. The light goes out when it is safe for her to release the button and allow the show to complete normally.

Show Control

Since there is a video system that needs tight integration, and it is a time-based show, the show-control consultant chose a time-oriented show-control system that has direct support for the model of video server. It can also, with various interfaces, take as input or output a number of protocols such as DMX, Sony 9-Pin, and so on.

APPROACH 1

Ralf takes the consultant's recommendation to set up a full-scale test at corporate headquarters two weeks before the trade show. The control computer is located backstage right next to the turntable controllers and the video and audio racks (see Figure 29.2).

The show controller runs the show off its internal clock, and the last few cues on the simplified event list are shown in Table 29.2.

Table 29.2 Xylenol Approach #1 Show-Control Script

Time Code	Action	Messages/Operations
00:03:20:18	"Put on a happy . . ."	(Soundtrack)
00:03:21:00	Turntable Warning Light On	DMX Out 21 to 100%
00:03:21:20	Smiley Face on Screen	(Video)
00:03:24:00	Audio Matrix Moves Sound to Rear	MIDI Show Control Sound Go Cue 1
00:03:25:00	Swoosh Sound Starts	(Soundtrack)
00:03:25:01	Lights 3 and 4 Dimmers to Full	DMX Oouts 11 and 16 to 100%
00:03:25:15	Turntable Rotate to Battery Position	Serial "C1⇐"
00:03:25:19	Matrix Swoosh Pan to Front	MIDI Show Control Sound Go Cue 2
00:03:26:00	Lights 3, 4 to Intermediate Position	Outs 12/17 to 50/50%
00:03:26:00	Lights 3, 4 to Intermediate Position	Outs 13/18 to 50/50%
00:03:27:00	Lights 3, 4 to Final Position	Outs 12/17 to 90/10%
00:03:27:00	Lights 3, 4 to Final Position	Outs 13/18 to 10/90%
00:03:30:00	Turntable Warning Light Off	DMX Out 21 to 00%
00:03:58:00	Houselights (Spots 1 & 2) to Full	Outs 1/6 to 100%
00:05:00:00	Reset to Top of Show and Wait for "Go"	Sony 9- Pin Stop

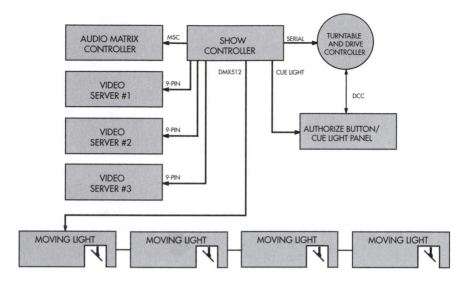

Figure 29.2   Put on a Happy Face: Approach 1 Block Diagram

The Results

The presentation goes very well; Mr. Schumaker from Germany and Michael from marketing are both dutifully impressed. Ralf barely hears the compliments, because he was awake all night getting the moving lights programmed. So he gives in to the show-control consultant's recommendation and rents a moving-light console that can accept MIDI Show Control messages. It is sent overnight and is programmed before the exhibit leaves the headquarters.

APPROACH 2

The system layout for the trade show is the same as what was built up in testing, with a few exceptions. Since the moving-light controller is so easy to program, Ralf adds a number of cues to the presentation, each triggered using a MIDI Show Control lighting message. The console is configured as MSC device 2, and the moving lights are connected (in a daisy chain) to the DMX 512 output of the console (see Figure 29.3).

The turntable sometimes takes just a bit more than 5 seconds to rotate, so if the attendant releases the button as soon as the indicator went out, the turntable will not fully complete its half rotation. So a second is added to the warning light-off time command (see Table 29.3).

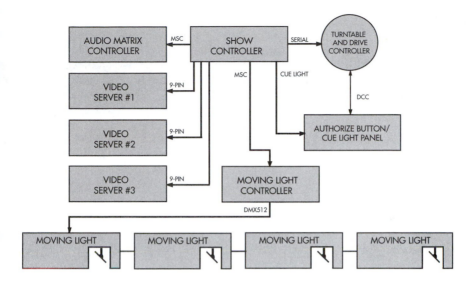

Figure 29.3 Put on a Happy Face: Approach 2 Block Diagram

Table 29.3 Xylenol Approach #2 Show Control Script

Time Code	Event	Action
00:03:20:18	"Xylenol is the one for you"	(Soundtrack)
00:03:21:00	Turntable Warning Light On	MSC Lighting Go Cue 101
00:03:21:20	Smiley Face on Screen	(Video)
00:03:24:00	Sound Pans Quickly to Rear	MIDI Show Control Sound Go Cue 1
00:03:25:00	Swoosh Sound Starts	(Soundtrack)
00:03:25:01	Lights 3 and 4 Dimmers to Full	MSC Lighting Go Cue 18
00:03:25:15	Turntable Rotate to Battery Position	Serial "C1⇐"
00:03:25:19	Swoosh Pan to Front	MIDI Show Control Sound Go Cue 2
00:03:25:27	Lights Pan to Front	MSC Lighting Go Cue 19
00:03:27:00	Lights Change to Yellow Color	MSC Lighting Go Cue 20
00:03:31:00	Turntable Warning Light Off	MSC Lighting Go Cue 100
00:03:58:00	Houselights to Full	MSC Lighting Go Cue 21
00:05:00:00	Reset to Top of Show and Wait for "Go"	

The Results

The presentation is the hit of the show. Prescriptions for Xylenol increase 50 percent in subsequent weeks, so Ralf gets a big raise. Ralf also contracts the show-control consultant a year in advance for the next show—Michael wants the models next year to be part of the presentation, interacting with it!

30

Film at 11

It's a crazy night in Massive Stadium. During "Comfortably Rich," the band's biggest hit, images of a flying poodle, edited perfectly to the song's beat, are showing on a giant circular screen. Video walls built into the set switch back and forth from prerecorded poodles to live views of the band. Throughout the song, sound effects and barks from the poodle footage emanate from the massive quad sound system. Then, suddenly, the drummer's riser lifts 20 feet into the air; this is the moment the crowd has been waiting for—the drum solo. As the riser's ascent slows, the poodle images disappear and the solo starts. As the drummer hits each of his drums, the huge array of moving lights dances precisely to the beat. At the end of his solo, the drummer plays the famous opening beats from "Young Rust," and as the drum riser returns slowly to earth, images of rust and money appear on the screens.

THE MISSION

Elderly rockers Purple Floyd want this spectacle recreated nightly for their final tour (the band had its first "final" tour 10 years ago). However, the band wants to minimize the effects of time-based media on its live performance—whenever possible, they want the ability to be live and spontaneous. The drum solo is a prime example: they want to switch smoothly from a time-based segment ("Comfortably Rich") to a spontaneous segment (the drum solo) and back to a time-based number ("Young Rust").

General Considerations

To start our system design process, let's apply the general questions:

1. What is the master control information source?

   In this case, it is the band itself. Ideally, the systems should sync to the band, but there must be some general constraints to achieve the synchrony the band desires.

2. Should the system be event-based, time-based, or a hybrid?

   The fact that the sequence includes synchronized prerecorded media means that at least part of the show will be time-based. The interactive drum solo, however, requires an event-based system, dictating either separate systems or a hybrid.

3. Does the system include life-threatening elements?

   The mechanized drum riser is definitely life-threatening.

THE EQUIPMENT

The band's longtime production manager is in charge of contracting the various people and companies that will supply and operate gear for the tour. He decides to bring in a show-control consultant to ensure that the critical sequences work correctly.

Lighting

The tour is designed entirely with moving lights, and since there are no conventional fixtures, there are no dimmer racks. The only connection between the front-of-house lighting-control console and the moving lights is a data cable, which communicates with the fixtures themselves.

The moving-light controller has a MIDI port. Each of the many console keys may be triggered using a particular MIDI message, or the system can be fired using MIDI Show Control commands. The electronic drum kit, however, puts out MIDI Note messages, so these messages will have to be processed and converted in order to trigger the console. The following looks have been programmed into the console for the drum solo:

Look	MSC Message	Drum/Note Number	Hex Note Number
1	Go Cue 1, List 10	Kick/C3	30h
2	Go Cue 2, List 10	Snare/D3	32h
3	Go Cue 3, List 10	High Tom/E3	34h
4	Go Cue 4, List 10	Mid Tom/F3	35h
5	Go Cue 5, List 10	Low Tom/G3	37h

Sound

Purple Floyd's massive quad sound system is controlled using a digital 1000-input console, which has a control surface out in the house and a processing rack backstage. Interconnection is via a proprietary console network based on Ethernet. A fiber-optic "snake," with a redundant backup system, has been run for additional audio, control, and backup. MIDI, SMPTE, and serial signals can also be sent in both directions out over this snake system.

Prerecorded audio for the video segments is stored on a hard-disk based system, which was selected to retain maximum flexibility in the field. The hard-disk system chases time code from the video for frame-accurate audio.

Video

Live video from the five cameras and playback sources is controlled by a video director located with all the video gear backstage. DVD players will provide all the standard definition prerecorded images for the video walls, while hard-disk based video servers will provide high-definition television (HDTV) to high-power video projectors for the big screen. The video server can chase time code; the DVD must receive serial commands. The video wall has a separate control system run by the video director.

Video Time-Code Scheme

The poodle film segment is 6 minutes, 23 seconds, and 4 frames long; the rust segment is 3 minutes, 25 seconds, and 20 frames long. Each prerecorded video segment in the show will be assigned a different time-code hour: the poodle segment is the third in the show, so it uses hour 3; the rust segment is next, so it uses hour 4.

Table 30.1   Purple Floyd Video Server Cue List

Time Code	Event
03:00:00:00	10 seconds preroll video black
03:00:10:00	Start of Poodle segment
03:06:33:04	End of Poodle segment
03:07:00:00	End of video black
04:00:00:00	10 seconds preroll video black
04:00:10:00	Start of Rust segment
04:03:35:20	End of Rust segment
04:04:00:00	End of video black

Table 30.2   Purple Floyd DVD Cue List

Time Code	Event	DVD Serial Command
03:00:00:00	10 Seconds pre-roll	Play
03:00:10:00	Start of Poodle segment	
03:06:33:04	End of Poodle segment	Still
03:06:35:00	Cue for Rust segment	Locate to 04:00:00:00
03:07:00:00	End of video black	
04:00:00:00	10 Seconds pre-roll	Play
04:00:10:00	Start of Rust segment	
04:03:35:20	End of Rust segment	Still
04:03:37:00	Cue for Next segment	Locate to 00:05:00:00
04:04:00:00	End of video black	

To make sure everything can sync up, 10 seconds of video black is added onto the head of each video segment, and also onto the tail (end) of each segment, to fill out to the next largest time-code minute. Table 30.1 and Table 30.2 show the time-code listing for the video servers and the DVDs.

Musical Synchronization

For everything to work seamlessly, the musicians somehow must lock themselves to the time code. The sound engineer feels that the most flexible option for generating a "click track"[1] is to use a programmable, MIDI-

---

[1]A click track is an audio track used to tell musicians when to start a song. The track is traditionally a series of metronome clicks starting a measure or two before the band should start; hence the name click track. Click tracks can also be vocal count-offs—"1 2 3 4 1 2 3 4 Go"—or drum patterns.

Time-Code-controllable drum machine. The drum machine was also selected because the drummer feels most comfortable syncing himself to a pattern of drum sounds rather than metronome clicks or voice counts. The production manager wanted to simply record the click track as an audio signal on the video, but the engineer pushed for the drum machine because the drummer could easily and intuitively reprogram it on-site if changes were necessary.

Once synced to a video segment, the drummer and the rest of the band can "float" a little bit within the timing of the segment, as long as they mostly stay in sync. To make the first transition from a time-based to a spontaneous segment, the drummer simply begins his solo as the "Comfortably Rich" film segment ends. When the drummer wants to end his solo, he signals the operators to start the next segment by playing a special beat pattern, which he never plays except at the end of the solo. The operators start the next segment, and the drummer is able to resync himself (and therefore the band) by listening (carefully) to the click track. A similar approach is taken to get into and out of guitar solos and the like.

Stage Machinery

The drum riser will lift to a preset position on receipt of a serial message. At the top position, an output contact is closed, indicating end-of-travel back to the controller. Another serial message causes the riser to reset to its down position. A special "authorize" button is located near the lift control, which the drum technician will press and hold when the drummer and all crew are in a safe position, enabling the effect.

SHOW-CONTROL SCRIPT

Although the video cue lists tell part of the synchronization story, the whole sequence is getting quite complicated now, so the production manager generates a script (see Table 30.3).

APPROACH 1

The production manager decides that the best way to run the system is to have one central controller talk to all the individual controllers. The consultant rents a commercial show-control system and configures it to generate SMPTE for the video and audio server systems. SMPTE is split using a time-code distribution amplifier/analyzer, supplied locally to the hard-disk system using a short cable, and also sent backstage to the video server.

Table 30.3 Purple Floyd Show-Control Script

Trigger	Event	Action
Manual	Comfortably Rich Preroll	Start Video Segment
8 Beats Before First Frame	Start of Click Track	Click Track to Drummer
03:00:10:00	Comfortably Rich Segment Start	
03:05:00:00 (Approx)	Check Riser Safety	
03:06:15:00 (Must be enabled)	Drum Riser Raises	
03:06:33:04	End of Song/Start of Solo	
Manual	Enable MIDI Drum Lights	Trigger Light Looks
03:06:35:00	Cue Film for Young Rust	Cue DVD for next segment
Manual	Disable MIDI Drum Lights	
Manual	Young Rust Preroll	Start Video Segment
Manual	Lower Riser	
8 Beats Before First Frame	Start of Click Track	Click Track to Drummer
04:00:10:00	Young Rust Segment Start	
04:03:35:20	End of Song/Segment	Cue DVD for next segment

MIDI Time Code is generated by the show-controller for the backstage drum machine and run over the fiber-optic line backstage. Serial commands are also sent from the show-controller to the DVD and drum riser backstage (see Figure 30.1).

To implement the drum-controlled moving lights, the consultant uses the fiber-optic line to send MIDI drum notes from backstage to the show controller, and writes a program that takes each MIDI note message and converts it to the proper MIDI message for the moving-light console.

The Results

The system is tested before the band arrives and works well. Each sequence is started with a single key-press on the show controller, which sends time code out to external devices, and then sends the individual MIDI messages and contact closures based on the time code.

The band has set aside two entire days of rehearsal to work on integrating themselves with the prerecorded segments, and this turns out to be a

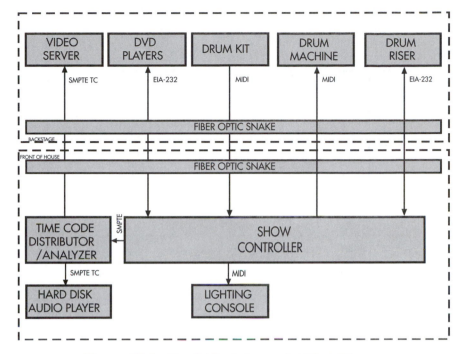

Figure 30.1 Purple Floyd: Approach 1 Block Diagram

wise decision. It takes a while to create a drum pattern acceptable to the drummer and to get his monitoring system working correctly. Through trial and error, each segment's MIDI Time Code start point for the drum machine is determined so that the film will appear to start exactly on the first beat of the music.

Everything is working beautifully. The consultant asks the production manager if the person who will be running the show-controller on the tour will be available soon for training. To this the production manager replies, "I thought you were running the system on the tour!" The consultant gets out his contract, points out the "no touring" clause, and the production manager goes running for his laptop to find an operator smart enough to handle the job. "Wait," says the consultant. "There's another way to do this."

APPROACH 2

Since the various system operators (lighting, video, back-line staff) will be on the tour anyway, the consultant suggests that they should run the system. Instead of using the show-controller to send SMPTE Time Code to all the slave devices, the video server, since it is easy to operate, will be the

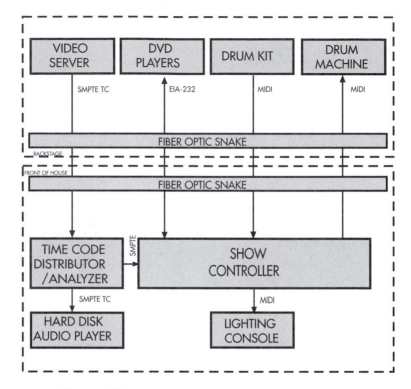

Figure 30.2 Purple Floyd: Approach 2 Block Diagram

master time-code source and operated by the video director. Time code from the server is sent through the TC distribution amp to the audio hard-disk player and to the show-controller, which converts the SMPTE to MTC for the drum machine and controls the DVD player at the appropriate time codes. The show-controller will also convert MIDI notes into commands for the interactive drum-solo lighting sequence. Since a roadie was already standing by the drum riser holding the enable button, and since operation of the riser system isn't really time-critical, the roadie will simply run the lift manually (see Figure 30.2).

The Results

This approach works well and, with a little practice, very smoothly. The production manager is also ecstatic since he now has one fewer crew, and he gives the show-control consultant a big bonus.

31

Ten-Pin Alley

The animatronic bowling pin beckons the crowd, "Hey kids, come over here and watch an amazing show with me, Bowly!" The house lights dim, and spectacular moving lights spring to life. "You too, grownups," says Bowly. A catchy bowling tune replaces the store's background music and sound effects, and a huge screen starts lowering into place. "Here we go!" shouts Bowly, and video images of dancing bowling pins fill the screen, cut precisely to the music beat. At the end of the 5-minute show, the house lights and regular background music restore, the screen retracts, and Bowly says, "Hey, thanks for coming, the next show will be in a few minutes. In the meantime, why not come inside and take a look around?" Video monitors around the floor, which had been relaying a feed from the show, spring back to life, and display live bowling highlights from around the world, intercut with real-time score updates from the adjacent bowling alley.

"Big Pete," president of 300 Score Entertainment (3SE), wants this sequence to take place every 30 minutes at "StrikeTown" bowling superstores/alleys in malls around the world. The flashy shows are designed to attract customers into the store, get them to stay a little longer, and maybe buy some StrikeTown sportswear or a new bowling ball, and later bowl a round, or dine and dance in the attached bar/restaurant complex.

THE MISSION

Big Pete has hired a design firm to produce the shows, and the firm will be producing the video and audio media in-house. The design firm's producer/

director is working with Big Pete's architect for scenic elements and has hired big-name Broadway lighting and sound designers to create the lighting and sound in the store. For the shows, freelance lighting, sound, animatronic, and show-control programmers are hired, and they will return two or three times a year to change the shows.

Big Pete has hired a general contractor (GC) to build the first StrikeTown. The GC has hired an entertainment lighting contractor to handle entertainment lighting systems; a scenery automation company to handle the large screens; an A/V contractor to handle audio, video, and control; and an animatronic character company to provide Bowly and his control system. On the A/V contractor's recommendation, Big Pete has hired a show-control consultant to coordinate the control of all the systems.

Shows will run automatically from a centralized "Scheduler" computer, which can be updated from corporate headquarters in Milwaukee over the corporate intranet or from the store manager's desktop. Shows can also be run manually from a touch-screen controller for special events, such as weddings, or appearances by famous bowlers with StrikeTown endorsements.

The bean counters of 3SE will allow only one maintenance person for all the technical systems in the store and the bowling alley. This person will be responsible for everything from the show systems, to a fancy elevator system to bring bowling balls up from the basement warehouse area, to the pin reracking equipment. Management decides that each system should run a full self-test every morning, and also respond to a simple "query" just before the start of each show, so that maintenance personnel can be alerted and shows cancelled if a system is not working properly. The system will have both a "day" mode when the store is open, and a "night" mode when the store is closed and show equipment is shut down.

General Considerations

To start our system design process, let's apply the general questions:

1. What is the master control information source?

   The Scheduler will start each show and will be responsible for scheduling day and night modes.

2. Should the system be event-based, time-based, or a hybrid?

   Each show will be "locked down" after programming, so the system can be time-based (but executed on an event basis).

3. Does the system include life-threatening elements?

   The large screen could be life-threatening.

THE EQUIPMENT

A wide variety of equipment needs to be connected and controlled for this system.

Scheduler

The Scheduler is going to be created, installed, and maintained by 3SE's information technologies (IT) department, since it is going to run on the corporate intranet. The IT department originally wanted to control all aspects of the show and store, but after hearing some war stories from the show-control consultant and GC, they realized that they would be getting in over their heads. So a separate system, specified by the show-control consultant, will run the shows and be triggered at the appropriate time by the Scheduler. The Scheduler will maintain a Web page on the corporate intranet for remote monitoring, and will offer Web-cam views of the store and backstage equipment room.

The Scheduler will send a variety of commands to the show-controller. Five minutes before show time, the Scheduler will send a "Warning Show #n" command, and later a "Go Show #n" message to start the show. Each command will be acknowledged by the show-controller, which will control everything associated with the show. Both the Scheduler and show-controller will be able to communicate with various store systems.

Show Video

Video is a key element of the shows. To ensure maximum flexibility, and to allow shows to be easily updated, video will be run off a hard-disk-based video server, which can have its contents updated over the corporate intranet. While the control connection to the server is via Ethernet, the server's designers decided not to reinvent the wheel and designed the server to accept Sony 9-Pin/Odetics commands over a link with the show-controller. The server has a balanced XLR time-code input and output and can chase or generate time code.

Each video segment is assigned a different time-code hour, and 5 minutes of video black is included at the head of segment before the actual show starts so that "Bowly" can start and run and other systems can roll up. One minute of video black fills out the end of each segment. Table 31.1 shows two typical show segments.

The show video projectors also need some control so that they can be configured, put into or taken out of "standby" mode at the start and end of each day, and queried before shows. The projectors have daisy-chainable EIA-422 ports.

Table 31.1 StrikeTown Video Server Media Layout

Time Code	Event
11:00:00:00	5 Minute Preroll Video Black
11:05:00:00	Start of "Bowling's Greatest Bloopers" Segment
11:09:04:25	End of Bowling Segment
11:10:04:25	End of Video Black
12:00:00:00	5 Minute Preroll Video Black
12:05:00:00	Start of "King Pin" Segment
12:10:01:00	End of "King Pin" Segment
12:11:01:00	End of Video Black

To test the entire video system—from server to projector—each morning, a special test pattern is rolled from the video server and projected on the screen. If the projector is on and working, the projector's light will activate a special photo sensor placed in the screen area. For the query check before each show, the video server will be sent a simple status message that it acknowledges, and then the projectors will be queried for lamp hours and on/off status.

Store Video

The store video systems have been contracted separately, and video for the 100 or so monitors around the facility is routed through an EIA-232 serial-controlled routing switcher. The switcher can route any of a number of satellite-received sports channels to the various monitors, put up logos, take graphics feeds for messages or score highlights from the alley, or take the video feed from the shows. No morning self-test is designed for the store video systems, but the switcher can respond with simple "ack"-like messages during the preshow checks.

Show Audio

Audio will be played off a multitrack hard-drive playback unit, which can chase SMPTE Time Code or accept MIDI Machine Control commands. The mix for the store will be accomplished through a computerized mixing matrix system, which can accept either MIDI Show Control commands, or chase SMPTE Time Code. All the amplifiers for the store are connected, monitored, and controlled from a control system made by the amp manufacturer.

For the full morning audio system test, a cue is fired in the matrix system playing a test tone to the speakers, and a small microphone in the store near the main speaker position is routed to a device that detects that specific tone and closes a relay. The contact closure from the relay is sent back to the show-controller. For the preshow query, the matrix is sent a MSC message to which it responds. The amplifier control system takes a serial message and responds with a status update.

Store Audio

The contract for store audio is separate from the show audio, and while similar equipment (amplifiers, etc.) is used in some parts of the system, a matrix system designed for permanent installations (rather than shows) is used. The store audio matrix system can call up presets or respond to simple queries over an EIA-232 link, or via SNMP commands over Ethernet. No morning self-test is designed for this system.

Animatronics

"Bowly" has his own control system, which can chase SMPTE time code, or be triggered by EIA-232 serial commands or contact closures. A programming panel is provided for inputting Bowly's moves, and a small audio deck with time-code output capability is also provided in the animatronic control rack, so that Bowly can be programmed "offline" separately from the show, and then integrated when his programming is complete.

For the morning self-test, a heavy-duty limit switch is discreetly positioned near Bowly, and when the test program is executed, Bowly simply hits the switch. For normal preshow checks, Bowly's control system responds with a simple "ack" command over the serial port.

Stage Machinery

The projection screen motion-control system takes serial commands over an EIA-232 link. Each 8-byte command consists of a command byte (typically 01h for "Go to position"), an acceleration time byte, a target velocity byte, 3 bytes representing target position (giving 24-bit precision), a deceleration time, and a CRC check. When the controller successfully completes the CRC check, the command is executed. A manual control panel with auto/manual lockout is provided, as is a complete E-Stop system.

The screen is housed in a vertical area closed to the public, accessible only via a locked door. For safety reasons, a sensor put on the door sends a signal to both the motion-control system and to the show-controller each time the door is opened. When the sensor is tripped, the screen, if moving, will stop, and the system has to be manually reset using a key-switch near the door before the screen will be allowed to move again.

The motion-control system is closed loop, with encoders mounted on the screen drum itself. But for the morning self-test, to be sure that the screen hasn't jammed or fallen off the drum, photo-sensors are positioned near the bottom of the screen's travel and near the top. During the morning check, the screens are run out (the screens come in during "night" mode to keep them stretched out), and each sensor is examined by the show-controller.

For the quick preshow self-test, the motion-controller moves the screen about an inch, looks for motion on its encoder, and then reports its status back to the show-controller.

Show Lighting

The show lighting system consists only of moving lights, and a controller is selected that is available in both a console version with full controls, and a rack-mount version with limited control. A full console is rented for show change-outs, and the show is then loaded into the rack-mount system for daily operation. The controller can chase SMPTE Time Code, or accept MIDI Show Control commands for cues.

For the system self-test, the same photocell sensors designed for testing the projectors are used. One at a time, cues are executed via MIDI Show Control, commanding each moving light to shine its beam on one of the photo sensors.

The console isn't capable of sending an "ack" in response to incoming MSC commands, so for the simple preshow test it will be commanded via MSC to execute a cue to turn on a DMX output, which is routed back to a DMX input on the show-controller.

Store Lighting

The contract for store lighting has been let separately from show lighting. The store system is fairly simple, with two general "looks": normal and show. The store controller can accept serial commands, and also acknowledge via a simple "Ack" for the preshow test. No morning self-test is designed for this system.

THE APPROACH

The show-control consultant picks a show-control system that can generate time code, chase it, send serial, MIDI, or other messages, send and receive

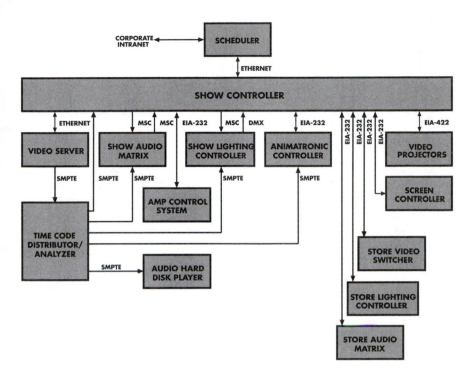

Figure 31.1 StrikeTown: Show-Control System Block Diagram

messages over Ethernet, and send or receive contact closures. The show-control consultant decides that an Ethernet connection should be used between the Scheduler and the show-controller, to leave room for future expansion. At the 5-minute warning, the Scheduler will send its control message via TCP/IP to the show-controller. The show-controller will then check each system, by sending various serial or MSC events to each of the subsystems, and wait for replies from each. If all the critical systems check OK, the controller sends a message back to the Scheduler saying that the show is standing by, and this is logged on the Scheduler's Web page. If the systems do not check out OK, the show-controller sends a message to the Scheduler detailing the problem, and the Scheduler can put this information on its Web page, send an E-mail, or even page maintenance personnel. The consultant decides that since without video there is no show, and since video is a linear, time-based media, the video server should generate time code for all the other show systems. It should also send TC back to the show-controller, so it can generate messages for systems like store audio and lighting, which cannot accept time code. Figure 31.1 shows the system block diagram.

SHOW-CONTROL SCRIPT

The show-control consultant generates a simplified show-control script, one segment of which is shown in Table 31.2.

Table 31.2 StrikeTown Typical Segment Show-Control Script

Trigger	Event	Action
5 Minutes Before Show Time	Show 12 5-Minute Warning	Scheduler Sends Message to Show-Controller (SC)
SC Receives Message	SC Tests Screen	SC Sends Serial Message to Screen System
Screen Replies	Screen OK or Not OK	SC Sends "Screen OK" (or "Show Abort") Message to Scheduler
Screen Test Complete	SC Tests Show Video	SC Sends Serial Message to Video Server
		SC Sends Serial Message to Projectors
Video Server and Projectors Reply	Video/Projectors OK or Not OK	SC Sends "Show Video OK" (or "Show Abort") Message to Scheduler
Show Video Test Complete	SC Tests Store Video	SC Sends Serial Command to Store Video
Store Video Replies	Store Video OK or Not OK	SC Sends "Store Video OK" (or "Not OK) Message to Scheduler
Store Video Test Complete	SC Tests Show Audio	SC Sends MSC Message to Show Sound Matrix
		SC Sends Serial Message to Amp Controller
Matrix and Amp Controller Reply	Matrix/Amp Controller OK or Not OK	SC Sends "Show Audio OK" (or "Show Abort") Message to Scheduler
Show Audio Test Complete	SC Tests Store Audio	SC Sends Serial Message to Store Audio
Store Audio Replies	Store Audio OK or Not OK	SC Sends "Store Audio OK" (or "Not OK") Message to Scheduler
Store Audio Test Complete	SC Tests Animatronics	SC Sends Serial Message to Animatronic Controller
Animatronic Controller	Animatronics OK or Not OK Replies	SC Sends "Animatronics OK" (or " Not OK") Message to Scheduler
Animatronic Test Complete	SC Tests Lighting	SC Sends MSC Message To Show Lighting

(continued)

Table 31.2 *(continued)*

Trigger	Event	Action
Show Lighting Replies	Show Lighting Contact Closure On or Off	SC Sends "Show Lighting OK" (or " Not OK") Message to Scheduler
Show Lighting Test Complete	SC Tests Store Lighting	SC Sends Serial Message to Store Lighting System
Store Lighting Test Complete	SC Evaluates If Critical Systems (Screen, Show Video, Show Audio) Are OK	SC Sends "Standing by for Show" Message to Scheduler, or Sends "Critical System Failure, Show Aborting," and Cancels Show
Show Time	Show 12 Go	SC Starts Video Segment 14
Start Of Show	Video Starts Rolling	Time Code Is Generated
12:00:00:00	Time Code Starts Rolling	
12:01:00:00	Bowly Starts Talking	TC Triggers Animatronics Preshow
12:04:00:00	Store Audio Starts to Fade Down	SC Sends Serial Message to Store Audio
12:04:30:00	Store Lighting Starts to Fade Down	SC Sends Serial Message to Store Lighting
12:04:55:00	Screen Lowers	SC Sends Serial Message to Screen System
12:04:58:00	Bowly Says, "Here We Go!"	
12:05:00:00	Show Starts	
Various	Show Lighting and Sound Chase Time Code	
12:10:01:00	Show Ends	
12:10:02:00	Screen Retracts	SC Sends Serial Message to Screen System
12:10:06:00	Store Lighting Starts to Fade Up	SC Sends Serial Message to Store Lighting
12:10:07:00	Store Audio Starts to Fade Up	SC Sends Serial Message to Store Audio
12:10:10:00	Bowly Finishes Speaking	SC Sends Serial "Rest" Command Sent To Bowly
12:11:06:00	End of Time Code	SC Sends "Show Complete" Message to Scheduler, and Systems Reset as Necessary for Next Show

The Results

The first StrikeTown opens in the country's largest mall in Minnesota, and is a huge success. The only problem is that the maintenance issues are too much for one person to handle, and a second full-time person, who deals only with show systems, store audio, and store video is added. The self-tests are still used by the new show maintenance person, but he now has time to schedule and coordinate maintenance since he doesn't also have to clear pin-jams in the bowling alley. Big Pete announces future StrikeTown locations in Las Vegas, Orlando, and Paris.

32

It's an Itchy World after All

Itchy and Scratchy wander onto the huge outdoor stage from opposite ends. Itchy, proclaiming his friendship, gives a bouquet of flowers to Scratchy, who is purringly happy. But, seconds later, Scratchy gives his trademark scream as Itchy shoots him off the stage with a large-caliber machine gun. Scratchy staggers back onstage to get a drink of water from a well, but Itchy sneaks in from the side and kicks Scratchy down the opening. The manic mouse then throws a hand grenade down after the crazy cat, and a huge explosion bellows out, spraying the audience with water. Moments later, a charred Scratchy appears at the mouth of the well, staggers across the stage, and lays down under a ledge to get a badly needed cat nap. Little does he know that he is sleeping on a bowling alley. Itchy, however, is happy to point this out, and quietly arranges nine warhead bowling pins around the napping cat. He then rolls a bomb down the alley, and you can guess what happens next—Strike!

THE MISSION

These are the first three segments (Scratchy's first three lives) of the Itchy and Scratchy Epic Stunt Spectacular, which is to be the main attraction at Duff Gardens, the internationally-known theme park located near Orlando, Florida. The attraction will purportedly show how action movies are made, using indestructible cartoon characters Itchy and Scratchy to demonstrate various stunts. The show, the biggest at Duff Gardens, will run five times daily during peak season, both day and night, with show lighting used for the nighttime shows. Mr. Burns, Duff's CEO, has taken a personal interest in the show, and so everyone is working hard to ensure that everything goes smoothly. Itchy and Scratchy are Duff's corporate icons, so no expense is spared.

While the attraction's construction is lavish, its operating costs will be rigidly controlled—systems are designed to minimize labor costs. The entire show will be run by one technical director (TD), one sound operator, and several pyrotechnicians who reload between shows.

General Considerations

Now, let's apply our general questions to get started:

1. What is the master control information source?

   This will vary: sometimes the time base will supply control information; other times the human operators and, for critical sequences, the actors onstage will provide control information themselves.

2. Should the system be event-based, time-based, or a hybrid?

   The show will be loosely time-based, with event-triggering for critical sequences.

3. Does the system include life-threatening elements?

   Definitely. All proper precautions should be taken.

THE EQUIPMENT

Equipment for the production is being supplied by a number of subcontractors, all working for WDI (Wacky Duff Illusions), Duff's in-house design and engineering department, which is designing and general contracting the show.

Show Control

Park management has standardized all operations in the park on the same commercially available show-control system, to facilitate maintenance, training, and updates. Park management systems will interface with the show-controller through a serial link, and this will allow the park's central control system to tell the show-controller whether to run day or nighttime versions of the show, or other functions, such as turning on work lights at specific times for cleaning, and so on.

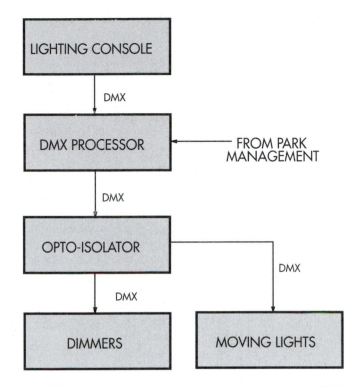

Figure 32.1 Itchy and Scratchy: Lighting System Block Diagram

Lighting

The lighting system will be built around a rack-mounted version of a large theatrical console. A normal console system will be used for the programming period, and then the show will be downloaded into the rack-mounted unit for show operation. Either version of the console can be driven via MIDI Show Control commands; output to dimmers and moving lights will be via DMX. A special processor in line between the console and dimmers provides interfacing for emergency systems (see Figure 32.1). This processor allows park management to bring up independently of the show, systems in the event of a park-wide or other emergency.

Slide Projectors

Three large-format projectors are used to generate massive images for the nighttime shows. One projector is used to show preshow images on a nearby water tower shaped like Itchy's mouse ears. The other two are used to dissolve images on a set wall, for sequence titles. Slide-changing for the systems is completely automated, and the system has a PC-based controller that can accept serial messages.

Sound

The sound system combines both playback and reinforcement technologies. The bulk of the sound system control is accomplished through the use of a computerized matrix sound controller, which triggers sound effects and controls all routing and gain manipulation for the system. Sounds come from three sources: a sequencer-based music system, an EPROM (read-only memory) system for sound FX and "dialogue," and several wireless mics, used by an announcer who pulls hapless victims out of the audience (see Figure 32.2). All the speakers are self-powered, and the manufacturer's remote monitoring system is used.

The sound controller runs in a cue-based mode like a lighting board. The controller handles all MIDI message generation for the sound system, and includes a large audio matrix for routing and gain manipulation. The controller's primary interface is a mouse and a monitor; for ease of operation, the operator also has a number of MIDI faders, which control the internal submasters for show-to-show adjustments.

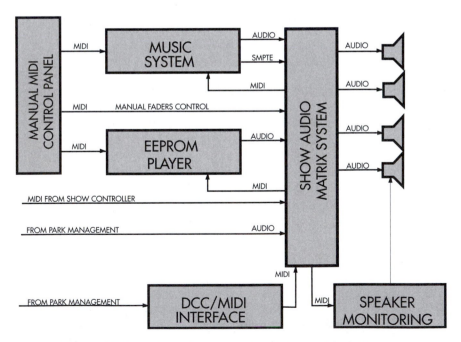

Figure 32.2   Itchy and Scratchy: Sound System Block Diagram

Instrumental music for each segment is generated in real time using a customized music sequencer. The actors essentially perform to this presequenced musical soundtrack, but special sequences have been built enabling the system to "vamp" on any measure of the music. In case anything goes wrong onstage, the sound operator can stretch each segment indefinitely if necessary. When activated, the music system provides time code to control other show elements; in vamp mode, the last valid time-code frame is repeated indefinitely.

Prerecorded sounds, such as the Itchy and Scratchy theme song and voiceover used to open the show, and all internal sound effects and dialogue come from an EEPROM-based system. Sounds from this system are triggered by MIDI Note messages from a panel controlled by the sound operator, or by the show-controller for certain effects such as the machine gun.

Also on this machine are the "dialogue" tracks. Itchy and Scratchy never speak in their cartoon nor in this show; they do, however, make certain sounds such as screams, whistles, and groans. Each individual sound is triggered manually by the sound operator to ensure proper synchronization regardless of what happens onstage. In rehearsal the actors pick certain moves to indicate to the operator when to trigger the sound.

Like the lighting system, the sound system has connections to park management. Special emergency paging lines can be made active at any time, and park background music and a general paging system are also included.

Mr. Burns went to a competitor's theme park and was disturbed when a character's dialogue came out of a speaker stage left when the actor was stage right. He asked his sound designer to prevent this problem at Duff Gardens, and the designer is using a feature of the sound system to position sound "images" at any location on the massive stage by varying the arrival time and gain characteristics of a number of discrete channels to zones covering the audience. This allows a laugh from Itchy to appear to come from Itchy no matter where in the audience you are sitting. For this production, the blocking is very predictable, so each localization point for the actor's moves is programmed in and triggered at specific times.

Effects

There are extensive pyrotechnic and other effects in this production, which will be controlled using a computer-based pyro controller that works in conjunction with a Programmable Logic Controller (PLC) and the human TD (technical director) for safety interlocks (see Figure 32.3).

The PLC determines whether the effect is safe to go based on the state of proximity detectors, and, most importantly, actor-operated safety switches. For dangerous effects, the actor must press and hold a button or buttons, indicating that he or she is in a safe position, or the effect will not be allowed to

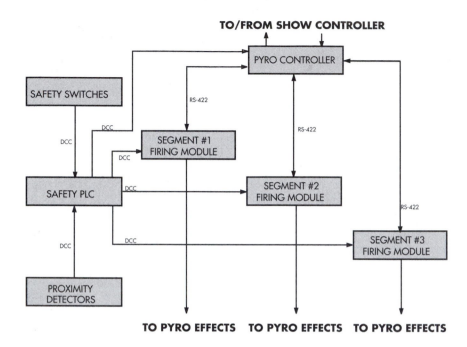

TO/FROM SHOW CONTROLLER

Figure 32.3 Itchy and Scratchy: Pyro System Block Diagram

operate. Until the effect is safe to go, the firing contacts to the actual effect are shorted by the PLC, ensuring that no matter what happens upstream in the pyro controller, the effect cannot fire until all is safe. Additional PLC outputs are used to report status back to the master controller and to a custom enabling panel in front of the technical director. Pyro cues are fired only if enabled by the TD.

For safety reasons (and to save money), pyro substitutes are used whenever possible. The well explosion, for example, is really a pneumatic "air cannon" effect, which simply blasts a tremendous amount of water out of the well in conjunction with a sound effect. The machine-gun bullet hits are also pneumatic. To keep things simple, the pyro controller fires both pyro and substitute pyro effects (although some subsystems are used with some of the substitute pyro effects).

Miscellaneous Systems

There are a number of custom systems for this production. The first is the machine gun used by Itchy. To give the actor maximum flexibility and to make the effect as believable as possible, the actor actually controls the machine-gun effects directly, using a special gun with a radio transmitter.

When the trigger is squeezed on Itchy's machine gun, a radio signal is sent to a receiver, which generates a MIDI message for the master show-controller. When enabled by the TD, the pneumatic bullet-hit effects are triggered, along with localized machine-gun sound effects. The machine-gun firing interval has been agreed on in advance after extensive testing and is programmed into each system.

Another special system is a cue-light controller for the actors backstage. Since the actors perform the show to the music, this controller indicates when certain actions, such as entrances, should occur. Large monitors backstage indicate at what time code each event should happen; red lights next to the monitor come on for a warning and turn off to indicate that the event should take place.

A similar system is implemented over the TD booth in the front of the house. A pair of green lights (one for backup) mounted on top of the TD booth indicates to the actor playing Itchy that Scratchy is safely in place for certain effects, such as the grenade and the machine gun.

THE APPROACH

Since so much money is being spent on the attraction, WDI does extensive testing in advance to ensure that as few changes as possible are made after construction begins. The general approach is to keep the show as time-based as possible, while staying flexible on any life-threatening elements. Each segment's time base is generated with the music, and the actors lock themselves to the music. If anything goes wrong, the sound operator simply "vamps" the music. Since the music is entirely instrumental, vamping a few bars might sound a little strange, but it will be acceptable (see Figure 32.4).

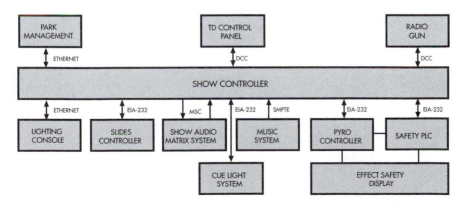

Figure 32.4   Itchy and Scratchy: Show-Control System Block Diagram

Each segment is started by the technical director when everything is in place and operational. The show-controller issues a Sound Go command, which starts the music sequencer, which in turn then generates time code, which is then used to trigger the actors' cuing system and light and localization cues for the entire sequence.

SHOW-CONTROL SCRIPT

WDI comes up with a detailed cue list for show planning (see Table 32.1). In addition to trigger sources and show-control messages, the list indicates who executes a particular effect. TD denotes that the technical director executes the effect; TC indicates that the effect is executed automatically based on the time code; SoundOp means that the sound operator takes the cue; and House Mgr. is the house manager in charge of the audience. This script applies to a nighttime show, including all lighting and slide commands; for the sake of simplicity, however, cue-light cues, system acknowledgments, and other messages are not included here.

Table 32.1   Itchy and Scratchy Stunt Show Cue List

Time Code	Event	Actions	Executed By	Control Messages
Segment #0	**Preshow**			
Event	TD starts preshow	Park background music up	TD	Sound Go Q00
		Sound localization preset		Localization Go Q00
		Preshow light look		Lights Go Q00
		Preshow slides up		Projection Go Q00
Event	10 minutes before show	"Please take your seats"	House Mgr.	Note A2 On/Off
Event	2 minutes before show	"Please take your seats"	House Mgr.	Note B2 On/Off
Event	TD starts show	Itchy and Scratchy Theme Song	SoundOp	Sound Go Q01
00:00:10:13	2nd measure of Music	Houselights to half	TC	Lights Go Q01
00:00:20:02	4th measure of Music	Houselights out	TC	Lights Go Q02
00:00:24:28	"Itchy" in Introduction	Slide of Itchy up/Pre Show out	TC	Projection Go Q01
00:00:32:07	"Scratchy" in Introduction	Slide of Scratchy dims up	TC	Projection Go Q02
00:01:02:23	Autostart Segment #1		TC	

(continued)

Table 32.1 *(continued)*

Time Code	Event	Actions	Executed By	Control Messages
Segment #1	**That Happy Cat**			
01:00:00:00	Segment starts	Flowers music Go/Entrance out	TC	Sound Go Q11
		"That Happy Cat" slides up	TC	Projection Go Q11
		Sound localization cue	TC	Localization Go Q11
01:00:10:00	Scratchy enters	Lights for Scratchy up	TC	Lights Go Q11
01:00:18:00	Scratchy moves center	Sound localization cue	TC	Localization Go Q12
		Scratchy whistling	SoundOp	Sound Go Q12
01:00:32:00	Itchy enters with flowers	Lights for Itchy up	TC	Lights Go Q12
		Itchy squeaking	SoundOp	Sound Go Q13
01:01:18:00	Itchy and Scratchy move center	Sound localization cue	TC	Localization Go Q13
01:02:03:00	Scratchy moves stage right	Sound localization cue	TC	Localization Go Q14
01:02:05:00	Itchy exits	Sound localization cue	TC	Localization Go Q15
01:02:30:00	Itchy enters with machine gun	Sound localization cue	TC	Localization Go Q16
		TD authorizes machine gun	TD	Pyro Standby Q 101
Event	Scratchy safely in place	Scratchy authorizes gun	Scratchy	Pyro Standing by Q101
01:02:32:00	Scratchy safely in place	Lights for Scratchy in place	TC	Lights Go Q13
Event	Itchy squeezes trigger	Machine gun bullet hits	Itchy	Pyro Go Q101/Standby102
		Machine gun sounds start	Itchy	Note C2 On
		Machine gun flashes	Itchy	Lights Go Q14
		Scratchy screaming sound FX	Itchy	Sound Go Q14
Event	Scratchy breaks photocell beam	Flowers music fade out	TD	Sound Go Q15
		Lights for Scratchy off	TD	Lights Go Q16
Event	Itchy releases trigger	Machine gun hits stop	Itchy	Pyro Go Q102
		Machine gun sounds stop	Itchy	Note C2 Off
		Machine gun flashes stop	Itchy	Lights Go Q15
Event	Itchy character laughs	Itchy laughing sound FX	SoundOp	Sound Go Q16

(continued)

Table 32.1 *(continued)*

Time Code	Event	Actions	Executed By	Control Messages
01:03:00:00	Itchy exits	Lights fade down	TC	Lights Go Q17
Segment #2	**Well and Truly**			
Event	Scratchy's head around corner	Well music go	TD	Sound Go Q21
02:00:00:00	Scratchy staggers onstage	Lights for Scratchy up "Well and truly" slide up	TC TC	Lights Go Q21 Projection Go Q21
02:00:10:00	Scratchy moves towards well	Sound localization cue	TC	Localization Go Q22
Event	Scratchy moaning	Moaning sound FX	SoundOp	Sound Go Q22
Event	Takes drink from well	Slurping sound FX	SoundOp	Sound Go Q23
02:00:30:00	Itchy enters	Lights for Itchy up	TC	Lights Go Q22
Event	Itchy kicks Scratchy down well	TD authorizes explosion Falling sound FX	TD TD	Pyro Standby Q201 Sound Go Q24
02:00:45:00	Scratchy down well	Lights focus on well	TC	Lights Go Q23
Event	Itchy laughs	Itchy laughing sound FX	SoundOp	Sound Go Q25
Event	Scratchy in safety position	Scratchy authorizes explosion	Scratchy	Pyro Standing By Q201
Event	Itchy throws grenade	TD fires explosion Lights for explosion Sound for explosion Well music out	TD TD TD TD	Pyro Q201 Go Lights Go Q24 Note D2 On/Off Sound Go Q26
02:02:00:00	Itchy walks offstage	Sound localization cue	TC	Localization Go Q23
Event	Itchy laughs	Itchy laughing sound FX	SoundOp	Sound Go Q27
02:02:05:00	Itchy walks offstage	Lights fade down	TC	Lights Go Q25
Segment #3	**Bowling for Scratchy**			
Event	Scratchy's head peers out well	Bowling music go	TD	Sound Go Q31
03:00:00:00	Scratchy climbs out of well	Lights for Scratchy "Bowling for Scratchy" slide Sound localization cue Scratchy moaning sound FX	TC TC TC SoundOp	Lights Go Q31 Projection Go Q31 Localization Go Q31 Sound Go Q32

(continued)

Table 32.1 *(continued)*

Time Code	Event	Actions	Executed By	Control Messages
03:00:10:00	Scratchy moves towards alley	Sound localization cue	TC	Localization Go Q32
03:00:20:00	Scratchy lies down	Lights focus on Scratchy	TC	Lights Go Q32
		Sound localization cue	TC	Localization Go Q33
		Purring sound FX Go	TC	Sound Go Q33
03:00:30:00	Itchy enters	Lights up on Itchy	TC	Lights Go Q33
03:00:33:00	Itchy moves towards alley	Sound localization cue	TC	Localization Go Q34
Event	Itchy arranges bowling pins	Standby for explosion	TD	Pyro Standby Q301
03:01:45:00	Itchy arranges bowling pins	Lights focus on Itchy	TC	Lights Go Q34
Event	Scratchy moves to safety	Scratchy authorizes explosion	Scratchy	Pyro Standing By Q301
Event	Itchy rolls bomb down alley	Bowling sound effects	SoundOp	Sound Go Q34
Event	Bomb ball hits pins	TD fires explosion	TD	Pyro Q301 Go
		Lights for explosion	TD	Lights Go Q35
		Sound for explosion	TD	Note E2 On/Off
		Purring sound FX stop	TD	Sound Go Q35
03:03:00:00	Itchy walks offstage	Sound localization cue	TC	Localization Go Q35
		Itchy laughing sound FX	TC	Sound Go Q36

Before each show, the pyro-technicians load all the pyro equipment and walk through the attraction with the actors to do a safety check. When the show is ready for the audience, the TD executes a cue on the controller that starts preshow mode. In this mode, special park background music is piped through the system, along with any park-wide paging or announcements. If the night show is being run, a preshow light look is brought up, and the Itchy and Scratchy slide is projected on the water tower. The house manager keeps in touch with the TD over a handset phone as the audience files in, and the sound operator triggers one announcement 10 minutes before show time: "Ladies and gentlemen, please take your seats. The Itchy and Scratchy Stunt Show will start in 10 minutes." Two minutes before show time, the house manager checks again and the sound op triggers another recorded announcement. At this point, the TD gets verbal confirmation over the headset that the actors are ready and calls places. When the house manager indicates that the audience is seated, the sound op starts the introduction sequence—the ever-popular Itchy and Scratchy theme.

As the house lights dim out, over the sound system can be heard the strains of the theme song: "They fight, they fight, they fight they fight they fight! Fight-fight-fight, fight-fight-fight! The Itchy and Scratchy Epic Stunt Spectacular!" Recorded along with the opening theme is time code, which is sent back to the master controller, which triggers the slide projectors as the recorded announcer introduces the popular animated characters. At time code 00:01:02:23, on the final downbeat, segment 1 is automatically triggered; the show-controller also switches to monitor the sequencing system for all subsequent time code.

The first sequenced music cue begins, the slides bring up the title of the first segment—"That Happy Cat"—and a localization preset cue is issued. At time 01:00:05:00, Scratchy's cue light comes on; at 01:00:10:00 the light goes off and Scratchy enters. The system takes an automatic localization cue as he moves center, and the sound op triggers a whistling cue as the actor turns his head toward the audience. Itchy is cued to enter and comes onstage with his bouquet of flowers. The sound op executes a "squeak" cue, and Itchy walks offstage. Several localization cues are then taken automatically.

Itchy then enters with the machine gun. As soon as the TD sees Itchy, he executes a cue telling the pyro system to stand by for cue 101. Scratchy moves to the correct position to go flying through a breakaway wall when hit by the bullets. To signal that he is ready, he stands on two switches mounted in the deck, one for each foot. These switches are wired into the pyro PLC, and when both switches are closed the PLC closes a contact to the pyro controller, which is indicated on the TD's control panel and received by the show-controller. When the master show-controller receives this message, the green lights on top of the booth come on, indicating to Itchy that everything is ready. As soon as Itchy pulls the trigger, a radio signal is sent, closing a contact closure at the show-controller. This triggers the machine-gun sound effects, special lighting, a scream sound for Scratchy, and the bullet hits. Scratchy crashes through the wall, and the sound op executes a cue that fades the flowers music out (although time code is still generated). The time code turns Scratchy's light look off and executes a localization cue. When Itchy releases the trigger, all the effects stop. Itchy moves his head in a way to signal the sound op to play a sadistic laugh cue and then walks offstage. A light cue is taken, leaving only a spotlight on the hole in the wall where Scratchy crashed through.

The audience is tense, but when they finally see Scratchy's bullet-ridden head peer around the corner, they give a big cheer. As soon as the sound op sees Scratchy's head, he starts segment 2, starting the sequenced "well" music; time code from the sequencer then starts the other elements. Scratchy moves toward the well, several light and localization cues are triggered automatically, and the sound op triggers a moan sound. As Scratchy leans into the well, the sound op triggers several manual slurping sounds, then Itchy's cue light goes out, he enters and kicks Scratchy down the well. The TD executes a cue that puts the explosion effect into standby, and the sound op triggers a falling and splash sound effect.

The actor playing Scratchy, of course, only falls about six feet and climbs into a special bunker to protect him from the explosion. Itchy dances around the top of the well to cover the time Scratchy needs to get into the safety position. When in place, Scratchy presses and holds an authorize switch in his bunker underneath the well, which signals the pyro controller, the TD, and the show-controller, which turns on the green lights on top of the booth. Itchy sees the green ready light and tosses the hand grenade down the well; the TD waits a moment and then executes a cue triggering the water-cannon effect, a light cue, an explosion sound effect, and a cue that fades out the "well" music. Sound localization and light cues are then taken automatically, the sound operator triggers a laughing cue, and Itchy walks offstage. The lights fade down, and finally Scratchy's charred head is seen over the top of the well. The TD then starts the next sequence.

The sound op triggers appropriate moaning cues, and other cues are taken automatically from the time code as Scratchy staggers over to the bowling alley. The sound op executes a purring cue as Scratchy lays down. Itchy's cue light goes off, and he enters. Itchy's act of arranging the large bowling pins is actually a diversion as Scratchy is moving to an explosion-proof bunker behind the alley. The TD executes a cue telling the pyro system to stand by, Scratchy presses and holds a safety switch, and the green cue light comes on. Itchy sees the light and rolls the ball down the alley. As the ball hits the pins, the TD triggers a command firing the huge explosion cue, the sound effect, light cue, and a sound cue that kills the purring sound. As Itchy walks offstage, the sound operator triggers another laughing cue.

The Results

We've covered only the first three of nine segments of the show, but the attraction is a rousing success, and people line up all day to get in! Mr. Burns says the show is "Excellent!"

Conclusion

The field of entertainment control is constantly evolving, and so I've focused here not on specific gear, but on the concepts underlying the equipment. The two really are inseparable, but as long as you learn *why* you are pressing a button, and not just to press it at such and such a time, that knowledge can easily transfer to another system. This is critical today—the only thing I can accurately predict is that you will someday have to learn protocols and standards not covered in this book. I hope, with the foundation offered here, that the learning process will not be too painful—in fact, it should be fun. That's why we're in this crazy business, right?

PREDICTIONS

Before making any new predictions in this second edition, I should evaluate my predictions from the first edition:

1. *Systems will continue to be integrated. That was an easy prediction! Integration of control systems for live performance is inevitable financially and desirable aesthetically. The ultimate goal of show control is to recreate accurately the vision of the director, designers, and performers onstage, night after night.*

Well that certainly happened, but to a lesser degree than I anticipated, at least in the world of live shows. However, more people today than ever need to understand entertainment control systems, so the information in this book is more relevant than ever.

2. *People will not be put out of work by show control technology. Labor unions may argue with me here, but people who are willing to learn these new technologies will continue to work; if you've read this far, you are certainly one of these people. I believe that the end result of show-control technology is more shows, staffed by fewer people. Show control has almost certainly made possible in many ways the explosion of theme parks across the country.*

Show control has also fueled the explosion of themed retail. I would venture to say that the entertainment control market has expanded dramatically in the last 5 to 6 years, and that more people are working in more venues than ever before. In general, new technology in entertainment seems to expand what can be done, not put people out of work.

3. *Humans will not be eliminated from the show control loop (any time soon). Control for live performance is too complicated to be completely automated yet—there are just too many variables. Many elements of production, and sound, in particular, will continue to have considerable human involvement for a long time to come.*

I believe this is still the case.

4. *The AES-24 protocol in development will radically change sound systems. . . .*

Well, many others and I were totally wrong about this one, but not for technical reasons. The standard was never completed primarily for political and commercial reasons, so we'll never be sure whether or not it would have worked as anticipated. However, as I've detailed, the need for wide-ranging, object-oriented interconnection of a variety of audio devices is less than it was before, since sound systems are increasingly centralized.

Here's a replacement prediction: ESTA "ACN" (or whatever its final name) could dramatically change lighting and entertainment control systems. The ESTA ACN task group differs from the AES committee in that it has highly motivated commercial forces behind it, and end-users and manufacturers are screaming for this new functionality. That's a dramatically different situation than we saw in the AES SC-10 effort. The only question now is when? ACN is already behind the original milestones set by the task group. If and when it is ever finished, ACN will certainly be included in a future edition of this book.

WEB SITE

I hope you have enjoyed this book and found it useful. If you have any comments, questions, or corrections (please, no hate mail), I'd like to hear them. Please check my Web site at:

http://www.zircondesigns.com

You can E-mail me from there, and I also have online resources such as company and standards contact information. Since companies move, merge, and go out of business all the time (especially these days), I'm not including printed company contact information in this book, but I do include a full listing with links on the Web site.

Thanks, and talk at you in the third edition!

John Huntington
March 2000
New York City

Useful Tables

DECIMAL/HEX/BINARY/ASCII

The following table shows numbers in several formats, and ASCII characters:

Table A.1 Decimal/Hex/Binary/ASCII Conversion *ASCII Characters*

Decimal	Hex	Binary	ASCII Characters
000	00	00000000	NUL—Null Character
001	01	00000001	SOH—Start of Header
002	02	00000010	STX—Start of Text
003	03	00000011	ETX—End of Text
004	04	00000100	EOT—End of Transmission
005	05	00000101	ENQ—Enquiry
006	06	00000110	ACK—Acknowledge
007	07	00000111	BEL—Bell
008	08	00001000	BS—Backspace
009	09	00001001	HT—Horizontal Tab
010	0A	00001010	LF—Line Feed
011	0B	00001011	VT—Vertical Tab

(continued)

Table A.1 *(continued)*

Decimal	Hex	Binary	ASCII Characters
012	0C	00001100	FF—Form Feed
013	0D	00001101	CR—Carriage Return
014	0E	00001110	SO—Shift Out
015	0F	00001111	SI—Shift In
016	10	00010000	DLE—Data Link Escape
017	11	00010001	DC1—Device Control 1
018	12	00010010	DC2—Device Control 2
019	13	00010011	DC3—Device Control 3
020	14	00010100	DC4—Device Control 4
021	15	00010101	NAK—Negative Acknowledgement
022	16	00010110	SYN—Synchronous Idle
023	17	00010111	ETB—End of Transmission Block
024	18	00011000	CAN—Cancel
025	19	00011001	EM—End of Medium
026	1A	00011010	SUB—Substitute
027	1B	00011011	ESC—Escape
028	1C	00011100	FS—File Separator
029	1D	00011101	GS—Group Separator
030	1E	00011110	RS—Record Separator
031	1F	00011111	US—Unit Separator
032	20	00100000	Space
033	21	00100001	!
034	22	00100010	"
035	23	00100011	#
036	24	00100100	$
037	25	00100101	%
038	26	00100110	&
039	27	00100111	'
040	28	00101000	(
041	29	00101001	)
042	2A	00101010	*

(continued)

Table A.1 *(continued)*

Decimal	Hex	Binary	ASCII Characters
043	2B	00101011	+
044	2C	00101100	,
045	2D	00101101	-
046	2E	00101110	.
047	2F	00101111	/
048	30	00110000	0
049	31	00110001	1
050	32	00110010	2
051	33	00110011	3
052	34	00110100	4
053	35	00110101	5
054	36	00110110	6
055	37	00110111	7
056	38	00111000	8
057	39	00111001	9
058	3A	00111010	:
059	3B	00111011	;
060	3C	00111100	<
061	3D	00111101	=
062	3E	00111110	>
063	3F	00111111	?
064	40	01000000	@
065	41	01000001	A
066	42	01000010	B
067	43	01000011	C
068	44	01000100	D
069	45	01000101	E
070	46	01000110	F
071	47	01000111	G
072	48	01001000	H
073	49	01001001	I

(continued)

Table A.1 *(continued)*

Decimal	Hex	Binary	ASCII Characters
074	4A	01001010	J
075	4B	01001011	K
076	4C	01001100	L
077	4D	01001101	M
078	4E	01001110	N
079	4F	01001111	O
080	50	01010000	P
081	51	01010001	Q
082	52	01010010	R
083	53	01010011	S
084	54	01010100	T
085	55	01010101	U
086	56	01010110	V
087	57	01010111	W
088	58	01011000	X
089	59	01011001	Y
090	5A	01011010	Z
091	5B	01011011	[
092	5C	01011100	\
093	5D	01011101	]
094	5E	01011110	^
095	5F	01011111	_
096	60	01100000	`
097	61	01100001	a
098	62	01100010	b
099	63	01100011	c
100	64	01100100	d
101	65	01100101	e
102	66	01100110	f
103	67	01100111	g
104	68	01101000	h

(continued)

Table A.1 *(continued)*

Decimal	Hex	Binary	ASCII Characters
105	69	01101001	i
106	6A	01101010	j
107	6B	01101011	k
108	6C	01101100	l
109	6D	01101101	m
110	6E	01101110	n
111	6F	01101111	o
112	70	01110000	p
113	71	01110001	q
114	72	01110010	r
115	73	01110011	s
116	74	01110100	t
117	75	01110101	u
118	76	01110110	v
119	77	01110111	w
120	78	01111000	x
121	79	01111001	y
122	7A	01111010	z
123	7B	01111011	{
124	7C	01111100		
125	7D	01111101	}
126	7E	01111110	~
127	7F	01111111	DEL
128	80	10000000	
129	81	10000001	
130	82	10000010	
131	83	10000011	
132	84	10000100	
133	85	10000101	
134	86	10000110	
135	87	10000111	

(continued)

Table A.1 *(continued)*

Decimal	Hex	Binary	ASCII Characters
136	88	10001000	
137	89	10001001	
138	8A	10001010	
139	8B	10001011	
140	8C	10001100	
141	8D	10001101	
142	8E	10001110	
143	8F	10001111	
144	90	10010000	
145	91	10010001	
146	92	10010010	
147	93	10010011	
148	94	10010100	
149	95	10010101	
150	96	10010110	
151	97	10010111	
152	98	10011000	
153	99	10011001	
154	9A	10011010	
155	9B	10011011	
156	9C	10011100	
157	9D	10011101	
158	9E	10011110	
159	9F	10011111	
160	A0	10100000	
161	A1	10100001	
162	A2	10100010	
163	A3	10100011	
164	A4	10100100	
165	A5	10100101	
166	A6	10100110	

(continued)

Table A.1 *(continued)*

Decimal	Hex	Binary	ASCII Characters
167	A7	10100111	
168	A8	10101000	
169	A9	10101001	
170	AA	10101010	
171	AB	10101011	
172	AC	10101100	
173	AD	10101101	
174	AE	10101110	
175	AF	10101111	
176	B0	10110000	
177	B1	10110001	
178	B2	10110010	
179	B3	10110011	
180	B4	10110100	
181	B5	10110101	
182	B6	10110110	
183	B7	10110111	
184	B8	10111000	
185	B9	10111001	
186	BA	10111010	
187	BB	10111011	
188	BC	10111100	
189	BD	10111101	
190	BE	10111110	
191	BF	10111111	
192	C0	11000000	
193	C1	11000001	
194	C2	11000010	
195	C3	11000011	
196	C4	11000100	
197	C5	11000101	

(continued)

Table A.1 *(continued)*

Decimal	Hex	Binary	ASCII Characters
198	C6	11000110	
199	C7	11000111	
200	C8	11001000	
201	C9	11001001	
202	CA	11001010	
203	CB	11001011	
204	CC	11001100	
205	CD	11001101	
206	CE	11001110	
207	CF	11001111	
208	D0	11010000	
209	D1	11010001	
210	D2	11010010	
211	D3	11010011	
212	D4	11010100	
213	D5	11010101	
214	D6	11010110	
215	D7	11010111	
216	D8	11011000	
217	D9	11011001	
218	DA	11011010	
219	DB	11011011	
220	DC	11011100	
221	DD	11011101	
222	DE	11011110	
223	DF	11011111	
224	E0	11100000	
225	E1	11100001	
226	E2	11100010	
227	E3	11100011	
228	E4	11100100	

(continued)

Table A.1 *(continued)*

Decimal	Hex	Binary	ASCII Characters
229	E5	11100101	
230	E6	11100110	
231	E7	11100111	
232	E8	11101000	
233	E9	11101001	
234	EA	11101010	
235	EB	11101011	
236	EC	11101100	
237	ED	11101101	
238	EE	11101110	
239	EF	11101111	
240	F0	11110000	
241	F1	11110001	
242	F2	11110010	
243	F3	11110011	
244	F4	11110100	
245	F5	11110101	
246	F6	11110110	
247	F7	11110111	
248	F8	11111000	
249	F9	11111001	
250	FA	11111010	
251	FB	11111011	
252	FC	11111100	
253	FD	11111101	
254	FE	11111110	
255	FF	11111111	

DMX UNIVERSES

Table A.2 DMX Universes

Address/Universe 1	2	3	4	Address/Universe 1	2	3	4
1	513	1025	1537	31	543	1055	1567
2	514	1026	1538	32	544	1056	1568
3	515	1027	1539	33	545	1057	1569
4	516	1028	1540	34	546	1058	1570
5	517	1029	1541	35	547	1059	1571
6	518	1030	1542	36	548	1060	1572
7	519	1031	1543	37	549	1061	1573
8	520	1032	1544	38	550	1062	1574
9	521	1033	1545	39	551	1063	1575
10	522	1034	1546	40	552	1064	1576
11	523	1035	1547	41	553	1065	1577
12	524	1036	1548	42	554	1066	1578
13	525	1037	1549	43	555	1067	1579
14	526	1038	1550	44	556	1068	1580
15	527	1039	1551	45	557	1069	1581
16	528	1040	1552	46	558	1070	1582
17	529	1041	1553	47	559	1071	1583
18	530	1042	1554	48	560	1072	1584
19	531	1043	1555	49	561	1073	1585
20	532	1044	1556	50	562	1074	1586
21	533	1045	1557	51	563	1075	1587
22	534	1046	1558	52	564	1076	1588
23	535	1047	1559	53	565	1077	1589
24	536	1048	1560	54	566	1078	1590
25	537	1049	1561	55	567	1079	1591
26	538	1050	1562	56	568	1080	1592
27	539	1051	1563	57	569	1081	1593
28	540	1052	1564	58	570	1082	1594
29	541	1053	1565	59	571	1083	1595
30	542	1054	1566	60	572	1084	1596

Address/ Universe1	2	3	4	Address/ Universe1	2	3	4
61	573	1085	1597	94	606	1118	1630
62	574	1086	1598	95	607	1119	1631
63	575	1087	1599	96	608	1120	1632
64	576	1088	1600	97	609	1121	1633
65	577	1089	1601	98	610	1122	1634
66	578	1090	1602	99	611	1123	1635
67	579	1091	1603	100	612	1124	1636
68	580	1092	1604	101	613	1125	1637
69	581	1093	1605	102	614	1126	1638
70	582	1094	1606	103	615	1127	1639
71	583	1095	1607	104	616	1128	1640
72	584	1096	1608	105	617	1129	1641
73	585	1097	1609	106	618	1130	1642
74	586	1098	1610	107	619	1131	1643
75	587	1099	1611	108	620	1132	1644
76	588	1100	1612	109	621	1133	1645
77	589	1101	1613	110	622	1134	1646
78	590	1102	1614	111	623	1135	1647
79	591	1103	1615	112	624	1136	1648
80	592	1104	1616	113	625	1137	1649
81	593	1105	1617	114	626	1138	1650
82	594	1106	1618	115	627	1139	1651
83	595	1107	1619	116	628	1140	1652
84	596	1108	1620	117	629	1141	1653
85	597	1109	1621	118	630	1142	1654
86	598	1110	1622	119	631	1143	1655
87	599	1111	1623	120	632	1144	1656
88	600	1112	1624	121	633	1145	1657
89	601	1113	1625	122	634	1146	1658
90	602	1114	1626	123	635	1147	1659
91	603	1115	1627	124	636	1148	1660
92	604	1116	1628	125	637	1149	1661
93	605	1117	1629	126	638	1150	1662

Address/ Universe 1	2	3	4	Address/ Universe 1	2	3	4
127	639	1151	1663	160	672	1184	1696
128	640	1152	1664	161	673	1185	1697
129	641	1153	1665	162	674	1186	1698
130	642	1154	1666	163	675	1187	1699
131	643	1155	1667	164	676	1188	1700
132	644	1156	1668	165	677	1189	1701
133	645	1157	1669	166	678	1190	1702
134	646	1158	1670	167	679	1191	1703
135	647	1159	1671	168	680	1192	1704
136	648	1160	1672	169	681	1193	1705
137	649	1161	1673	170	682	1194	1706
138	650	1162	1674	171	683	1195	1707
139	651	1163	1675	172	684	1196	1708
140	652	1164	1676	173	685	1197	1709
141	653	1165	1677	174	686	1198	1710
142	654	1166	1678	175	687	1199	1711
143	655	1167	1679	176	688	1200	1712
144	656	1168	1680	177	689	1201	1713
145	657	1169	1681	178	690	1202	1714
146	658	1170	1682	179	691	1203	1715
147	659	1171	1683	180	692	1204	1716
148	660	1172	1684	181	693	1205	1717
149	661	1173	1685	182	694	1206	1718
150	662	1174	1686	183	695	1207	1719
151	663	1175	1687	184	696	1208	1720
152	664	1176	1688	185	697	1209	1721
153	665	1177	1689	186	698	1210	1722
154	666	1178	1690	187	699	1211	1723
155	667	1179	1691	188	700	1212	1724
156	668	1180	1692	189	701	1213	1725
157	669	1181	1693	190	702	1214	1726
158	670	1182	1694	191	703	1215	1727
159	671	1183	1695	192	704	1216	1728

Address/Universe 1	2	3	4	Address/Universe 1	2	3	4
193	705	1217	1729	226	738	1250	1762
194	706	1218	1730	227	739	1251	1763
195	707	1219	1731	228	740	1252	1764
196	708	1220	1732	229	741	1253	1765
197	709	1221	1733	230	742	1254	1766
198	710	1222	1734	231	743	1255	1767
199	711	1223	1735	232	744	1256	1768
200	712	1224	1736	233	745	1257	1769
201	713	1225	1737	234	746	1258	1770
202	714	1226	1738	235	747	1259	1771
203	715	1227	1739	236	748	1260	1772
204	716	1228	1740	237	749	1261	1773
205	717	1229	1741	238	750	1262	1774
206	718	1230	1742	239	751	1263	1775
207	719	1231	1743	240	752	1264	1776
208	720	1232	1744	241	753	1265	1777
209	721	1233	1745	242	754	1266	1778
210	722	1234	1746	243	755	1267	1779
211	723	1235	1747	244	756	1268	1780
212	724	1236	1748	245	757	1269	1781
213	725	1237	1749	246	758	1270	1782
214	726	1238	1750	247	759	1271	1783
215	727	1239	1751	248	760	1272	1784
216	728	1240	1752	249	761	1273	1785
217	729	1241	1753	250	762	1274	1786
218	730	1242	1754	251	763	1275	1787
219	731	1243	1755	252	764	1276	1788
220	732	1244	1756	253	765	1277	1789
221	733	1245	1757	254	766	1278	1790
222	734	1246	1758	255	767	1279	1791
223	735	1247	1759	256	768	1280	1792
224	736	1248	1760	257	769	1281	1793
225	737	1249	1761	258	770	1282	1794

Address/ Universe1	2	3	4	Address/ Universe1	2	3	4
259	771	1283	1795	292	804	1316	1828
260	772	1284	1796	293	805	1317	1829
261	773	1285	1797	294	806	1318	1830
262	774	1286	1798	295	807	1319	1831
263	775	1287	1799	296	808	1320	1832
264	776	1288	1800	297	809	1321	1833
265	777	1289	1801	298	810	1322	1834
266	778	1290	1802	299	811	1323	1835
267	779	1291	1803	300	812	1324	1836
268	780	1292	1804	301	813	1325	1837
269	781	1293	1805	302	814	1326	1838
270	782	1294	1806	303	815	1327	1839
271	783	1295	1807	304	816	1328	1840
272	784	1296	1808	305	817	1329	1841
273	785	1297	1809	306	818	1330	1842
274	786	1298	1810	307	819	1331	1843
275	787	1299	1811	308	820	1332	1844
276	788	1300	1812	309	821	1333	1845
277	789	1301	1813	310	822	1334	1846
278	790	1302	1814	311	823	1335	1847
279	791	1303	1815	312	824	1336	1848
280	792	1304	1816	313	825	1337	1849
281	793	1305	1817	314	826	1338	1850
282	794	1306	1818	315	827	1339	1851
283	795	1307	1819	316	828	1340	1852
284	796	1308	1820	317	829	1341	1853
285	797	1309	1821	318	830	1342	1854
286	798	1310	1822	319	831	1343	1855
287	799	1311	1823	320	832	1344	1856
288	800	1312	1824	321	833	1345	1857
289	801	1313	1825	322	834	1346	1858
290	802	1314	1826	323	835	1347	1859
291	803	1315	1827	324	836	1348	1860

Address/ Universe 1	2	3	4	Address/ Universe 1	2	3	4
325	837	1349	1861	358	870	1382	1894
326	838	1350	1862	359	871	1383	1895
327	839	1351	1863	360	872	1384	1896
328	840	1352	1864	361	873	1385	1897
329	841	1353	1865	362	874	1386	1898
330	842	1354	1866	363	875	1387	1899
331	843	1355	1867	364	876	1388	1900
332	844	1356	1868	365	877	1389	1901
333	845	1357	1869	366	878	1390	1902
334	846	1358	1870	367	879	1391	1903
335	847	1359	1871	368	880	1392	1904
336	848	1360	1872	369	881	1393	1905
337	849	1361	1873	370	882	1394	1906
338	850	1362	1874	371	883	1395	1907
339	851	1363	1875	372	884	1396	1908
340	852	1364	1876	373	885	1397	1909
341	853	1365	1877	374	886	1398	1910
342	854	1366	1878	375	887	1399	1911
343	855	1367	1879	376	888	1400	1912
344	856	1368	1880	377	889	1401	1913
345	857	1369	1881	378	890	1402	1914
346	858	1370	1882	379	891	1403	1915
347	859	1371	1883	380	892	1404	1916
348	860	1372	1884	381	893	1405	1917
349	861	1373	1885	382	894	1406	1918
350	862	1374	1886	383	895	1407	1919
351	863	1375	1887	384	896	1408	1920
352	864	1376	1888	385	897	1409	1921
353	865	1377	1889	386	898	1410	1922
354	866	1378	1890	387	899	1411	1923
355	867	1379	1891	388	900	1412	1924
356	868	1380	1892	389	901	1413	1925
357	869	1381	1893	390	902	1414	1926

Address/ Universe 1	2	3	4	Address/ Universe 1	2	3	4
391	903	1415	1927	424	936	1448	1960
392	904	1416	1928	425	937	1449	1961
393	905	1417	1929	426	938	1450	1962
394	906	1418	1930	427	939	1451	1963
395	907	1419	1931	428	940	1452	1964
396	908	1420	1932	429	941	1453	1965
397	909	1421	1933	430	942	1454	1966
398	910	1422	1934	431	943	1455	1967
399	911	1423	1935	432	944	1456	1968
400	912	1424	1936	433	945	1457	1969
401	913	1425	1937	434	946	1458	1970
402	914	1426	1938	435	947	1459	1971
403	915	1427	1939	436	948	1460	1972
404	916	1428	1940	437	949	1461	1973
405	917	1429	1941	438	950	1462	1974
406	918	1430	1942	439	951	1463	1975
407	919	1431	1943	440	952	1464	1976
408	920	1432	1944	441	953	1465	1977
409	921	1433	1945	442	954	1466	1978
410	922	1434	1946	443	955	1467	1979
411	923	1435	1947	444	956	1468	1980
412	924	1436	1948	445	957	1469	1981
413	925	1437	1949	446	958	1470	1982
414	926	1438	1950	447	959	1471	1983
415	927	1439	1951	448	960	1472	1984
416	928	1440	1952	449	961	1473	1985
417	929	1441	1953	450	962	1474	1986
418	930	1442	1954	451	963	1475	1987
419	931	1443	1955	452	964	1476	1988
420	932	1444	1956	453	965	1477	1989
421	933	1445	1957	454	966	1478	1990
422	934	1446	1958	455	967	1479	1991
423	935	1447	1959	456	968	1480	1992

Address/ Universe 1	2	3	4	Address/ Universe 1	2	3	4
457	969	1481	1993	490	1002	1514	2026
458	970	1482	1994	491	1003	1515	2027
459	971	1483	1995	492	1004	1516	2028
460	972	1484	1996	493	1005	1517	2029
461	973	1485	1997	494	1006	1518	2030
462	974	1486	1998	495	1007	1519	2031
463	975	1487	1999	496	1008	1520	2032
464	976	1488	2000	497	1009	1521	2033
465	977	1489	2001	498	1010	1522	2034
466	978	1490	2002	499	1011	1523	2035
467	979	1491	2003	500	1012	1524	2036
468	980	1492	2004	501	1013	1525	2037
469	981	1493	2005	502	1014	1526	2038
470	982	1494	2006	503	1015	1527	2039
471	983	1495	2007	504	1016	1528	2040
472	984	1496	2008	505	1017	1529	2041
473	985	1497	2009	506	1018	1530	2042
474	986	1498	2010	507	1019	1531	2043
475	987	1499	2011	508	1020	1532	2044
476	988	1500	2012	509	1021	1533	2045
477	989	1501	2013	510	1022	1534	2046
478	990	1502	2014	511	1023	1535	2047
479	991	1503	2015	512	1024	1536	2048
480	992	1504	2016				
481	993	1505	2017				
482	994	1506	2018				
483	995	1507	2019				
484	996	1508	2020				
485	997	1509	2021				
486	998	1510	2022				
487	999	1511	2023				
488	1000	1512	2024				
489	1001	1513	2025				

System Troubleshooting Guidelines

In this appendix are some general rules of thumb I use when troubleshooting a system.

1. Know how to use test equipment! Test equipment such as oscilloscopes and multimeters are designed to let you look inside a system. Looking inside, you can often see the problem quickly.
2. Before starting to troubleshoot, be sure that:
   a. You have a signal flow diagram.
   b. You understand the signal flow through the system.
   c. You can conceptually break down the system into functional parts.
   d. You have a known test signal source (CD Player, Signal Generator, etc.).
3. Don't panic! Ninety-nine percent of problems are simple power, configuration, or connection problems. Entertainment control equipment is mostly very reliable, but connections, cabling, and power can cause many problems.
4. Try to cure the problem and not the symptom. There are times when taking a shortcut to cure a symptom rather than a problem is a necessary course of action—such as 5 minutes before show time. But I've

found such shortcuts will come back to bite you eventually, so go after the problem whenever possible.

5. Verify the test signal source! Test your test equipment. (Is your meter or tester in the right mode?)
6. Quantify the problem:
   a. Is no signal coming out of the system at all?
   b. Is a distorted signal coming through?
   c. Is a signal that is somehow changed coming through?
   d. Is the system working as anticipated?
   e. What part of the system is not working as anticipated?
7. Check the obvious:
   a. Is each device in the system powered up and turned on? Ensure that all the power and other indicator lights are showing correct operation.
   b. Are all the connectors connected properly?
   c. Are the output and input indicator lights or meters for each device in the system indicating correct signal function?
   d. Will the system work as designed?
8. For test purposes, simplify the system as much as possible—bypass any unnecessary equipment or features.
9. Determine "Verified," "Unverified," and "Suspect" devices. Verified devices are those you can determine to be working; unverified are those you have not tested. "Suspect" devices are those devices that you have tested but don't seem to be working as expected. Go through the system until you have verified every device.
10. Isolate the problem until you locate the malfunctioning device.
11. Take a break. If you get stumped, walk away and clear your head—walk around the block, go have lunch. Oftentimes, clearing your head leaves room for a new solution, or at least a new troubleshooting direction.

Contact Information

Here are an important mailing list, a list of major standards-making bodies, and a list trade associations important in the live entertainment industry. Contact information for all the companies mentioned in the book may be found at http://www.zircondesigns.com, as well as a complete and up-to-date list of organizations and much more.

MAILING LIST

Show Control Mailing List

http://archives.talklist.com/forms/show-control/index.html

This mailing list, started and maintained by Charlie Richmond of Richmond Sound Design, is an invaluable resource for all things related to entertainment control systems.

ENTERTAINMENT ORGANIZATIONS

Audio Engineering Society

60 East 42nd Street, Room 2520
New York, NY 10165-2520
(212) 661-8528
Fax: (212) 682-0477
http://www.aes.org

AES is the international society for audio engineering and technology. This large organization develops standards, publishes *The Journal of the AES*, and sponsors a number of annual trade shows and meetings.

Entertainment Services and Technology Association (ESTA)

875 Sixth Avenue, Suite 2302
New York, NY 10001
(212) 244-1505
Fax: (212) 244-1502
http://www.esta.org

ESTA is a trade organization for dealers, manufacturers, consultants, and end-users, and is now the key organization for the creation of live entertainment industry standards.

International Association of Amusement Parks and Attractions (IAAPA)

1448 Duke Street
Alexandria, VA 22314 USA
(703) 836-4800
Fax: (703) 836-4801
http://www.iaapa.org

IAAPA is the association for theme park and other related industries. It runs an enormous (and fun) annual trade show.

International Laser Display Association (ILDA)

4301 32nd Street West, Suite B-23
Bradenton, Florida 34205
(941) 758-6881
Fax: (941) 758-1605
http://www.ilda.wa.org

ILDA is the association for entertainment use of lasers.

MIDI Manufacturers Association (MMA)

P.O. Box 3173
La Habra, CA 90632-3173
Fax: (714) 736-9775
http://www.midi.org

MMA developed and maintains all the MIDI standards, including MIDI, MSC, MMC, and MTC.

National Systems Contractor Association (NSCA)

419 First Street SE
Cedar Rapids, IA 52401
(319) 366-6722
Fax: (319) 366-4164
http://www.nsca.org

The NSCA is the trade association for systems contractors, including audio and video. They host an annual trade show, offer a variety of educational programs, and offer a number of benefits to their members.

Professional Lighting and Sound Association (PLASA)

38 St. Leonards Road, Eastbourne
East Sussex BN21 3UT, UK
+44 (0) 1323 410335
Fax: +44 (0) 1323 646905
http://www.plasa.org/

PLASA is an international trade association for entertainment based in the United Kingdom and is a counterpart to ESTA. PLASA hosts a major annual trade show.

Society of Motion Picture and Television Engineers

595 West Hartsdale Avenue
White Plains, NY 10607
(914) 761-1100
Fax: (914) 761-3115
http://www.smpte.org

SMPTE is the engineering organization for video and motion pictures. They publish the SMPTE Time-Code standards and a host of others. SMPTE offers an annual trade show and a number of other regional meetings.

Themed Entertainment Association (TEA)

P.O. Box 11148
Burbank, CA 91510-1148
(818) 843-8497
Fax: (818) 843-8477
http://www.themeit.com

TEA is the association for themed entertainment.

United States Institute for Theatre Technology

6443 Ridings Road
Syracuse, NY 13206-1111
(315) 463-6463
Fax: (315) 463-6525
http://www.usitt.org

USITT published DMX512 (which is now maintained by ESTA) and has continued work on all facets of theatrical design and technology. USITT sponsors an annual convention, held at various sites throughout the United States, and publishes a journal—*TD&T* (*Theatre Design and Technology*).

OTHER RELATED ORGANIZATIONS

American National Standards Institute (ANSI)

11 West 42nd Street
New York, NY 10036
(212) 642-4900
Fax: (212) 398-0023
http://web.ansi.org

ANSI is the "administrator and coordinator of the United States private sector voluntary standardization system." ESTA is affiliated with ANSI.

Electronics Industries Association (EIA)

Telecommunications Industry Alliance (TIA)

2500 Wilson Boulevard, Suite 300
Arlington, VA 22201
(703) 907-7700
Fax: (703) 907-7727
http://www.eia.org
http://www.tiaonline.org/

EIA and TIA work together on many standards for interfacing, such as the popular EIA/TIA serial standards.

Institute of Electrical and Electronic Engineers

3 Park Avenue, 17th Floor
New York, NY 10016-5997
(212) 419-7900
Fax: (212) 752-4929
http://www.ieee.org

The IEEE is another major standards-making body. One of the standards generated by IEEE is 802.3—Ethernet.

National Fire Prevention Association

1 Batterymarch Park
P.O. Box 9101
Quincy, MA 02269-9101
(617) 770-3000
Fax: (617) 770-0700
http://www.nfpa.org/

NFPA is the organization that created the National Electric Code, the Life Safety Code, and many other important safety standards.

Bibliography

Here are some books I find useful (most of these are on my bookshelf). Be sure to check http://www.zircondesigns.com for an up-to-date list.

GENERAL ENTERTAINMENT TECHNOLOGY

Ballou, Glen M. *Handbook for Sound Engineers: The New Audio Cyclopedia*. Boston: Focal Press, 1990. ISBN 0-240-80331-0. This is an expensive, and now slightly dated, bible of audio. But the basics of audio have not changed, so the book is still very useful.

Bracewell, John L. *Sound Design in the Theatre*. Englewood Cliffs, NJ: Prentice Hall, 1993. ISBN 0-13-825167-3. Self-published now by the author, this is an excellent book on theatrical sound design.

Campbell, Drew. *Technical Theatre for Nontechnical People*. New York: Allworth Press, 1999. ISBN 1-58-115020-2. This is a great introductory book to the world backstage.

Cunningham, Glen. *Stage Lighting Revealed: A Design and Execution Handbook*. Cincinnati, OH: Better Way Books, 1993. ISBN 1-55870-290-3. Covers stage lighting.

Entertainment Services and Technology Association. *Introduction to Modern Atmospheric Effects*. New York: Entertainment Services and Technology Association. (See ESTA contact information in Appendix C.)

Entertainment Services and Technology Association. *Recommended Practice for Ethernet Cabling Systems in Entertainment Lighting Applications*. New York: Entertainment Services and Technology Association.

Entertainment Services and Technology Association. *Supplement to the Recommended Practice for Ethernet Cabling Systems in Entertainment Lighting Applications*. New York: Entertainment Services and Technology Association. These excellent consensus-created documents are extremely useful for anyone in entertainment technology.

Giddings, Phillip. *Audio Systems Design and Installation*. Boston: Focal Press, 1990. ISBN 0-240-80286-1. This is an amazingly detailed and comprehensive book, useful for anyone who installs or designs any kind of system.

Glerum, Jay. *Stage Rigging Handbook*. Southern Illinois Press, 1997. ISBN 0-809-31744-3. This is the stage rigging "bible."

Grob, Bernard. *Basic Television and Video Systems*. New York: McGraw Hill, 1984. ISBN 0-07-024933-4. A solid textbook for video technology.

Hartwig, Robert L. *Basic TV Technology*, Third Edition. Boston: Focal Press, 1990. ISBN 0-240-80417-1. Covers video fundamentals in an easy-to-understand format.

Holden, Alys, and Sammler, Ben. *Structural Design for the Stage*. Boston: Focal Press, 1999. ISBN 0-240-80354-X. A great book on structures.

Mezey, Phiz. *Multi-Image Design and Production*. Boston: Focal Press, 1988. ISBN 0-240-51740-7. Though a bit dated, this is one of the few books that covers multi-image production.

Moody, James. *Concert Lighting: Techniques, Art, and Business*, Second Edition. Boston: Focal Press, 1997. ISBN 0-240-80293-4. Mr. Moody has been in the business a long time, and this book brings those years of experience to the reader.

Shelley, Steven Louis. *A Practical Guide to Stage Lighting*. Boston: Focal Press, 1999. ISBN 0-240-80353-1. This is a great book on lighting, written by a very experienced Broadway designer.

Thompson, George. *Focal Guide to Safety in Live Performance*. Boston: Focal Press, 1993. ISBN 0-240-51319-3. This is an excellent book on live performance safety.

Vasey, John. *Concert Sound and Lighting Systems*, Third Edition. Boston: Focal Press, 1999. ISBN 0-240-80364-7. This book covers, as you might expect, concert sound and lighting systems.

Watkinson, John. *The Art of Digital Audio,* Second Edition. Boston: Focal Press, 1994. ISBN 0-240-51320-7. This is a highly detailed exploration of the details of digital audio.

White, Glenn D. *The Audio Dictionary,* Second Edition. Seattle: University of Washington Press, 1987. ISBN 0-295-97088-X. An excellent (and very inexpensive) reference for all aspects of audio.

GENERAL SMPTE AND MIDI

Ratcliff, John. *Time Code: A User's Guide*, Third Edition. Boston: Focal Press, 1993. ISBN 0-240-51539-0. An excellent book, and one of the few that extensively covers timecode systems and applications in detail for many applications.

Rumsey, Francis. *MIDI Systems and Control*. Boston: Focal Press, 1990. ISBN 0-240-51300-2. An excellent book on MIDI that goes well beyond the basics for sound and musical applications.

DATA COMMUNICATIONS/NETWORKING

Anderson, Don. *FireWire System Architecture,* Second Edition. Reading, MA: Addison-Wesley, 1999. ISBN 0-201-48535-4. This is a very detailed book on 1394/FireWire.

Axelson, Jan. *Parallel Port Complete*. Madison, WI: Lakeview Research, 1999. ISBN 096-508191-5. This is a great "hands-on" book that also gives a lot of detailed technical information.

Axelson, Jan. *Serial Port Complete*. Madison, WI: Lakeview Research, 1999. ISBN 096-508192-3. The follow-up to the parallel port book, this is a great "hands-on" book that also gives a lot of detailed technical information on serial interfacing. Includes information on RS-422 and 485, which is rare.

Campbell, Joe. *C Programmer's Guide to Serial Communications*. Carmel, IN: Howard W. Sams, A Division of Macmillan Computer Publishing, 1987. ISBN 0-672-22584-0. You don't need to be a C programmer to get a lot out of this book. Mr. Campbell writes in a very easy, nonintimidating style; the first half (before the programming) of this book provides a wealth of information for anyone interested in Serial Communications.

Goble, William M. *Control Systems Safety Evaluation and Reliability*, Second Edition. Research Triangle Park, NC: Instrument Society of America, 1998. ISBN 1-55617-636-8. This is an interesting book, but it contains enough math to make my head hurt.

Grier, Richard. *Visual Basic Programmer's Guide to Serial Communications*. Seattle: Mabry Software, 1998. ISBN 1-890422-25-8. This is a great book for hands-on experimenting with Visual Basic and serial ports.

Lampen, Stephen H. *Wire, Cable, and Fiber Optics for Video and Audio Engineers*. New York: McGraw Hill. ISBN 0-07-038134-8. This is an excellent book for anyone involved in wire and cable. And that means nearly everyone in our industry!

McDowell, Steven, and Seyer, Martin D. *USB Explained*. Upper Saddle River, NJ: Prentice Hall, 1999. ISBN 0-13-081153-X. This is a very strange and poorly organized book. However, it has a lot of information and about 100 pages of useful control signals at the end that have almost nothing to do with USB.

Putman, Byron W. *RS-232 Simplified*. Englewood Cliffs, NJ: Prentice-Hall, 1987. ISBN 0-13-783499-3. A good book on RS-232, from an engineering standpoint.

Sechweber, William L. *Data Communications*. New York: McGraw-Hill, 1988. ISBN 0-07-001097-8. This book is a bit dry and somewhat dated now, but it covers comprehensively this broad subject. It also includes a few things not included by Stallings, below.

Stallings, William. *Data and Computer Communication*, Sixth Edition. Upper Saddle River, NJ: Prentice Hall, 1999. ISBN 0-130-84370-9. This is an excellent introduction to data communications with an amazing amount of information. One of many "bibles" Stallings has written.

Stevens, W. Richard. *TCP/IP Illustrated, Volume 1: The Protocols*. Reading, MA: Addison-Wesley, 1994. ISBN 0-201-63346-9. This is a fantastic book. I bought several books when trying to learn about TCP/IP, but I was lost on the subject until I read this book (recommended by Jim Janninck). Sadly, the author recently died, but the information should be current for some years to come. We can only hope that someone as thorough will pick up the book and cover IP6.

Straw, R. Dean, editor. *The ARRL Handbook for Radio Amateurs*. Newington, CT: American Radio Relay League, annually. ISBN 0-87259-183-2. This is an excellent practical bible on communications and electronics. Written for radio "hams," it is useful for anyone interested in practical electronics.

Thompson, Laurence M. *Industrial Data Communications*. Research Triangle Park, NC: Instrument Society of America, 1997. ISBN 1-55617-585-X. This is a good introduction to industrial data communications, but it lacks some of the detail of the Stallings books. However, it covers some topics that Stallings does not.

Index